Library of
Davidson College

STEPHEN AND BLOOM
AT LIFE'S FEAST

LINDSEY TUCKER

# STEPHEN AND BLOOM AT LIFE'S FEAST

*Alimentary Symbolism
and the Creative Process
in James Joyce's "Ulysses"*

OHIO STATE UNIVERSITY PRESS: COLUMBUS

Selected excerpts from *A Portrait of the Artist as a Young Man* by James Joyce. Copyright 1916 by B. W. Huebsch. Copyright renewed 1944 by Nora Joyce. Definitive text Copyright © 1964 by the Estate of James Joyce. Reprinted by permission of Viking Penguin Inc., the Executors of the James Joyce Estate, and The Society of Authors as the literary representitive of the Estate of James Joyce.

All quotations from James Joyce's *Ulysses* are copyright © 1914, 1918, by Margaret Caroline Anderson and renewed 1942, 1946, by Nora Joseph Joyce. Reprinted by permission of Random House, Inc., The Bodley Head Ltd., and the Society of Authors as the literary representative of the Estate of James Joyce.

Quotations from *Musical Allusions in the Works of James Joyce,* by Zack Bowen, are reprinted by permission of the State University of New York and the author.

Copyright © 1984 by the Ohio State University Press
All Rights Reserved.

*Library of Congress Cataloging in Publication Data*

Tucker, Lindsey, 1936–
  Stephen and Bloom at life's feast.

  Bibliography: p.
  Includes index.
  1. Joyce, James, 1882–1941. Ulysses. 2. Joyce, James, 1882–1941—Allegory and symbolism. 3. Creativity in literature. 4. Food habits in literature. 5. Dinners and dining in literature. 6. Digestion in literature. 7. Body, human, in literature. I. Title.
PR6019.O9U747  1984         823'.912                    84-2342
ISBN 0-8142-0361-2

FOR ZACK

CONTENTS

| | | |
|---|---|---:|
| ONE | Introduction | 1 |
| TWO | Stephen | 11 |
| THREE | Bloom | 45 |
| FOUR | Stephen and Bloom | 89 |
| FIVE | Conclusion | 145 |
| | Notes | 157 |
| | Selected Bibliography | 167 |
| | Index | 173 |

# *ACKNOWLEDGMENTS*

My debt to many fine teachers and scholars is extensive. My largest debt is to my husband, Zack Bowen, to whom I owe my interest in, and understanding of, Joyce. His long hours of reading and editing, his advice, and his enthusiasm have played a major role in the creation of this book. I also owe much to the insights of George Michael Evica at the University of Hartford for awakening my interest in the study of ritual, myth, and archetype.

I am also grateful to the members of the faculty at the University of Delaware who saw me through the dissertation that was the basis of this study, especially Jerry Beasley, Kevin Kerrane, and Ellen Pifer. And final thanks must go to those special Joyceans, Bonnie Scott, James F. Carens, and Father Robert Boyle for all their help and inspiration along the way.

# ONE  *Introduction*

All of James Joyce's fiction has the creative process itself as one of its central concerns. Of the three major image clusters that Joyce employs as analogues for this process, the first two, already clearly recognized and fully discussed by scholars, are the image of the artist as priest and the artist as alchemist.

The artist's role as priest is most memorably defined in *A Portrait of the Artist as a Young Man* where he is described as "a priest of eternal imagination transmuting the daily bread of experience into the radiant body of everliving life."[1] Since ritual is the means whereby the priest performs transformative acts, Joyce's knowledge about, and use of, Catholic liturgical elements have been the subjects of a number of studies.[2]

The second dominant image cluster involves Joyce's use of alchemical techniques and process. Alchemy is an especially useful analogue for creativity because, like the mass, it involves transformations of substances, the reconciliation of such oppositions as body and spirit, the relatedness of all things.[3]

A third image cluster that pertains to the creative process involves body functions. Joyce himself was clear about the importance of the body in his work. To Frank Budgen he described *Ulysses* as, among other things, "The epic of the human body," and continued, "In my book the body lives in and moves through space and is the home of a full human personality." When Budgen protested, "But the minds, the thoughts of the characters," Joyce replied, "If they had no body they would have no mind. . . . It's all one."[4]

Nevertheless, whereas critics have been aware of Joyce's interest in bodily processes, attention has usually focused on them as examples of naturalistic detail; beyond that, it has been the reproductive and sexual aspects rather than the digestive ones that have elicited the most comment. Certainly though, Stuart Gilbert's early study made clear that Joyce relates body organs to the structure of *Ulysses*.[5] However, no full study has been done on the function of the digestive processes as they relate to the creativity and language. Yet the relationship is there because Joyce uses both ritual and alchemy as sources for imagery when he speaks of the creative process, and both ritual and alchemy are grounded in alimentary functions. The hermetic maxim that all functions are reflections of one another and that the lowest is a paradigm of the highest is also an assumption that seems implicit in Joyce's work.

Joyce's attention to meals and the digestive process, as well as his careful delineating of the responses of Bloom and Stephen to functions of the body, are two ways in which he comments on the creative process, on aesthetic and kinetic types of creativity, and on the fertility and wholeness of the characters themselves. Furthermore, and perhaps more important, Joyce's attention to the transformational properties of language, style, and narrative techniques derive from his awareness of the role played by the alimentary process in relation to the so-called higher activities of the mind.

Of course, any discussion involving body processes brings to the fore the question of whether some of Joyce's material (and interests) are scatological. Certainly his letters to Nora Barnacle, composed during a prolonged absence during the months of August and December 1909, serve as compelling if distasteful testimony to such inclinations, for Joyce's rather passionate declarations are punctuated by references to excremental matters as well.[6] Indeed, it is often difficult to separate alimentary symbolism from its anal component, and the presence of anality in Joyce's work has been a cause of both concern and comment among critics. Clive Hart, in his noted study of *Finnegans Wake*, feels called upon to say, "I think I must offer some explanation, if not an apology for the consistently scatological nature of interpretations which follow," and observes that Joyce's fascination with the scatological borders on "an obsession": "There can be no denying that Joyce found everything associated with evacuation unusually pleasurable." Yet Hart also feels that although *Finnegans Wake* may be the dirtiest book in the language, "a curious and unaccustomed beauty radiates from the imagery contained in the descriptions of the genital and anal regions of the primal Mother and Father figures . . . a beauty which is distilled by verbal alchemy from obscene scrawls on the 'oozing wall of a urinal.'"[7] Hart's important realization of the beauty created by "verbal alchemy" is perhaps the key to Joyce's use of such images, and maybe exactly what lifts his interest beyond the merely scatological. *Finnegans Wake* is not the exception, and all his early works give evidence of this same concern, although in less extravagant ways.

Mark Shechner, in his psychoanalytic study of *Ulysses*, argues for the work as a self-analysis of its author and is very much aware of the importance of the body as both source and influence in the making of Joyce's art. He makes this interesting statement: "If it is true that patterns of moral, psychological, and artistic behavior may be systematically modeled after primitive patterns of compromise around areas of body conflict, then we should be able to discover a stylistic paradigm in any artist's life and work."[8] Suggesting that "we can construct a consistent and far-reaching theory of Joyce's art around the dialectic of anal control," Shechner uses dominance/subordination, shame/self-esteem, and most important, spatial modalities of open and closed to describe Stephen as essentially a closed character with a retentive temper, whose major use of control is via language. Bloom, he argues, is an open character with an "eliminative temper."[9] I think these categories are not only valid but helpful, and a close study of texts will show that these dynamics are frequently present.

It was Freud, of course, who focused on lower body functions as determining later social behavior. Although many of his conclusions have come to be considered too reductive, his basic postulates have been recognized as valid by many analysts, and their ideas about the relationship of alimentary functions to behavior should perhaps be summarized here. The infant's earliest experience of the world outside is the via the mouth, through which he *incorporates* his experience, i.e., nursing. This mode of incorporation grows more complicated and involves breathing, biting, grasping, touching—all of which are based on the primal need to breath, drink, eat, and thus to grow. The anal zone, the second important zone at this age of consciousness, involves a more complicated set of responses because there are alternating and contradictory impulses present—namely, retention and elimination. The child's response to this function and its conflicts is closely connected to its achievement of some sort of autonomy and self control.[10]

For Freudians, alimentary consciousness is presexual and superseded by the genital stage of development, but the Jungians seem to see both stages as coexistent. Erich Neumann, a Jungian whose insights on this subject have done much to shape my thinking in regard to the presence of alimentary images in *Ulysses*, says that the primary unity "remains the foundation of our existence even after our consciousness, grown independent with the separation of the systems, has begun to elaborate its scientifically objective view of the world," and adds, furthermore: "It cannot be stressed enough that eating and food—as the symbolism of language, myth, dream and fairytale show time and time again—signify a manner of interpreting the world and integrating oneself with it."[11]

Important to this discussion is the concept of sin and evil in relation to the body. For early consciousness, before the separation of systems, the mouth and anus are not seen as higher and lower, but are of equal importance, and the anus is viewed in positive terms as creative.[12] However, as the individual assumes an erect posture, the lower body pole is reduced in importance; anal smells and functions are rejected as disgusting, then as evil. It is particularly a characteristic of Judeo-Christian culture that the upper-spirit-world is magnified and that the lower-body-world is rejected. And original sin is associated then in its most basic meaning with the inferiority of the individual, whose body functions, his elimination in particular, become identified with the elimination of evil. This negative evaluation establishes itself in the conscious mind as a division between body and self which causes anxiety. This anxiety in turn causes some individuals to see themselves as infected by evil, particularly their own evil. The result is a fragmentation of consciousness, the creation of a threatening death-hell-lower world.[13] This summary seems to me to most aptly describe Stephen's problems with sin and anality so memorably depicted in chapter 3 of *A Portrait of the Artist as a Young Man*.

The psychoanalytic school views this conflict and repression of the anal stage as the cause of creativity. In other words, the creation of art is the result of the sublimation of the anal stage. However, this theory does not do justice to Bloom's essentially creative nature and to his ability to accept the world. A Jungian interpretation would tend to view art, not in a negative way, but as "one among many creative continuations of the anal stage that has been preserved and integrated with the individual's development as a whole."[14] Furthermore, Freudian approaches have developed, for the most part, from an extensive study of abnormal and pathological behaviors. A Jungian approach allows us to interpret Bloom's so-called feminine aspects and his fondness for excrementa as evidence of his receptive and expressive nature.

Happily, two new studies have used Freudian insights and analytical techniques to more expansive ends. Sheldon R. Brivic's *Joyce Between Freud and Jung*, uses, as the title suggests, both approaches. Brivic, in stressing Joyce's uses of both Freud and Jung, argues that Freud is useful when examining the developing mind of Joyce, or rather, its unconscious content, and Jung is helpful in showing Joyce's more rational or conscious purposes. Brivic suggests that Joyce's use of Jung really comes into play as Joyce, in his own growth "from a world of frustration to one of transcendence," finds Jung's mythic system helpful in the construction of his own.[15] Valid as this argument may be, I feel that Brivic still gets trapped in reductive and judgmental readings of the characters, seeing Bloom, for example, as having three fundamental drives: "his masochism, his cuckoldry and an attraction to inanimate matter and the tendency toward inanimate matter in life."[16] In *The Transformation Process in Joyce's "Ulysses,"* Elliott B. Gose, Jr., deals more positively with Joyce's debt to Freud by focusing for the first half of his book, on Joyce's fascination with the ideas of Giordano Bruno.[17] Bruno has long been recognized as an important influence on Joyce's thought, but Gose's study is the most thorough to date. Seeing nature as a divine substance that is possessed of both spiritual and material components, Bruno offers Joyce a new mode of vision, taking him beyond the doctrines of Catholicism and the equally inhibiting precepts of the Platonic system. Bruno turns mutability into a positive feature, emphasizing it as a transformational process. By doing so, Bruno, according to Gose, influences Joyce in three key areas: "in his [Joyce's] ability to embody in his fiction a sense of the happenings of nature as interconnected, of the everyday as containing the eternal, of mind as microcosmos."[18] In his section on Freud and

Joyce, Gose again liberates both Joyce and his characters from the narrower kind of Freudian interpretations. Bloom's behavior is thus explained in Brunian terms by Bloom's awareness of, and participation in, physical cycles—things becoming one another, birth, death, decay. In Freudian terms, Bloom escapes this "reality" through sexual fantasies, but undergoes a healthful purgation in "Circe."

I have suggested earlier that ritual is a relevant ingredient in any discussion of alimentary symbolism. This is because it is through ritual, as practiced by primitive peoples, that we see the earliest knowledge of the world expressed in terms of body symbolism. Ritual is, of course, an objectification of psychic processes, but it imitates the functions of the body, too, and lends order and structure to all life processes. It is not, until later, an abstract set of concepts, but is instead a set of life-serving actions involving participation in natural rhythms, and it is the more elemental nature of ritual that Joyce seems to recognize.

In the fields of anthropology and comparative religion, much work has been done in this century on the universal patterns of religious practices, some of which Joyce was also familiar with. Sir James Frazer's *The Golden Bough* is perhaps the most influential and well-known study in this area. Although there is no explicit evidence that Joyce was acquainted with Frazer, John Vickery sees Joyce as using the Christ figure in anthropological contexts and argues that Joyce indeed saw Christian rituals as existing in a recognizable pattern in older religions, especially those patterns that involve the dying and reviving god, priest/kings, and scapegoat figures.[19] Furthermore, Vickery notes that Joyce had in his personal library such works as Jane Harrison's *Mythology*, Ernst Renan's *Les Apôtres*, Lucien Lévy-Bruhl's *L'Âme primitive*, and *L'Experience mystique et les symboles chez les primitifs*, among others.[20]

Other later work done on the nature of ritual is also pertinent to this discussion because it also stresses the essential quality of the alimentary component. Theodor Gaster, for example, breaks down ritual into two main divisions, rites of *kenosis* or emptying, and rites of *plerosis* or filling. The former involves rites of mortification, as exemplified in Lenten periods, fasts, a state of suspended animation, rites of purgation characterized by the expulsion of evil, both moral and physical, from the community. The latter involves rites of invigoration, in which an attempt is made to reestablish fertility, and rites of jubilation, which include a communal feast.[21]

Language is another major factor to be considered when discussing alimentary symbolism. That speaking is founded in the dynamics of the alimentary zone may be taken for granted more than understood, but Ernst Cassirer outlines the connection between eating and speaking in a helpful way:

> It is above all in certain consonants and groups of consonants that a specific sensous tendency is manifested. In the very first babblings of children a sharp distinction is evident between sound groups of essentially "centripetal" and essentially "centrifugal" tendency. The *m* and *n* clearly reveal the inward direction, while the explosive sounds *p* and *b*, *t* and *d* reveal the opposite trend. In one case the sound indicates a striving back to the subject; in the other, a relation to the "outside world," a pointing or rejection. The one corresponds to the gestures of grasping, of attempting to draw close, the other to the gestures of showing or thrusting away.[22]

Out of the need to objectify the internal in terms of space, Cassirer argues, human consciousness reproduces analogically what it experiences internally; hence there is a metaphorical relationship between language and body.

This relationship was early discerned by Giambattista Vico, a seventeenth century Italian humanist whose work, *The New Science*, was of particular interest to Joyce. (Numerous critical studies have been done on Joyce's use of Viconian cycles of history, etymology, and language.[23]) Discussing the origins of language, for example, Vico postulated that it evolved from gesture, that man then created interjections (passionate monosyllabic sounds). These sounds were followed by pronouns (since interjections were the venting of one's own passions, pronouns were necessary).[24]

Of particular importance here is Vico's focus on all creative processes—intellectual and linguistic—as extensions of human consciousness and human corporeality. Not only does he view psychological cause as dominant over physical, but his argument for the existence of a common language was accompanied by a belief that "words are carried over from bodies and from the properties of bodies to signify the institutions of the mind and spirit."[25] He goes to say "in all languages the greater part of the expressions relating to inanimate things are formed by metaphor from the human body and its parts and from the human senses and passions." In elaborating on what he calls his "imaginative metaphysics" that precedes so-called rational metaphysics, Vico, in the same passage, concludes that man "becomes all things by *not* understanding them . . . he makes the things out of himself and becomes them by transforming himself into them."[26] That Vico's imaginative approach to language was perhaps the cause of Joyce's absorbing interest in him can hardly be disputed.

Jeanne McKnight, in another psychoanalytic study that focuses particularly on Stephen, sees him as threatened by madness and as using language for control because, she says, he is unable "to locate the boundaries of his own ego, his own self, and subsequently feels endangered by things which he perceives will swallow him up."[27] Stephen's fear of being "eaten" causes him to create words for the purpose of controlling his view of the world. She concludes: "Expression is Stephen's way of bringing himself into the world, and in the metaphor of expression are linked the ideas of speaking (language), asserting one's idenitity (being 'born'), and pressing out (excreting) all the beauty which is inside,"[28]

One final and most important ingredient that is present in language and is vital to the practice of ritual acts as well as the creation of art is memory. We know that memory is a vital element in ritual because the act of remembering a primal event, one involved with the creation of mankind, the creation of man's fertility, is the moving force behind the ritual act. It is through memory that man and his cosmos are renewed and become vital organisms again.

Vico called memory "the Mother of the Muses" and saw it as having three functions. First, says Vico, memory remembers things; second, it alters and imitates these things; third, it invents; it gives those things a "new turn or puts them into proper arrangement and relationship."[29] This last creative aspect of memory, involving not merely retention, but the creation of a new form, is the determinant of the creative ability of both Bloom and Stephen. For example, Stephen's view of life is re-created anew in each chapter of *A Portrait*, and Bloom's most meaningful acts of creation operate not in terms of his linguistic ability so much as his memory of Molly and Howth.

What I want to emphasize here, however, is the association of memory and the digestive processes. Like digestion, memory involves the taking in of experience in the creation of a new form, and Cassirer explains the process in an interesting passage using body references, usually reproductive it is true, as metaphors for consciousness and its acts:

> In order to remember a content, consciousness must previously have possessed itself of that content in a way differing from mere sensation or perception. The mere repetition of the given at another time does not suffice; in this repetition a new kind of conception and formation must be manifested. For every "reproduction" of a content embodies a new level of reflection. By the mere fact that it no longer takes this content as something simply present, but confronts it in imagination as something past and yet not vanished, consciousness, by its changed *relation* to the content, gives both to itself and the content a changed ideal of meaning.[30]

Stephen's obsession with images of devouring is tied to the memory of his dead mother, and memory forces him to translate threatening alimental images into language that nonetheless retains traces of the alimental. Bloom's memory is not only activitated by eating, but this activating is itself expressed in alimental terms. In "Oxen of the Sun," for example, the narrator speaks of Bloom's "cud of reminiscence." Bloom's most fertile and meaningful creation involves his and Molly's lovemaking on Howth where Molly feeds him an already-chewed seedcake. That this memory should invigorate Bloom throughout his day is neither sentimental nor ironic. Bloom's re-creation of the fertile and transformative act of eating is a fictional demonstration of the dynamic ritual.

It is the relationship among these elements—the alimentary process, language, ritual, and art—that will be discussed in the following chapters, and we shall see how Joyce creates both the form and content of *Ulysses* through a use of, and a recognition of, man's ingestive, transformative, and eliminative functions.

Since *Ulysses* seems to move from a naturalistic, stream-of-consciousness style that focuses on the minds of Stephen and Bloom to a more self-conscious, parodic one that includes them both and is dominated by other voices, I have chosen to discuss Stephen and Bloom separately and then jointly as they come together in the later episodes.

To that end, chapter 2 deals only with Stephen. To fully account for Stephen's negative reactions to food, his fear of being devoured, and his tendency to translate troublesome aspects of nature into language, I have found it necessary to include in chapter 2 some comments on *A Portrait of the Artist as a Young Man.*

Chapter 3 deals with Bloom and his particularly assimilating nature. Chapter 4 treats episodes in which Stephen and Bloom are both present. Chapter 5 is a conclusion that uses the "Penelope" episode as a final statement on Joyce's attitude about the relationship of digestive processes to art.

# TWO  *Stephen*

### *Alimentary Imagery in "A Portrait"*

Before discussing alimentary symbolism in *Ulysses*, it may be helpful to look briefly at *A Portrait of the Artist as a Young Man*, where important alimentary images link the emergent artist of *A Portrait* with that of *Ulysses*.

We know that Stephen's growth as an artist is keyed to the Eucharistic image of the priest who transmutes "the daily bread of experience into the radiant body of everliving life."[1] (All subsequent references to *Portrait* are cited parenthetically in the text.) This image of the mass, spiritualized as it is, is grounded originally in the process of digestion. It is evolved to express the ingestion of the divine being which will effect a miraculous transformation and provide a different kind of nourishment for those who participate in the rite. It is not the physical origins of this image that seem important to Stephen, however. Nevertheless, the alimentary process is present, and the fact that it lies beneath the surface is significant in itself, for we know that Stephen's need to keep instinct and body functions repressed and the equally strong need to bring them to consciousness generate the tensions that are important to Stephen's (and Joyce's) kind of language and art.

However, we also recall that the artist/priest metaphor is not the final word about the alimentary process, for we also have Stephen's definition of Ireland as the "old sow that eats her farrow" (203). These two images vividly exemplify the nature of Stephen's psychological problems and suggest the cause of his rigid dualism. To fail to become the artist is to become devoured by country, church, and mother. Yet to become the artist is to become immersed in unconscious energies that are usually viewed as female, that is, the qualities usually associated with the female principle: instinct, emotion, biorhythmic processes.

As mentioned in the previous chapter, both Mark Shechner's and Jeanne McKnight's studies present illuminating psychoanalytical backgrounds for both novels and are particularly helpful in their discussions of Stephen's problems. Both writers also draw on Philip Slater's important work on mother-son relationships in the Greek family, to which Irish families bear some significant similaritities. Indeed, Slater coins an interesting term that seems to describe Stephen's problem accurately, namely the "oral-narcissistic dilemma," the "desire to merge and the desire to be free and separate." Slater goes on to say that this conflict "originates in a failure to negotiate successfully the transition from the infantile state of total narcissism and total dependence to one involving an awareness of the separate existence of others,"[2] Slater also says that "the desire for symbiosis is matched by a fear of submergence implying loss of individuality and identity."[3]

In another important psychoanalytic analysis of Joyce's work, Chester G. Anderson correlates events in Joyce's childhood with events in *A Portrait* and argues that the past is never relinquished: "In spite of his complex and intricate use of sublimation, projection, repression," he says of Joyce, "the repressed would return again and again in new forms, demanding new defenses."[4] Shechner, McKnight, and Anderson emphasize the oral factors of Stephen's problem, his fear of being devoured, and his creation of language as bulwark; Anderson's analysis deals most strongly with the oral basis of Stephen's needs. He associates Stephen with the child whose Oedipal conflict leads him to an oral sadistic stage in which he fantasizes the ingestion of the mother. As Anderson explains it, the child, "his sucking libido unsatisfied and unsatisfiable, fantasizes destroying the mother's breast and eating his way through the flesh of her innards to devour the contents."⁵ However, Anderson's (and Freud's) heavy emphasis on the sadistic aspects of childhood fantasy is qualified by such Jungians as Erich Neumann who denies sadism or castration as components of the oral stage. To view the mother as an object of gratification is, Neumann says, "a genuine objective element in the primal situation, not an infantile projection."⁶

In any case, Stephen's attitude about food, his tendency to relegate digestive functions to a lower world that is both attractive and threatening, is our main concern here. It is also important to note the relationship of the digestive process to his later attitudes about sin and hell, as well as his projection of devouring attributes on both male and female figures that he sees as threatening to him. Also significant is Stephen's use of earthy and excremental images to explain the basis of art and his use of the dynamics of peristalsis in relation to language.

The mention of food can't help but call to mind the famous Christmas dinner scene in chapter 1 where the young Stephen is first allowed to sit at dinner with the adults. The scene carries such heavy psychological, religious, and sexual reverberations in addition to the political ones that the role of food seems obvious and literal. Yet in the battle between Dante, Mr. Casey, and Simon, food serves as an important commentary.

As the quarrel begins, for example, Simon is giving Stephen a generous amount of sauce for his turkey. As the meal continues and the argument between Dante and the men intensifies, Simon attempts to break the tension by asking "Who's for more turkey?" (31). But he also seems to be undercutting Dante's obsessive concerns with more spiritual matters. Dante, worried about his insult to a priest, ignores the question and continues on the topic dearest to her: "Nice language for any catholic to use!" As the conflict worsens, Simon's attention to the dinner increases: "He heaped up the food on Stephen's plate and served uncle Charles and Mr Casey to large pieces of turkey and splashes of sauce. Mrs Dedalus was eating little and Dante sat with her hands in her lap" (32).⁷ Dante is hardly mollified when Simon next cuts off the turkey tail and offers it as the "pope's nose." When there are no takers, Simon says, "I think I had better eat myself" (33). But Simon is defeated by the women's hostility, and his dinner is, he admits, "spoiled." Getting angrier, he next attacks a priest, the "tub of guts up in Armagh. . . . You should see that fellow lapping up his bacon and cabbage of a cold winter's day" (33). He continues to use food as a weapon against the women, or at least Dante, as he eats with features twisted into a "grimace of heavy bestiality" and makes "a lapping noise with his lips" (33).

But the real attack against Dante comes with Mr. Casey's story about the "very famous spit," offered, as Simon puts it, to "help us to digest" (34). The story is about a drunken old woman who screams accusations about Parnell and Kitty O'Shea at Casey. The hostility against Dante, implicit in the story, is deepened as Simon gnaws on a bone and tears "some meat from it with his teeth" (36). Then the old woman utters her denunciation of Kitty in "a name that I won't sully . . . your ears . . . by repeating," Casey says. His reaction is memorable: "She stuck her ugly old face up at me when she said it and I had my mouth full of tobacco juice. I bent down to her and *Phth!* says I to her like that" (36).

Behind the story's crudeness we can see the life-affirming men fighting rather pathetically, and in symbolic terms whose full import they fail to understand, against the life-denying women (who not coincidentally evince little appetite), first by drawing attention to eating and thereby to things of the body, and second by telling a story whose denouement has implicit sexual overtones. Furthermore, the spitting suggests a rejection rather than an assimilation, an inverted ejaculation, and is a comment upon what the men have been denied. Sheldon R. Brivic is right in saying that the spitting scene is the "height of . . . male assertiveness," but it is a pathetic assertiveness indeed.[8] Beyond her embodiment as the church and the sterility of Ireland, Dante is also representative of the Terrible Mother. The scene reflects in rather remarkable terms the deep tensions, political, religious, but especially sexual, that permeate the household.

Thus at a dinner that celebrates the birth of Jesus and the birth, in broader terms, of the new sun (after the midwinter solstice), Stephen too is born into a new awareness. After the meal he tries to write a poem about Parnell. But his important reaction to the scene is more subtle. Stephen dismisses the physical act of spitting as "not nice" (37), and he goes on to ponder language. Neither the abundance of gravy on his plate nor the violence at the table reflected through the spit story seem to interest him so much as the question of what *name* the woman had called Kitty O'Shea. Language is, of course, one way in which Stephen will insulate himself against disturbing, and usually physical, aspects of his experience. Sometimes he will directly change food into a word. During his illness at Clongowes for example, he is fascinated by Brother Michael's pun, ("butter you up") on the toast brought to the sick Stephen. As he views the trussed turkey, Stephen ponders on why the word *turkey* also meant pandybat: "Why did Mr. Barrett in Clongowes call his pandybat a turkey?" (30)

At this point in his life, Stephen, although ambivalent, seems to be more sympathetic with his father who represents an energy he is initially attracted to. Another dinner scene suggests these basically positive feelings: "Stephen had been awaiting his father's return for there had been mutton hash that day and he knew his father would make him dip his bread in the gravy" (71). Early in *A Portrait*, food seems more often mentioned in connection with men like his father, Mr. Casey, or Uncle Charles and seems to remind him pleasantly of natural life. In chapter 2, in the scene with Uncle Charles, eating and elimination are mentioned in conjunction with rhetoric as Uncle Charles, with lofty diction and pompous preparation, announces he will "repair to" the outhouse. His offering of an apple to Stephen ("They're good for your bowels"61), may be accepted, but Stephen does reject his religiosity and his overblown rhetoric.

There are other occasions in the early part of *A Portrait* where Stephen seems to retain pleasant associations with food and matters related to body functions and earth. Sometimes he is even moved by them. Anderson's argument that Stephen rejects food when he is rejected or defeated seems a valid one when Stephen's response to *acceptance* by his peers, for example, is examined.[9] After his conference with Father Conmee and his victory over Father Dolan, the natural world seems less threatening. Hailed by his peers as a hero, he is suddenly aware of "the smell of the fields in the country where they digged up turnips to peel and eat them when they went for a walk to Major Barton's" (59).

Stephen's drive in the milk car is also a pleasant experience for him. His view of the cows "at grass" is positive. But when autumn comes and the cows are driven home, he has a different impression of them. In the cowyard there are "foul green puddles and clots of liquid dung and steaming brantroughs" (63) that momentarily "sicken" him. Again, he will deal with his fears, and the life of the milkman will become appealing enough for him to think of again. A second passage contains some of the rare alimental images to be found in *A Portrait* and foreshadows the time when, in the Martello tower, Stephen will create stories from the figure of the milkwoman. But here his identification with the milkman dominates, and he is not yet old enough to reject this common mode of life: "He thought it should be a pleasant life enough, driving along the roads every evening to deliver milk, if he had warm gloves and a fat bag of gingernuts in his pocket to eat from" (64).

By the time Stephen has moved to Dublin, however, such feelings have been altered. Doubtless his emergent sexuality, coupled with his Catholic upbringing, have everything to do with this change, but also important is Stephen's developing awareness of his father's downward path in life. Where his father was associated positively with food and natural life processes (in contrast to his mother's more spiritual nature), this natural life takes on the characteristics of "squalor," a word Stephen will use many times to describe his environment, and natural life comes to signify for him ugliness, decay, bondage, and death.

Since Stephen has seen his father swallowed up by Ireland, church, and family, it is not surprising that his own fears of being devoured grow keener as he grows older. In fact, the motif of devouring remains a dominant one in both *A Portrait* and *Ulysses*.

It is in chapter 3, where his sexuality and consequent guilt dominate his consciousness, that Stephen seems most cognizant of eating: "He hoped there would be stew for dinner, turnips and carrots and bruised potatoes and fat mutton pieces to be ladled out in thick peppered flourfattened sauce. Stuff it into you, his belly counselled him" (102). Now he eats with "surly appetite" (111), feels "his belly crave for its food" (102), clears "thick scum from his mouth with his tongue" (111). He feels he has "sunk to the state of a beast that licks its chaps after meat" (111). His sense of self-abhorrence increases as he sees his soul "fattening and congealing into a gross grease" (111).

It is in this state of mind that Stephen, during the retreat, is to ingest the sermon of Father Arnall. This sermon, on death, judgment, hell, and heaven, is most memorable for its description of hell. If we look beyond the horror and the implicit sadism of its content, we find the sermon dominated largely by images of ingestion and elimination. The association of evil and the Christian hell with anality is acknowledged by most psychologists. What is also important is the aspect of sadism involved in the elimination of evil. Neumann might be speaking of Arnall when he says: "The Christian . . . who imputes to the saints so nauseating a pleasure in the sufferings of their fellow men is obviously avenging himself on the saints for repressing his own chthonian aspect."[10] That the struggle is against the lower body pole is most obvious in this type of Christian doctrine and severely intensifies Stephen's problem of assimilating the world and his lower self.

Father Arnall begins with one ingesting pair—Adam and Eve—who both ate to receive knowledge and thereafter fell. The price paid for their "epistemophelia" was their exile from Eden and their need to "earn their bread in the sweat of their brow" (118). Certainly their fall is replicated in the life of Stephen, whose family struggles every day to get enough to eat. Even the dangers of language are involved in this fall, for it was the "poison" of the serpent's "eloquence" "poured" into Eve's ear that was the cause of it all (118). Hell is, of course, the great devourer that *"has enlarged its soul and opened its mouth without any limits"* (117). Hell is also a maw with "boundless fire raging in its very vitals" (121). It eats but is never sated. Stephen seems deeply moved by this image. In this fantasy he is fearful of being eaten; he imagines his body first as dying, then as a corpse placed in a "long hole in the ground . . . to feed the mass of its creeping worms and to be devoured by scuttling plumpbellied rats" (112), to be "eaten with flames, gnawed by vermin" (132).

Besides these devouring motifs, Father Arnall's sermon focuses on hell in excremental terms. He speaks of the stench of hell as comprised of "all the filth of the world, all the offal and scum of the world," and of hell as a "vast reeking sewer" where the bodies of the damned themselves exhale . . . "a pestilential odour" (120). He also speaks of the damned whose tastes are tortured "with foul matter" (122).

Stephen can't help but be influenced adversely by such images since they reinforce his own sense of his soul as a "foul swamp of sin" (114), that as a "beast in its lair . . . had lain down in its own filth" (115). As his sense of his own sinfulness increases, the excremental imagery becomes stronger: "The sordid details of his orgies stank under his very own nostrils" (115).

The natural world is described in a similar fashion. Stephen views the rainy Dublin day in this manner: "It would rain forever, noiselessly. The water would rise inch by inch. . . . All life would be choked off, noiselessly: birds, men, elephants, pigs, children: noiselessly floating corpses amid the litter of the wreckage of the world" (117).

This passage is dominated by images of floating bodies, rising water that chokes life; in other words, the world, like hell, is a sewer. The references to noiselessness are interesting because Stephen seems to associate a lack of noise, words, language, with mystery and secrecy, ultimately with process and qualities of the female principle.

In any case, he returns to his room "to be alone with his soul" (136), a hounded and almost hysterical Stephen, who sees the "leprous company of his sins" (137) closing around him. Finally, in a description that suggests the operation of peristalsis, we are told: "The senses of his soul closed. They closed for an instant and then opened. He saw" (137).

What Stephen sees is a truly excremental vision that blends images of the natural world, body functions, and affirms the animal or chthonic nature of man:

> A field of stiff weeds and thistles and tufted nettlebunches. Thick among the tufts of rank stiff growth lay battered canisters and clots and coils of solid excrement. A faint marshlight struggled upwards from all the ordure through the bristling greygreen weeds. An evil smell, faint and foul as the light, curled upwards sluggishly out of the canisters and from the stale crusted dung.
>
> Creatures were in the field. . . . Goatish creatures . . . trailing their long tails behind them (137).

Yet even this essentially visual and essentially eliminative vision contains references to language: "Soft language issued from their spittleless lips. . . . They moved in slow circles, circling closer and closer to enclose, to enclose, soft language issuing from their lips, their long swishing tails besmeared with stale shite, thrusting upwards their terrific faces" (138). Here upper and lower body poles, so rigidly separated in consciousness, merge. All lower body functions, already rendered evil, have thrown their characteristics off onto language that now carries connotations of dirt and evil. Mouths excrete and language becomes associated with dung. Stephen's vision of language contrasts markedly with that of the preacher who has earlier spoken of Christ as "the Eternal Word" (118). Different also is Stephen's own use of words, his "foul long letters" that he writes and leaves in the grass for girls to find (116).

This inversion, by which basically creative functions become imaged as evil, is paralleled in Stephen's physical reaction. The gluttony that marked his immersion in the world of natural instincts is transformed; he now experiences "the reeking odour pouring down his throat, clogging and revolting his entrails" (138), and is forced to vomit.

His phobia regarding ingesting is thus given a more explicit rationale. Clearly Stephen is unable to assimilate his own instinctive nature, for that nature is too closely linked to the Dublin world of squalor, to the instinctual wisdom he fears, and against which he erects his bulwarks of intellectual, bookish wisdom. His resistance is manifested, not so surprisingly, in terms of choking, clogging. Into the washstand that must, in his mind, be associated with the wash basin at the Hotel Wicklow and the word *suck*, Stephen vomits, that is, he allows his body's substance to be sucked from him. At the same time, his vision is reduced in power, and his forehead is cold and damp.

It is inevitable that under these conditions, Stephen must confess, or vomit up his sins, and his act is described in particularly evacuative terms: "His sins trickled from his lips, one by one, trickled in shameful drops from his soul festering and oozing like a sore, a squalid stream of vice. The last sins oozed forth, sluggish, filthy. There was no more to tell" (144). Thus in a complex train of associations, Stephen has transformed normal ingestion, transformation, and elimination into a metaphorical state in which his mouth and soul become orifices of elimination. The stream of vice produced in this confession lacks any element of creativity that, on a psychological level, is usually associated with the eliminative functions. Stephen not only is unable to assimilate his experience, he is also unable to transform it and must expel it.

Nevertheless, the act of expelling, even in this rather inverted form, is a kind of purge, and at the end of this chapter, as Stephen sits by the fire in his own kitchen, he views food in a more neutral manner. He observes: "On the dresser was a plate of sausages and white pudding and on the shelf there were eggs. They would be for the breakfast in the morning after the communion in the college chapel. White pudding and eggs and sausages and cups of tea. How simple and beautiful was life after all!" (147). At communion the next day, his eating is regarded in somewhat different terms. It is now God whom he wishes to assimilate; incorporeal substance cannot harm him:

*Corpus Domini nostri.*

Could it be? He knelt there sinless and timid: and he would hold upon his tongue the host and God would enter his purified body (146).

Chapter 4 reflects the same neutral, mortifying moods. Certainly Stephen's attitude toward the passions indicates how real his sense of mortification, of being emptied, is. He is, for example, unable to "harbour," that is, he is unable to contain,"passions" (149). We are told that "a brief anger had often *invested him*, but he had never been able to make it an abiding passion and had always felt himself *passing out of it* as if his very body were being divested with ease of some outer skin or peel'" (149, italics mine).

In this chapter, each of his senses is mortified. The gluttony he has indulged in (or imagines himself indulging in) that is both a feature of guilt and a condition of it is replaced by mortification of his sense of taste, and he now diverts his mind from food. His sense of smell poses other problems that suggest that his new mode of existence will be shortlived. This sense, the one least respected by man and the most highly developed in animals, is the one that Stephen still possesses and even values to a high degree. Indeed, he likes smells and is so comfortable with them that he must seek out particularly bad ones in order to successfully mortify this sense, finally discovering a certain "stale fishy stink" (151) to which he can subject himself.

Stephen is so removed from life and bodily processes at this point that he can only picture himself as a celebrant: "It was as in the pictures of the mass" (159). Even the sacrament, which involves ingestion, of course, becomes problematic. It fails to truly enter him and seems to "have turned into dried up sources" (152). Furthermore, he finds that "his actual reception of the eucharist did not bring him the same dissolving moments of virgin selfsurrender" (152).

Yet finding that a purely mystical type of surrender will not succeed, that stasis in terms of body functions as well as in terms of psychic life is destructive, he recognizes his need for surrender and dissolution. This need seems to remain a threat to him, and his attempt to transform it into an intellectual state does not diminish its power or presence: "The idea of surrender had a perilous attraction *for his mind* now that he felt his soul beset once again by the insistent voices of the flesh which began to murmur to him again" (152, italics mine).

Thus the "grave and ordered and passionless life" (160) he envisions after the Prefect's proposal is a passing fantasy. The unrest in him is too great, and as he contemplates this life, he begins to 'ingest' the sights and smells of another one: "His lungs dilated and sank as if he were inhaling a warm moist unsustaining air and he smelt again the warm moist air which hung in the bath in Clongowes above the sluggish turfcoloured water" (161). He realizes that he will not join the priesthood, that he is destined to be "elusive of social or religious orders" (162), and yet, in spite of this disturbing vision of the future, life, even the squalid life of Dublin, calls to him in positive ways: "The faint sour stink of rotted cabbages came towards him from the kitchengardens on the rising ground above the river. He smiled to think that it was this disorder, the misrule and confusion of his father's house and the stagnation of vegetable life, which was to win the day in his soul" (162).

He returns to his own kitchen where a description of a simple dinner table's contents takes on aspects of desolation: "The last of the second watered tea remained in the bottoms of the small glassjars and jampots.... Disgarded crusts and lumps of sugared bread, turned brown by the tea which had been poured over them, lay scattered on the table. Little wells of tea lay here and there on the board and a knife with a broken ivory handle was stuck through the pith of a ravaged turnover" (163). Stephen's strange view of the remnants of a family meal certainly reinforces Anderson's argument that his attitude toward food is phobic.[11] Yet the wording is vivid and also suggests that he can assuage his fears and pain in regard to the uglier aspects of life by means of language.

That his mind is moving in this direction we can see during his walk along the strand. Here he views himself as the artist "forging anew in his workshop out of the sluggish matter of the earth a new soaring impalpable imperishable being" (169). Although this newly awakened purpose seems to reflect sublimation more than anything else (for the end result will be a body "purified in a breath and delivered of incertitude and made radiant and commingled with the element of the spirit" (169), still, Joyce makes us see his Icarian fall, his failure to abandon the "dull gross voice of the world" (169). The cries of his swimming comrades "O, cripes, I'm drownded!" bring us back. Nevertheless, Stephen does momentarily overcome his fear of water, and as he wades, his soaring thoughts become diverted from sky to sea, finally merging as he observes: "The water of the rivulet was dark with endless drift and mirrored the high-drifting clouds" (170). And again: "He felt above him the vast indifferent dome and the *calm processes* of the heavenly bodies; and the earth beneath him, the earth that had borne him, had taken him to her breast" (172, italics mine). If earth and sky, matter and spirit, are not reconciled in Stephen's mind and heart, they suggest at this moment a benign environment and supply him with comforting symbols of nurturing.

By chapter 5 there is an acknowledgement of the need to accommodate the uglier sides of life described at the end of chapter 4, and in the opening scene there are images of food, water and excrement: "He drained his third cup of watery tea to the dregs and set to chewing the crusts of fried bread that were scattered near him, staring at the dark pool of the jar. The yellow dripping had been scooped out like a boghole and the pool under it brought back to his memory the dark turfcoloured water of the bath in Clongowes" (174). The image of the "turfcoloured" water appears many times and is obviously associated both with process (cycles of decay, dissolution, birth, and integration) and liquidities that describe the female principle. Other images repeat this association. The lane that Stephen walks through is "waterlogged" with "heaps of wet rubbish" and "mouldering offal" (175). The "rainsodden earth" gives off a "mortal odour," "a faint incense rising upward through the mould from many hearts" (184).

Besides his environment, Stephen has difficulties accepting his male companions without projecting upon them threatening aspects involving eating as well as the mouth and teeth. This important motif is carried over into *Ulysses* and appears most predominantly in "Telemachus." Even in chapter 5, Stephen's companions are almost always associated with natural processes or with eating. One lean student possesses an "open moist mouth" (196); another gulps down "the spittle in his throat as if he were gulping down the phrase" (198); and another has a "pallid bloated face" (210). Stephen accuses Lynch of eating pieces of "dried cowdung" as a boy (205). Even Stephen's attempt to define beauty is thwarted by food. In a conversation with Lynch and Cranly, he says to Lynch: "Do you remember the night? Cranly lost his temper and began to talk about Wicklow bacon" (207). Later he admonishes Lynch: "Art," he tells him, "is the human disposition of sensible or intelligent matter for an esthetic end. You remember the pigs and forget that" (207). Stephen's juxtaposition of the subject of art with Cranly's eating points up the general tendency he has to create his world in terms of polarities—himself against Cranly, art against physical process. He would naturally, therefore, see Cranly's eating and preference for discussing food as standing opposed to him, to matters dealing with art and the intellect.

It is not surprising that Cranly, as his closest friend and his most formidable opponent, is associated with food in a number of places. He is first seen dislodging "a figseed from his teeth on the point of his rude toothpick" (229). Cranly is also described as rooting "at his gleaming uncovered teeth," and as "sucking at a crevice in his teeth" (230). Throughout the pair's conversation (234-39), we have no less than five references to Cranly's fig chewing. As Stephen enters the group he sees that "Cranly had taken another dried fig from the supply in his pocket and was eating it slowly and noisily" (234). As the boys' conversation continues, Cranly continues to eat, at one point "holding out what remained of the halfchewed fig," which he jokingly offers to another (235). The fig is then described as "munched pulp" (235), a detail that is meaningless by itself but one to be reconsidered in the light of Molly's chewed seedcake. The development of the latter in *Ulysses* stems from Joyce's interest in the image as a commentary on nurturence and knowledge.

The conflict between Cranly and Stephen becomes intensified as Stephen tells Cranly that he has refused to make his Easter duty. Although Cranly's reproach is softened by his allowing that religious doubts can be overcome, a disturbed Stephen replies, "I do not wish to overcome them" (239). This reply causes Cranly to take out another fig and Stephen protests: "Don't please. You cannot discuss this question with your mouth full of chewed fig," upon which Cranly, throwing the fig into the gutter, disclaims, "Depart from me, ye cursed, into everlasting fire" (239), an act reminiscent of Stephen's rejection of food in chapter 3. Stephen still views physical ingestion as incompatible with the intellectual kind.

Cranly challenges him still further, however, and probably comes closest to making Stephen confront the nexus of the problem when he explains to Stephen his reluctance to "communicate": "You are not sure of that too, because you feel that the host too may be the body and blood of the son of God and not a wafer of bread? And because you fear that it may be?" (243). Stephen's answer is affirmative. "I feel that and I also fear it," he says, and Cranly, pursuing the question, asks, "But why do you fear a bit of bread?" (243). Stephen's reply is, "I imagine . . . that there is a malevolent reality behind those things I say I fear" (243). What he fears is the "chemical action which would be set up in my soul" (243). Below the metaphorical language, the fear of ingestion has been transformed into a fear of cannibalism that, paradoxically, involves not only Stephen's ingestion of the divine body, but a chemical reaction whereby he himself would be dissolved.

Later in his diary entries, he will bring up Cranly and the figs one more time. In his transformation of the earlier scenes, Stephen now projects Cranly as a John the Baptist figure. Having thus somewhat neutralized Cranly's threatening aspects by making him a precursor figure to the coming of Stephen, Cranly's food is poetically transformed too; "He eats chiefly belly bacon and dried figs. Read locusts and wild honey" (248). Yet for the harbinger of Christ, this food represents a fasting act more than the kind of ingestion we might normally associate with Cranly. By rendering Cranly in Biblical and mythic terms and his acts as a mortification rite, Stephen has, once again, created in the name of art a psychic shield.

Besides these male companions whose threatening features involve alimentary imagery, there is Stephen's attitude toward kissing to be considered. As a young boy, Stephen seems confused by the act. At Clongowes he is teased because "he kisses his mother every night" (14) and when he denies that he does so, he is teased anyway. The ambivalence of both his and the boys' feelings seems to disturb him: "He felt his whole body hot and confused in a moment. What was the right answer to the question?" (14). It is interesting that his body plays so dominant a role in his reaction here, although his mind, as always, gains dominance eventually. The result is a lot of thought about the subject of kissing: "What did that mean, to kiss? You put your face up like that to say goodnight and then his mother put her face down. That was to kiss. His mother put her lips on his cheek; her lips were soft and they wetted his cheek; and they made a tiny little noise: kiss" (15). Since we know that Stephen is made uncomfortable by both softness and wetness, and we also know that the "tiny little noise" may be associated in Stephen's mind with the disturbing word *suck* as well as with Dante's "noise after dinner" (11), we might infer that kissing here is not totally comfortable for him.

Later, Stephen's ambivalence about kissing seems more explicit. At one point he muses on the "language of memory" revealing "kind gentle women" with "sucking mouths" (233). In his encounter with the prostitute, we are told that "his lips would not bend to kiss her"

(101). This sentence is repeated twice. And yet Stephen also wants "to be held firmly in her arms, to be caressed" (101). He thus seems to desire surrender, to want to be absorbed while at the same time recoiling from the embrace. When he finally does surrender to the kiss, his emotions are profound: "He closed his eyes, surrendering himself to her, body and mind, conscious of nothing in the world but the dark pressure of her softly parting lips. They pressed upon his brain as upon his lips as though they were the vehicle of a vague speech" (101). Although Stephen seems to close his eyes and surrender his mind, he never abandons his cognitive processes that are his protection against total absorption. That her lips press on his brain indicates how conditional his surrender really is. Bearing in mind what has been said about Stephen's use of language as a defense against engulfment, we can note here, as in a number of instances, that women are associated with some kind of speech to which Stephen lacks access. I think Stephen's reference to the mute speech of women, or, as in this case, the "vague speech" of the woman's lips, is indicative of his deepest fears. Obviously women have some hold on a kind of language that he does not possess.

Closely linked to eating and kissing is Stephen's fascination with the image of the bat. A number of years ago William York Tindall, in a discussion of *Chamber Music*, noted that Joyce endowed "bats and the softness of a kiss" with the "inescapable suggestion of vampirism."[12] Joyce's apparent interest with the female as bat figure derives from the basically alimental character of the image. First, the kiss has long been known to have its basis, not in affection between the sexes, but in eating. As Robert Briffault has observed, "Sexual attraction, sexual 'hunger' as it has been aptly called, is a form of veracity. The object of the male cell in seeking conjunction with the female cell is primarily to improve its nutrition, in the same manner, and by virtue of the same fundamental impulse as it seeks food."[13] Vampirism is also associated with eating and cannibalism as well as with the domain of the Terrible Mother. Thus this image seems to suggest that for Stephen, female figures never truly become *animas* but retain their associations with the mother. Despite his efforts to render his females into bird figures, they never really transcend their associations with earth.

Joyce's most important use of the bat image in *A Portrait* emerges from the story of Davin's encounter with the strange country women. Although Stephen is only told of the event, it seems to move him.

That the woman is an archetypal figure is evident from the fact that she offers Davin a mug of milk, that she is bare-breasted, apparently pregnant, and that she invites him into her cottage for the night. Stephen thinks of this woman as a "batlike soul waking to the consciousness of itself in darkness and secrecy and loneliness" (183). "Batlike soul" seems almost a contradiction in terms since the bat is an animal associated with eating as well as flying, but the soul usually transcends both darkness and abodes like caves where a bat would live. The woman seems to represent elemental energies. She offers nourishment and sexual gratification, but to enter her darkness is to be devoured. Davin would not be the only one to decline her invitation.[14]

Despite Stephen's recourse to language as a protection against the devouring tendencies of country, church and mother, his use of language and his thoughts about the creative process contain a good deal of alimentary symbolism. Of course Stephen tries to make his brain take over all the functions of his body. At one point he envisions his "soul shrivilled up," as he walks "on in a lane among heaps of dead language" (178-79). This internal conflict does not cause him to create, but seems instead to suggest a sterile elimination to him: "His own consciousness of language was ebbing from his brain and trickling into the very words themselves which set to band and disband themselves in wayward rhythms" (179). What he creates is a verse that begins, "*The ivy whines upon the wall*" that he immediately characterizes as "drivel" (179). But he raises the word *ivy* to *ivory* and attempts thereby to remove from it all of its earth-associated and organic nature so that "The word now shone in his brain, clearer and brighter than any ivory sawn from the mottled tusks of elephants" (179).

When he is not relegating the digestive process to his brain, he is still struggling to "express from lumps of earth" (189) his sense of beauty. He says to Lynch that through the understanding of things, the artist must "try slowly and humbly and constantly to express, to press out again, from the gross earth, or what it brings forth, from sound and shape and colour which are the prison gates of our soul, an image of the beauty we have come to understand" (207). McKnight, picking up on Stephen's use of the word *express* rightly observes: "Language also becomes an excrescence, and through language the artist can express himself, press himself out of a confining space. Parturition and peristalsis seems fused together."[15] But Stephen the artist and Joyce the artist are not synonymous. Stephen, who is "wounded . . . to think that he would never be but a shy guest at the feast of the world's culture," striving to "forge out an esthetic philosophy" (180), is not the complete artist that Joyce is. Stephen prefers aesthetics to kinesis; Joyce knows that kinesis is necessary, for he is Leopold Bloom as well. The problems of creativity rely on the body for solution, and Joyce's "epic of the body," *Ulysses*, offers a fuller and more satisfying comment on that important relationship between body and the creative process.

## *Ulysses*

It is quickly apparent that the Stephen of *Ulysses* is still characterized by his fear of being devoured and a tendency to conceptualize body functions. That is, Stephen's physical functions become analogues of spiritual ones, since functions of the lower body pole are still associated with sin. Thus, turning these functions into a language of metaphor, Stephen diminishes their threatening nature. "Telemachus" is dominated both by the figure of Buck Mulligan and the image of Stephen's dead mother. We learn early that Stephen's guilt over his mother's death is connected to his rebellion against the Church and his self-imposed exile from Ireland. In "Telemachus," the mother figure is, therefore, a complex of images and is associated with the "snotgreen sea," the "scrotumtightening sea,"[16] the sea that drowns. (All subsequent references to *Ulysses* are cited parenthetically in the text.)

Another prominent, devouring figure that Stephen has to contend with is Mulligan, whose threatening aspect is manifested in part by the many references to his mouth or to his eating. It is no accident that "Toothless Kinch" (22) sees himself pitted against "Chrysostomos" (3), "golden mouth" Mulligan. So dubbed because his teeth are "glistening" with "gold points," (3) Mulligan's mouth is commented upon a number of times. For example, Stephen notices his "curling shaven lips," his "edges of . . . white glittering teeth" (6), his "white teeth" (13). We also hear a lot about Mulligan's plumpness. He has a "plump face" (6) and a "wellfed voice" (5), and unlike Stephen, seems to eat a lot. At breakfast Stephen watches him fill "his mouth with a crust thickly buttered on both sides" (15).

Mulligan is also a "mocker," a "usurper" and a "false priest," and it seems clear in this chapter that part of his threat to Stephen derives from the fact that he is both an assimilating and expressive figure. We are far more aware of his eating than we are of Stephen's, for it is Mulligan who sings, chants, laughs, eats, and drinks. In exuberance, he even combines song, language and food in typically saturnalian verse:

> *O, won't we have a merry time*
> *Drinking whisky, beer, and wine,*
> *On coronation,*
> *Coronation day?*
> *O, won't we have a merry time*
> *On coronation day?* (11)

It is also clear that Mulligan is the maker of language. He intones his "ballad of Joking Jesus" (as Stephen tells Haines) "three times a day, after meals" (19). His recitation of the *Introit* during the opening paragraph, when he raises his shaving bowl and razor, suggests his parody of the mass, of course, but the bowl is also a container that has associations with Stephen's mother.

It is less the chalice that Stephen imagines, a *vas mirabili* of transformation, than it is the bowl into which she vomits bile. Also, Mulligan's razor is the attribute of "Kinch"—an implement now turned against Stephen.

Mulligan's threatening aspects are also illustrated by the large number of references to aggressive behavior or pointed objects. Besides his pointed teeth, his slice of bread is "impaled" on a knife. He is seen "hewing thick slices from the loaf," and we are told that he "hacked through the fry on the dish and slapped it out on three plates" (12).

Perhaps the most threatening aspect of Mulligan involves more intangible concerns, especially those involving process, that is the manifestation of energy in growth, maturation, and decay, all the transformations that involve man and the cosmos. When Mulligan calls Stephen "dogsbody" (6), and also refers to his mother as "*beastly dead*" (8), he is outraged. Previously, in *A Portrait,* Stephen has been able to acknowledge to Lynch, "We are all animals. I also am an animal" (206), but the idea never sits well with him. The suggestion of his animal nature, which also implies the omnipresence of process, leads to questions about boundaries constructed by the intellect. Mulligan, in these instances and throughout this episode, seems to function as a kind of mediator, both for the mother figure and for the process for which she stands.

For example, Mulligan is called "Mercurial Malachi" (17), both here and later on in "Circe," and as he begins his dive off the fortyfoot, the image of Mercury is used again. He is described as "fluttering his winglike hands, leaping nimbly, his Mercury's hat quivering in the fresh wind that bore back to them his brief birdlike cries" (19). Mulligan, like Mercury, is a trickster figure, an archetypal personification of the dissolution of boundaries. Like all trickster figures, he is comfortable in water; yet he is also a bird; he dives and ascends, paralleling the ability of the trickster figures to pass between heaven and the underworld, to have both animal and human parts. Stephen's great fear of dissolving boundaries, expressed metaphorically in his hatred of water, his fear of sexuality, his guilt over his mother, is thus projected onto the figure of Mulligan who can save men from drowning, who wears priestly robes that suggest the blending of sexes as well as the blending of the sacred and profane.[17]

Mulligan's association with the *omphalos*, usually taken to mean the navel and which is also associated with things phallic, has some interesting antecedents in the myth of Heracles. The word *omphalos* derives from *Omphale*, the name of the queen who held Heracles captive. During his captivity, Heracles often dressed in women's clothes. Robert Graves observes that the later interpretations of the myth saw the *omphalos* as "the seat of female desire" and Heracles as the slave of a domineering woman. But the earlier meaning, he says, involves ritual practices in which Heracles was a deputy of the queen and assumed her garments as he assumed her functions.[18] These interpretations shed some light on Mulligan's function as a priest. It is he who loves the sea, who reminds Stephen of his "sin" against his mother, who becomes associated in Stephen's mind with guilt. Mulligan's role as a mediator also seems to be suggested by the fact that, as Mulligan tells Stephen, his aunt "won't let me have anything to do with you" (5). Mulligan's subservience and his aunt's role as punisher of Stephen seem strange unless we view the aunt and Mulligan as servants of the archetypal mother. Mulligan's association with the goddess is also suggested by the fact that he is comfortable with fluids, with change.

In any case, it is Mulligan's reproach that calls to memory Stephen's dream about his mother. Stephen's vision involves mostly smells—"odour of wax and rosewood, her breath, that had bent upon him, mute, reproachful, a faint odour of wetted ashes" (5). But it is also significant that the mother is envisioned as mute, that there is always the suggestion of secrecy about her, that Stephen speaks of "her secrets," of "love's bitter mystery" (9), and of "mute secret words" (10). Her only expression in "Telamachus" seems to be her vomiting of "greenish sluggish bile" (5).

In this chapter, Stephen's fear of being eaten becomes also a fear of drowning, and this fear intensifies as the chapter progresses. Stephen says to Mulligan, "You saved men from drowning. I'm not a hero, however" (4). The phrase "five fathoms" recalls Shakespeare's drowning man in *The Tempest* when Stephen imagines a "swollen bundle" with a "puffy face, salt white" (21). Here, assimilation seems associated not with life but with death. The seawater then becomes a "deep jelly" (21); when the sea darkens to a "deeper green" (9), it brings back to the memory of his mother and the green bile. His silent accusation, "Ghoul! Chewer of the corpses!" (10), may be uttered at God, at nature, or at process, but it is also followed immediately with, "No, Mother. Let me be and let me live" (10). To Stephen's associative mind, the mother, not God, is the devourer because it is she who symbolizes silence, darkness, mystery—nondifferentiated consciousness, the sea.

The morning breakfast in the tower seems a normal occurrence and an example of naturalistic detail, But it serves as the focus of tension between Mulligan and Stephen and is a scene that seems to awaken the artistic nature in Stephen. It is, of course, dominated by Mulligan who is described as a kind of alchemist (the intellectual counterpart of the trickster figure): "In the gloomy domed livingroom of the tower Buck Mulligan's gowned form moved briskly about the hearth to and fro, hiding and revealing its yellow glow. Two shafts of soft daylight fell across the flagged floor from the high barbicans: and at the meeting of their rays a cloud of coalsmoke and fumes of fried grease floated, turning" (11). Mulligan is the one who frys the breakfast, carries "dish and a large teapot" to the table, and orders the other two: "Kinch, wake up. . . . Bread, butter, honey. Haines, come in. The grub is ready. Bless us, O Lord, and these thy gifts. Where's the sugar?" (12). When he demands, "I want Sandycove milk," the old milkwoman appears almost on cue. Perhaps his nature as trickster figure is best exemplified on all levels when, changing his voice to old Mother Grogen's, he quips, "When I makes tea I makes tea. . . . . And when I makes water I makes water" (12). Not only does he dissolve boundaries in terms of voice and sex, but tea becomes urine; eating and elimination are transformed linguistically in terms of a pun into the complements they are.

Mulligan has ordered Stephen to pour tea, and Stephen is also forced to pay the milkwoman, but aside from his three cups of tea and Mulligan's accusation, "You have eaten all we left, I suppose" (17), we have no view of Stephen eating. We are told he has eaten the remains. Remains become associated with his mother and also later with the husks of swine, eaten by the Prodigal son.

What Stephen does during the meal demonstrates again his tendency to transform meals and eating into words or metaphor. When Mulligan teases him about his monthly bath, the subject of washing causes Stephen to think of Ireland. "All Ireland," he says, "is washed by the gulfstream" (16). As he utters these words, he is pouring honey over his slice of bread. The suggestion seems to be that Ireland, washed by the gulfstream, is not cleansed or rejuvenated. Honey, a pure food that inhibits the growth of bacteria, that inhibits, in other words, decay, is poured over the bread the way Stephen's art will be poured over the daily bread of existence. But here the image does not seem to suggest any real transformation, that any true art will result, and the question of whether Stephen will change that bread into a "radiant body" seems to receive a negative answer. Instead, we have Stephen saying, in reference to Mulligan, "I eat his salt bread" (20). This is a reference, Weldon Thornton tells us, from the "Paradiso" where it is predicted that Dante will partake of the suffering of others and that being exiled, he will prove "how salt the savour is of other's bread."[19]

As we will see presently, the old milkwoman does suggest some hope for Stephen, but Mulligan patronizes her, tasting her milk at her bidding, saying "If we could only live on good food like that . . . we wouldn't have the country full of rotten teeth and rotten guts. Living in a bogswamp, eating cheap food and the streets paved with dust, horsedung and comsumptives' spits" (14). The image of death, decay, and excrement and even the reference to rotting teeth must cause Stephen an uncomfortable moment of identification. Symbolically, his mouth is full of decay because he cannot assimilate the squalor of Ireland, and yet this is what he must learn to do if he is to be the artist.

For Stephen the milkwoman is threatening. He first sees the doorway "darkened by an entering form" (13) who is "old and secret," "maybe a messenger," "a witch on her toadstool" (13) Yet although the scene disturbs him, he develops some interesting images about her. She is a "lowly form of an immortal serving her conqueror and her gay betrayer" (14)—Haines and Mulligan. But she is also, as Stephen repeats, "a messenger from the secret morning" (14), the personification of energy from the unconscious who serves to awaken something in Stephen. It is out of this breakfast that Stephen will begin to make his art. His vision of the old woman with the "old shrunken paps" is also a vision of that woman "crouching by a patient cow at daybreak in the lush field," the witch with "wrinkled fingers quick at the squirting dugs" (13-14). Although she is old and dried up, she can supply rich milk. She is not just a figure of death, associated with Stephen's mother; she is the substance of Stephen's art, an energizing image, the figure he must first assimilate and render harmless.

In "Nestor," where memory and history are dominant concerns, Stephen contends with Deasy and another kind of stasis—that produced by history, which is also an inhibitor of process but at the same time a betrayer of life and therefore of truth. As in "Telamachus," Stephen indicates an aversion to process and a preoccupation with the mouth in terms of certain kinds of language.

Stephen's first conflict with history, however, is in relation to his students who exemplify process to him. For example, he notices one student, Armstrong, whose satchel is filled with figrolls, crumbs that "adhered to the tissues of his lips," and his "sweetened boy's breath" (24). Other students also have "breaths, too, sweetened with tea and jam" (25).

But Stephen feels removed from these boys; their laughter suggests to him their lack of innocence. They ingest figrolls; he ingests knowledge. Memory creates for him the library of St. Genevieve where "he had read, sheltered from the sin of Paris," and he thinks, "fed and feeding brains about me" (25). As Stephen continues, "in my mind's darkness a sloth of the underworld, reluctant, shy of brightness, shifting her dragon scaly folds," (25), we see again that for him natural functions carry the stamp of sin, and feeding becomes a mental process. Feeding the brain means starving the mind's darkness, which is imaged as female. The threat of being devoured must come to his mind now because his train of associations involves drowning and devouring. Talbot recites the verse of "Lycidas," "*Sunk though he be beneath the watery floor*" (25), and Stephen recalls Aristotle's phrase that "floated out into the studious silence of the library" (25). His thoughts about his mind's darkness are countered by Talbot's further recital about "Him that walked on the waves" (26). Stephen fears being sunk to the watery floor; he depends on words "to float" him so that he, like Jesus, can walk the waves.

Stephen next creates a special kind of language. For those who couldn't understand, Jesus spoke in parables. Stephen speaks in riddles. But his riddle is not a legitimate one. It is unanswerable and confusing to the students:

> *The cock crew*
> *The sky was blue:*
> *The bells in heaven*
> *Were striking eleven.*
> *Tis time for this poor soul*
> *To go to heaven* (26).

The boy's question, "What is that?" seems to ask whether the poem is, in fact, a riddle at all. Although the students appear interested in the answer, it is really Stephen who needs to know it. His conclusion, "The fox burying his grandmother under a hollybush" (27) is certainly not enlightening. Most critics see the lines as an attempt by Stephen to rid himself of guilt over death of his mother. Certainly the displacement of mother for grandmother is tenable, but more than an attempt to bury any crime, it seems necessary for Stephen/Christ/fox to bury the threatening aspects of the mother who stands for all threats to his identity. It is also an attempt on Stephen's part to control his animal nature through language. The poem, with its rigid form and meter, provides a safe structure for the dangerous energies evoked by the images of the fox and the death of his mother.

Still the images of process haunt him. The boys explode into activity, fleeing him for the hockey game in a "clamor of . . . boots and tongues" (27). Their noise replaces Stephen's obscure language. One child, however, remaining behind, intensifies his feeling of engulfment. This child, Sargent, has, like the young Stephen, "misty glasses weak eyes" and cheek "dull and bloodless" with a mark of ink upon it "recent and damp as a snail's bed" (27). "Like him was I" (28), Stephen thinks as the boy's image revives his musings about art. Instead of being rendered immortal by fading into his art, Stephen is forced to face himself as a fragile but very alive child; the ink on the boy's face has not made beautiful language, but has become a "stain," a "snail's bed" (27). Then the boy himself becomes a snail with "weak watery blood." The implications of process refuse to remain buried. "Was that then real?" Stephen asks himself, recalling his mother's "prostrate body" (27). Again his mind pulls back the image of the fox. This time the language is more powerful, truly evocative: "On a heath beneath winking stars a fox, red reek of rapine in his fur, with merciless bright eyes scraped in the earth, listened, scraped up the earth, listened, scraped and scraped"(28). Critics have long suspected that the fox is trying to uncover as much as he is trying to bury.[20] But it is not so much Stephen's misdeeds that he must disinter as the knowledge he needs to be creative. The rapine nature of Stephen and the fox involves a need to descend into mystery, in Jungian terms, to undergo a urobouric descent. This descent is a symbolic return to the womb whereby the hero, if he survives, is born again, but this time becomes the father himself.

Garrett Deasy represents another example of the refusal of the past to be buried. With his hoarding tendencies and his materialism, he indeed manifests "all the traits of a typically anal-retentive personality," as Suzette Henke suggests.[21] And he also represents another threat to Stephen. Mulligan was all digestion and expression; Deasy hoards, and his expression is characterized by flatulence. Mulligan is active, Deasy represents stasis; Mulligan represents fluidities, Deasy represents solids.

Deasy's interest in the mouth and its words is particularly sterile and life-denying. "Do you know," he asks Stephen, "what is the proudest word you will ever hear from an Englishman's mouth?" The answer is "*I paid my way*" (30). Beyond the materialistic values implicit in the answer, Stephen is disturbed by the boastful language. Furthermore, for him, Englishmen are the heirs to the Roman watercloset and victims of indigestion. The association of words with things monetary is also alien to him. Deasy is, of course, full of words, but they are only rhetorical clichés. He tells Stephen loftily, "We are a generous people but we must also be just" and Stephen answers, "I fear those big words" (31). Deasy's linguistic creation is, appropriately, an editorial on foot and mouth disease. Again, Joyce enjoys blending language with content. Deasy says to Stephen, "Mark my words," and later on adds, "I don't mince words, do I?" (33). Mincing words is an alimentary metaphor and is exactly what Deasy does do. He is affected, and his rhetoric is constipated and choppy. An example: Speaking of his cure for foot and mouth disease, he says, "Now I'm going to try publicity. I am surrounded by difficulties, by . . . intrigues, by . . . backstairs influence." (33). His accusation that the Jews "eat up the nation's vital strength" (33) is ironic since Deasy is himself dessicated, eaten up, and yet, according to him, there are no Jews in Ireland.

James H. Maddox makes the point that Stephen and Bloom think of "the world of process as essentially feminine."[22] In "Nestor" this idea is pointed up in negative terms in Deasy's projections on powerful—therefore threatening—women such as Cassandra, Eve, Helen, Kitty O'Shea. What these projections also signify is the deficiency of his own feminine nature. His anal retentiveness, suggesting on a physical level the absence of fluidity, marks him as psychologically rigid. He is reminiscent of Mr. Duffy of "A Painful Case" and here personifies for Stephen the dangers of repression, atrophied intellect, meaningless rhetoric, as well as the dangers of getting caught—emotionally, intellectually, and linguistically—in linear time and in surface, or ego consciousness.

J. Mitchell Morse has stated, in his discussion of the "Proteus" episode, that if Stephen is to be a serious artist, he must experience the beast; he must "become identified with the beast, mere nature, the universe, the unconscious and indifferent all-embracing all," but that he must be "neither put off nor absorbed."[23] Thus, "Pan's hour, the faunal noon" (49), that Stephen seems to recognize as a time when boundaries dissolve, is the time in which he must deal with his own dissolution of, or reconciliation with, matter, a task necessitated by the dictates of process. This struggle inevitably involves body functions, some of which are digestive.

As usual, food and ingestion are often disguised or sublimated by Stephen, and when direct references to food appear in his thoughts, they are usually associated with people whose lives and minds are much different from his own, people who tend to be simple, whose natures are more animal and instinctual. Thus we find Stephen recalling food in connection with Paris, where its citizens are "globbers" who "fork spiced beans down their gullets" (42). He recalls "eating your groatsworth of *mou en civet*, fleshpots of Egypt" and being "elbowed by belching cabmen" (41). The unappetizing stew, the reference to *fleshpots of Egypt* (a phrase used by the sorrowful children of Israel upon their exile from the land where "we did eat bread to the full,")[24] suggests Stephen's ingestion of Paris life and is also accompanied by a disgust that is similar to the kind that Bloom will experience as he watches the eaters in the Burton. Stephen also recalls from his Paris stay "moist pith of farls of bread," the "kerchiefed housewife" "a saucer of acetic acid in her hands," and Yvonne and Madeleine . . . shattering with gold teeth *chaussons* of pastry, their mouths yellowed with the *pus* of *flan breton*" (42). The acetic acid suggests the bowl of bitter waters associated with Stephen's mother, and the gold teeth are reminiscent of Mulligan's.

Stephen also recalls his meeting with Kevin Egan, the Irish nationalist (a man not unlike his own father), in terms of eating. He describes Egan as follows: "Around the slabbed tables the tangle of wined breaths and grumbling gorges. His breath hangs over our saucestained plates, the green fairy's fang thrusting between his lips" (43). This scene conveys Stephen's disillusionment with the romantic and sentimental personalities of his father and Egan.

His reverie on Uncle Richie Goulding contains another food reference that also suggests his association of food with the common people like his father. In his imagination he sees himself going to Richie's house and being offered "a rich of a rasher fired with a herring" (39). But Richie's house is a house of "decay," and it seems clear that Stephen further associates food with the world of poverty and decay. He also, of course, associates eating with devouring females. In "Proteus" he refers to Queen Victoria twice as the "old hag with the yellow teeth" (43, 50).

Sometimes Stephen makes food and language blend in sound. Recalling his meeting with Egan's son Patrice, he thinks: "lapped warm milk with me in the bar MacMahon. Son of the wild goose, Kevin Egan of Paris. My father's a bird, he lapped the sweet *lait chaud* with pink young tongue, plump bunny's face. Lap, *lapin*" (41). Again Stephen focuses on plumpness and on animal qualities, but out of these animal and assimilative images he creates language.

For the most part, process in Stephen's consciousness involves a sense of devouring, and the eating function is transformed into a vast symbol of devouring by nature. One aspect of this symbol involves Stephen's childhood fascination/revulsion with the word *suck*. In *A Portrait* it is sound, the swallowing aspect of the basin full of water and its threatening whiteness that moves him. In "Proteus" Stephen seems to encounter the word as a force especially associated with his mother and the process of eating.[25] In the opening lines of the chapter, he sees himself "walking into eternity" (37). He also sees the two cocklepickers are in the same predicament as he is with "splayed feet sinking in the silted sand. Like me, like Algy, coming down to our mighty mother" (37). Later he thinks of Sandymount strand as "unwholesome sandflats" that "waited to suck his treading soles" (41). This phrase, perhaps with a pun intended, followed by a description of the sand as "breathing upward sewage breath" (41), leaves no doubt that he views the mouth as associated with the downward-pulling tendency of earth, an orifice associated more with decay than the new growth. There is also a porter bottle standing up "stogged to its waist, in the cakey sand dough" (41). Personified as a sentinel, the bottle has also been swallowed by this "isle of dreadful thirst" just as Stephen may become swallowed by a country that drinks up its people's vitality. When he gets even nearer the sea, so that it even covers his boots, he thinks of his feet again sinking "slowly in the quaking soil" and commands himself to "turn back" (44). He does turn back to the tower where Mulligan and Haines wait in the "cold domed room" but, neither returning nor surrendering, we are told that he lifts, "his feet up from the suck and turned back by the mole of boulders" (44).

Sitting on his "stool of rock" he encounters now the "bloated carcass of a dog" (44). Stephen seems to call up a number of images of bloating (the drowning man is also bloated), and the associations of bloating with death, although natural enough, also shows his inclination to mark ingestion in yet another negative way. People who eat, in his mind, are men like his father and Richie, or drowned men who have eaten the sea, or the dog, bloated by decay—the stopping of process, also sunk in sand. Surely this image serves to objectify Stephen's fears for himself, and it is at this point that he makes his interesting metaphor about sand and language. He thinks,"These heavy sands are language tide and wind have silted here" (44). Although the dog has been partially swallowed by sand, sucked under too, the sand can also be a medium; in its dynamic relationship to the two other elements—water and air—it becomes a signature, the medium through which the elements express themselves.

The live dog that next appears on the scene is just as threatening to Stephen in real terms as the dead dog has been in metaphorical ones. Its behavior is especially interesting and foreshadows Stephen's. It approaches the carcass of the dead dog, and its actions are translated into interesting language by Stephen: "He stopped, sniffed, stalked round it, brother, nosing closer, went round it, sniffing rapidly like a dog all over the dead dog's bedraggled fell. Dogskull, dogsniff, eyes on the ground, moves to one great goal. Ah, poor dogsbody. Here lies poor dogsbody's body" (46). Interestingly, the language of Deasy and Mulligan seems to preside over the body of Stephen's image which is sunk in mud and bloated by the sea. But what seems to lie here is his deadened intellectual self, his fragmentizing intelligence, while the living dog and its instinctual energy seem actually to grow out of the dead.

As the dog changes again, so also does Stephen's view of it. It urinates on a rock and Stephen notes: "His hindpaws then scattered sand: then his forepaws dabbled and delved. Something he buried there, his grandmother. He rooted in the sand, dabbling, delving and stopped to listen to the air, scraped up the sand again with a fury of his claws, soon ceasing, a pard, a panther, got in spouse-breach, vulturing the dead" (46-47). The last phrase makes explicit Stephen's fear that he is really the eater of the dead, that the burial of his hostility toward his mother is countered by his need to disinter that hostility and confront the fears upon which is based.[26]

Despite his protests in "Circe," "Cancer did it, not I" (580), he does view himself as responsible for his mother's death, and his guilt is depicted in digestive terms.

Then the images of the dog, alive and dead, coalesce and aid Stephen in producing a vision of process imaged also in terms of eating. He makes a history grounded in the physical nature of things, in which: "A school of turlehide whales stranded in hot noon, spouting, hobbling in the shallows. Then from the starving cagework city a horde of jerkined dwarfs, my people, with flayers' knives, running, scaling, hacking in green blubbery whalemeat. Famine, plague and slaughters. Their blood is in me, their lusts my waves. I moved among them on the frozen Liffey" (45). Beginning with a history of a slaughter, Stephen then dissolves past time by establishing himself as protean, as a part of process, as he takes the attributes of Mulligan and Deasy as his own. Out of them he makes, at least temporarily, a new substance of himself. Nevertheless, he does remain separate, saying, "I spoke to no-one: none to me" (45).

The dog remains threatening, a "dog of my enemy," and Stephen narrates his experience as it happens: "I just simply stood pale, silent, bayed about." This last phrase, linking the baying of the dog with the waters that surround him, causes him to think of Mulligan who has "saved men from drowning and you shake at a cur's yelping" (45). Perhaps, he thinks, he could save someone. "I am not a strong swimmer. Water cold soft. When I put my face into it in the basin at Clongowes. Can't see" (45). Now his thoughts are literally drowned in water images. Not to be able to see is to surrender ego consciousness to the unconscious. This surrender is imaged in the drowning man and the mother. Both figures merge in his thoughts: "A drowning man. His human eyes scream to me out of horror of his death. I . . . With him together down . . . I could not save her. Waters: bitter death: lost" (46). Again his efforts to be a hero like Mulligan fail, and the drowning man represents both the mother he could not save and the self who is afraid to drown in powerful if repressed feelings. This drowning-man image continues to play an important role in "Proteus," and I shall return to it later. First, however, some other images of woman need mention.

The cocklepickers Stephen first sees are transformed into midwives. Like the old milkwoman, their association with process is cast in a negative light. Like the milkwoman, they connote mystery. "What has she in that bag?" Stephen asks. But his answer is, a "misbirth" (37). He next contemplates Eve's navel-less "belly without blemish bulging big" (38). This image too becomes negative and the belly becomes a "womb of sin" (38).

Memory of his mother causes him to remember Mulligan's aunt, and he chants a little song called "Hanigan's Aunt," which he, of course, in keeping with the chapter, has changed. Zack Bowen points out that the song, about a domineering woman, has final lines that Stephen doesn't sing but which may be relevant to his resentment of his mother and his dislike of process. These are:

> But still, I'd like to add—
> If Hanigan isn't about—
> That when we plant Mat Hanigan's Aunt,
> We won't be too put out.[27]

Stephen's omission of these lines may indicate that the planting metaphor as well as the song's ambiguous attitude toward the aunt hits too close to home.

In any case, the cocklepickers change again to become gypsies, and the woman (now there is a man and a woman) takes on aspects of a temptress. Stephen imagines her "calling under her brown shawl from an archway where dogs have mired" (47). This fantasy is a foretaste of "Circe" and combines the squalor of Dubin and the sinfulness of women with dog's excrement—all the elements with which Stephen must come to terms. Interestingly, the woman does evoke more than a few lascivious lines. As she passes him she becomes metamorphosed into Woman, fallen Eve, tracking "across the sands of all the world" (47). His muse, his temptress figure, moving across sand suggests that he needs her to chart, to make a path of language in those sands which will serve as his signature, his medium. But again the image fades into that of his mother, and he thinks: "Bridebed, childbed, bed of death, ghostcandled. *Omnis caro ad te veniet.* He comes, pale, vampire, through storm his eyes, his bat sails bloodying the sea, mouth to her mouth's kiss" (47–48).

Especially important here is the significance of kissing. Always an ambivalent act for Stephen, it is a sign of surrender, a sign of lust, but beyond that it retains its most primitive character. The pale vampire image is assumed to be an image of death, of course. Shechner observes that Stephen views the moment of his mother's expiration as a "ghostly kiss," by the "hangman God."[28] God as the pale vampire is needed a threatening image for Stephen, especially since he changes Hyde's life from "mouth to her mouth's kiss" to "mouth to my mouth" (The poem Stephen composes on the strand on a piece of paper torn from Deasy's editorial does not appear until the "Aeolus" chapter). Shechner, pondering homosexual implications in this line change, argues that Stephen may be indulging in his own kiss of death fantasy, but may also be "witness to the murderous kiss *and* the deadly incubus *and* the victim of murderous oral rape."[29] Shechner seems to give the lines too much emphasis here, and I am not sure that Stephen's view of the vampire as male or female matters in a chapter where sex changes seem appropriate. I think the image is masculine here because breath is associated with the creator/father and the masculine principle. Nevertheless, Stephen still shows us a consciousness terrified of being devoured by elemental energies. Here the threat is neither earth nor water but air. The rumination continues, and the phrase alters again to "mouth to her womb. Oomb, allwombing tomb. His mouth moulded issuing breath, unspeeched: ooeeehah: roar of catactic planets, globed, blazing, roaring, wayawayawayawayawayaway. Paper" (48). Breath is "unspeeched." It involves the upper body pole. While urinating he creates a wave-speech, and the lower body pole becomes the source of creation. Both poles create language out of matter, and it seems as if Stephen has achieved, at least for the moment, some reconciliation of opposites.

Body functions are particularly in evidence of this episode. Stephen thinks about Arius, the "illstarred heresiarch" who dies in a watercloset with "clotted hinderparts" (38). Stephen still associates sin with excrement. But his urination seems a positive act, making its own statement about his encounter with elemental energy. Although he still views process as "to no end gathered: vainly then released, forth flowing, wending back" (49-50), he nonetheless evolves a language out of his urination that shows us a Stephen who does not seem to be repressed or intellectualizing, as his language seems to grow out of the act itself. The passage must be quoted in full:

> In long lassoes from the Cock lake the water flowed full, covering greengoldenly lagoons of sand, rising, flowing. My ashplant will float away. I shall wait. No, they will pass on, passing chafing against the low rocks, swirling, passing. Better get this job over quick. Listen: a fourworded wavespeech: seesoo, hrss, rsseeiss, ooos. Vehement breath of waters amid seasnakes, rearing horses, rocks. In cups of rocks it slops: flop, slop, slap: bounded in barrels. And, spent, its speech ceases. It flows purling, widely flowing, floating foampool, flower unfurling. (49)

Stephen's own water "covering greengoldenly lagoons of sand," is of course a correlative of his own writing, the creation of language on sand by the tides it replicated in his symbolically fructifying act. For a moment, he thinks of his ashplant that might "float away." Nevertheless, and in spite of the risk of being seen by the cocklepickers, he continues. He turns to hear a new language, a "wavespeech." This "breath of waters"—air metamorphosed into water—becomes visual forms of animals, "seasnakes" and "rearing horses" as well as inanimate matter, rocks. His fructifying waters, joining with the sea, create both sound and sights. When they cease to make language, they still retain action—flowing on, becoming a "flower unfurled." The passage seems a remarkably comprehensive one. In it we have seminal waters identified with air in an almost Heraclatian transformation/ rotation of elements.

This momentary reconciliation of the ego with the unconscious, the solitary with the unitary, does not keep Stephen from evoking his darkest vision of the drowning man. On the contrary, it may be what allows him to face the nature of sea change and make language an evocation process. Having imagined the "corpse rising saltwhite from the undertow" (50) he imagines himself instrumental in bringing it up. I think his imaginary role is important. To counter Mulligan's ability to save men from drowning, Stephen will pull drowned men to the surface: "Bag of corpsegas sopping in foul brine. A quiver of minnows, fat of a spongy titbit, flash through the slits of his buttoned trouserfly. God becomes man becomes fish becomes barnacle goose becomes featherbed mountain. Dead breaths I living breathe, tread dead dust, devour a urinous offal from all dead" (50).[30] Besides the recognition of the uglier sides of process, in the symboliotic nature of all life with its inevitable cannibalism, Stephen seems aware of his own role as a "chewer of corpses" as the "pale vampire." It is this unpleasant fact of reciprocity on the alimentary level that Stephen needs to assimilate to become the artist. And, in fact, assimilation does seem to begin in "Proteus."

It is probably no coincidence that after this harrowing vision Stephen says, "Come, I thirst" (50). Although there may be some reference to the crucifixion and Christ's thirst on the cross, I think his words indicate a thirst for life that has suddenly become more physical and less intellectual.

Stephen performs one other interesting act before the chapter ends. He picks his nose and deposits the mucus on a rock. There are a number of interpretations of Stephen's act. Richard Ellmann views it as a sign of his acknowledgement of the corruption in life.[31] Ruth von Phul, arguing that the rocks themselves allude to the church, views the act as a kind of purge. Stephen, she says, defiles the church, but at the same time, since the dried mucus represents a blockage of breath, "he is purged, having freed himself of that which threatened life itself—impeding the flow of air into and breath from his being—in an ambigous symbolism of the *pneuma* as Holy Spirit."[32] This interpretation is ingenious but tenable. I think the nosepicking is a kind of purge, but it is also a creative act. There have been numerous references to mucus in "Telemachus." The "snotgreen sea" and its relationship to the "green sluggish bile" convey mostly negative associations. But here ciations. But here I think the nosepicking accomplishes with one form of matter what the urination has accomplished with another.

Stephen has bestowed his own creative products—liquid and solid— on nature. He has impregnated the sea with his own waters, and he has joined his mucus to earth.

Some positive changing has transpired in this chapter. Stephen has created poetry: he has confronted his worst fears and transformed them into language. Turning his face "over a shoulder, rere regardant" (51), he again acts out, in a gesture, what he has also enacted in his imagination; he has not only looked backward, he has looked beneath.

Later, in "Scylla and Charybdis," Stephen attempts to structure his psychological troublings in terms of an intellectual schema. The conflict between Aristotelian logic, dogmatism and rationalism (the rock), and Platonism and mysticism (the whirlpool), are convenient Odyssean frames of reference, but they are also two elemental female symbols of devouring too, and they suggest that although the intellectual sides may be clearly drawn, the psychological ones underlying them remain cloudy and unresolved. If the ethereal, formless, less-than-rational systems imaged in the whirlpool are threatening to Stephen, Stephen's Artistotelian temperament and education only form another species of monster. Underneath these conflicting systems lies Stephen's abiding concern with process.

Even here process underlies all. The library contains "coffined thoughts," and "mummycases, embalmed in spice of words" (193). The corpse of John Shakespeare "rots and rots" (207). Stephen, too, continues to change: "Molecules all change," he thinks, "I am other now" (189). Later he reflects, "We, or mother Dana, weave and unweave our bodies . . . from day to day" (194). His thoughts on fatherhood, art, and on the figure of Shakespeare as personification of problems related to both, also involve process. When A. E. describes art as a relevation of ideas, "formless spiritual essences" (185), Stephen translates his phrase into: "Formless spiritual. Father, Word and Holy Breath. . . who suffers in us every moment. This verily is that. I am the fire upon the altar. I am the sacrificial butter" (185). Obviously his attempts to gain ascendency over process through an identification with the Christ/Logos fails, and sacrifice involves again an alimentary metaphor. Later he links art with process and also with a female activity when he thinks that like our bodies, "so does the artist weave and unweave his image" (194).

Intellectual bulwarks suggested by the rock are not enough to solace Stephen. Fatherhood remains a "mystical estate" (207) founded on incertitude. *Amor matris* may be more certain but hardly less threatening. Blavatsky's elementals and A. E. 's "living mother" are no less disturbing than the wounding/destroying figures of Venus and Ann Shakespeare.

However, amidst this atmosphere of intellectual debate, a lone figure, who has himself just come from a reflection upon the "mesial grooves" of the goddesses, arrives. So they appear, Stephen and Bloom, together yet alone in their cogitations, Stephen pondering on cerebral essences, Bloom on alimentary essentials.

# THREE *Bloom*

It is that perennial barfly Lenehan who expresses what we will quickly come to know about Leopold Bloom: "He's not one of your common or garden . . . you know. . . . There's a touch of the artist about old Bloom" (235). And it is his "art" in the larger sense of the word, his ability to create out of his humanity, that is perhaps responsible for putting Bloom at the center of the novel.

David Hayman suggests that Bloom's many identifications with Christ, Moses, the Wandering Jew, Elijah, and Shakespeare—as well as with God as artist/creator—are due to his comprehensive and comprehending nature: "Bloom is the 'lord of things as they are,' not only in the sense that he is supremely aware of pragmatic reality but also in Stephen's Aristotelian sense that his soul or 'form of forms' incorporates more since it apprehends more of Dublin than any other soul in the book."[1] Hayman's use of the word *incorporate,* which Webster's defines as "to form or combine into one body or uniform substance as ingredients," is a useful one because it emphasizes Bloom's integrating abilities.

William M. Schutte's study of Bloom as artist, which concentrates mostly on "Lestrygonians," discusses Bloom's integrating abilities in terms of language, his perception of meaning, and his "ability to shape perceptions with the aid of the 'right' words into a unified and meaningful whole."[2] Again, in Schutte's words we have the suggestion of the importance of wholeness and integration to the function and meaning of Bloom himself. However, both Hayman and Schutte fail to see that Joyce's use of food is more than a Homeric parallel, that it is connected to language and all transformational processes. Schutte apologizes for the numerous food references in "Lestrygonians," describing them as "an intrusive element . . . designed to satisfy the Odyssean parallel"[3]; and Hayman calls Joyce "playfully Homeric."[4]

Of course the Homeric parallels are important, but their true significance lies in the emphasis that the Greeks placed on the relationship of food to culture. Stuart Gilbert, in discussing Joyce's use of Victor Bérard's theories (*Les Phéniciens et l'Odyssée*), notes that, "the food a nation eats is, to a certain extent, the criterion of its civilization, just as the library of an educated man is usually the index of his mental make-up."[5]

William York Tindall was more sensitive to the importance of digestive processes in Joyce's view of the world, but even he is apologetic: "It is true that Joyce notices digestion and excretion. But in *Ulysses* these harmless necessary facts, taking their place in his celebration of mankind, are no more important, and no less, than they are in daily life."[6]

Yet recognition of Bloom's ability to incorporate, to ingest his experience, is displayed first in his attitudes toward food and its digestion, and this ability is the basis of his thought processes, his verbal creativity, and his attitudes toward fertility. Frank Budgen tells us "Joyce in Zurich was a curious collector of facts about the human body, especially on that borderland where mind and body meet, where thought is generated and shaped by a state of the body." Joyce himself, in discussing a letter from a reader who wanted more of Stephen and less of Bloom in the novel, also told Budgen, "Stephen no longer interests me to the same extent. He has a shape that can't be changed."[7] Bloom's changing shape is doubtless dictated by his fuller awareness of the body and his more complete nature. Thus, throughout Bloom's chapters, as well as some others where he is less in evidence, we see digestive processes acting as a correlative, a signal, and sometimes a parody of the so-called higher processes.

"Calypso" is a chapter of beginnings and therefore reflects body processes on their more elemental level. We are certainly aware of the presence of emptying and filling in this episode, and it is interesting also that the early pages focus more on ingestion and the mouth and the later pages on expulsion and the anus. Along with this elemental dynamic, the episode seems to have a number of images relating to liquids—water, milk, blood, urine—and these too, as opposed to solids, are of a more elemental nature.

There are a number of motifs in "Calypso" that will be developed in later chapters—the waste land, Bloom's concerns about process, his own symbolic sterility. Bloom's use of memory as a creative agent, as well as the creation of language in general, emerges as an important concern. Nevertheless, these elements remain in the background. Bloom seems inclined in both "Calypso" and "Lotus Eaters" to avoid his problems.

I have suggested that the dominant image in the early pages of "Calypso" is that of the mouth as it relates to the act of ingestion. For example, in the opening lines we are told that he likes "the inner organs of beasts"—thick giblet soup, nutty gizzards, a stuffed roast heart, liver slices fried with crustcrumbs, fried hencod's roes," and especially "grilled mutton kidneys which give to his palate a fine tang of faintly scented urine" (55). His affinity with things alimentary—ingestive and eliminative—is thus established in this opening passage. The importance of the body in relation to the mind is also suggested by the fact that at his moment "kidneys were in his mind" (55), and he is, of course, fixing meals for both Molly and the cat.

Mouth images are present as he sets the kettle on the fire and observes its spout: "cup of tea soon. Good. Mouth dry" (55). When the cat appears, she makes Bloom aware of her presence by way of mouth, and he slakes her thirst with a dish of milk. As he watches her, more images of food come to mind: "He listened to her licking lap. Ham and eggs, no. No good eggs with this drouth. Want pure fresh water. Thursday: not a good day either for a mutton kidney at Buckley's. Fried with butter, a shake of pepper. Better a pork kidney at Dlugacz's. While the kettle is boiling. She lapped slower, then licking the saucer clean"(56). His thoughts remain on ingestion as he observes that even the tongue of the cat, with its "porous holes" (56), ingests. As he walks out to buy his pork kidney, he has a fantasy about Turko the Terrible and the Orient where he might "drink water scented with fennel, sherbet" (57).

Bloom even converts smells into liquids. As he passes Larry O'Rourke's he smells porter on the air: "From the cellar grating floated up the flabby gush of porter. Through the open doorway the bar squirted out whiffs of ginger, teadust, biscuitmush" (57). The curate he sees "swabs up" the place and rinses empties, and his duties lead Bloom to consider a larger problem—the "general thirst" of Dublin. This thirst, on a literal level the one for liquor ("Good puzzle would be cross Dublin without passing a pub"[58]), is countered by another kind of thirst, a cultural one, one experienced by other Dublners and Bloom himself. But Bloom avoids these thoughts now and concentrates on converting barrels of porter into profits until he can turn his mind from this kind of abstracting process back to food. When he arrives at Dlugacz's, he looks at the meat through the window and imagines even these in terms of liquids. The kidney oozes bloodguts (59), and "the shiny links packed with forcemeat fed his gaze and he breathed in tranquilly the lukewarm breath of cooked spicy pig's blood" (58-59). Also, the pork kidney he purchases is a "moist tender gland" (60).

This presence of liquids and thirst bring another dominant image of this episode to the fore, namely that of the waste land . Not only has Bloom noticed the proliferation of pubs across Dublin and the town's general thirst, but he also mentioned a drouth (57). The presence of a waste land remains in his consciousness as he reads his newspaper and the item about the Palestinian plantation of Agendath Netaim, planted with eucalyptus trees. This vision becomes enlarged to include the "orangegroves and immense melonfields" (60) of Jaffa, a fertile picture of the Near East that is always related to thoughts of Molly (melons will later be associated with Molly's buttocks). But his momentary vision of fertility and nourishment is replaced by a bleaker one:

> No, not like that. A barren land, bare waste. Vulcanic lake, the dead sea: no fish, weedless, sunk deep in the earth. No wind would lift those waves, grey metal, poisonous foggy waters. Brimstone they called it raining down: the cities of the plain: Sodom, Gomorrah, Edom. All dead names. A dead sea in a dead land, grey and old. Old now. It bore the oldest, the first race. A bent hag crossed from Cassidy's clutching a noggin bottle by the neck. The oldest people. Wandered far away over all the earth, captivity to captivity, multiplying, dying, being born everywhere. It lay there now. Now it could bear no more. Dead: an old woman's: the grey sunken cunt of the world.
> Desolation.
> Grey horror seared his flesh. (61)

In this vision, both lake and rain water have become poisonous; fish, with their association of food and fertility, are absent; not only is the image of the displaced Jew present, but uprootedness, a state of being disconnected, separated from a source of nourishment, dominates Bloom's mood. The emergence of the old milkwoman on the scene—perhaps the same milkwoman encountered by Stephen during his breakfast in the Tower—blends the Near East with Dublin and blends also all rootless people of the world—Dubliners as well as Bloom. Dead lands, configured by fallow females, have become "the grey sunken cunt of the world." Not for the last time does Bloom meditate on the chaotic and destructive side of process, the stream of life. This sense of the meaninglessness of existence will recur several times throughout the day, but later he will have means of dealing with it.

The horror he feels now is also expressed in terms of liquids, however. Oils slide along his veins; his blood is chilled: "Age crusting him with a salt cloak" implies the absence of the life-giving aspects of the sea and stresses the vegetation-killing properties of salt (61).

Later, after he has eaten and feels invigorated, he returns to this image of the waste land with a different attitude. Standing in his own garden, before going to defecate, he imagines his own fertile "waste" land, grown from his own feces, watered by his own urine, and he thinks: "Scarlet runners. Virginia creepers. Want to manure the whole place over, scabby soil. A coat of liver of sulphur. All soil like that without dung. Household slops. Loam, what is this that is?" (68). Obviously creation here is envisioned in totally organic terms, and also in terms of his own body.

After experiencing the horror of his second wasteland vision however ("Morning mouth. Bad images" [61]) Bloom returns home to more positive images of liquidities and nourishment. He imagines: "the gentle smoke of tea, fume of the pan, sizzling butter. Be near her ample bedwarmed flesh. Yes, yes" (61).

More images of liquids occur as he prepares breakfast. He tilts the kettle to "let the water flow in," watches "the lump of butter slide and melt," feeds the cat the blood of the pork kidney (62).

Molly sits under the Picture *The Bath of the Nymph,* an image of liquidities herself. Bloom sees "large soft bubs, sloping within her nightdress like a shegoat's udder. The warmth of her couched body rose on the air with the fragrances of the tea she poured. . . . Her full lips, drinking, smiled. Rather stale smell that incense leaves next day. Like foul flowerwater" (63).

The image of the foul flowerwater, coming after he has learned of Boylan's four o'clock visit, is a correlative of his own sense of sterility and decay. Caught in a world of liquid consciousness, his own ego seems to be sustained in amniotic fluid in a female world which, although positive and nourishing for a time in life, can also become destructive. Such an evolution of consciousness appears to be at least suggested here and is more fully developed in "Lotus Eaters," which also emphasizes Bloom's vegetative, hence passive, nature and diminished ego consciousness.

A number of important patterns involving food, fertility, and creativity are suggested in this opening episode. One involves Bloom's tendency to view people in terms of food. Throughout his day, he will continue to do this, especially with women. Here for example, the pork butcher has "blotchy fingers sausage pink," and the girl is viewed as "sound meat there like a stallfed heifer" with "moving hams" (59).

Food will also inspire Bloom to play with words throughout the day. Now, for example, as he watches the girl at Dlugacz's walk off with her sausages, he thinks: "for another: a constable off duty cuddles her in Eccles Lane. They like them sizeable. Prime sausage. O please, Mr Policeman, I'm lost in the wood" (60).

One of Bloom's most creative acts will involve memory, and his most complex and rich ones occur in conjunction with eating. Here, in the morning, he eats a kidney, an important visceral organ that carries long-standing symbolism. Neumann observes: "The liver and kidneys are visceral centers of great importance to psychic life. . . . But all visceral centers, which also function as affective centers controlling sexuality, are already centers of a higher order."[8]

Thus, after his breakfast and during his reading of Milly's letter, Bloom recalls the morning she was born—obviously a time of fertility. More particularly, he recalls the midwife, a "jolly old woman. Lots of babies she must have helped into the world" (66). Here the image, momentarily at least, remains positive, and woman appears in a more fruitful role.

But, as I have suggested, process haunts Bloom constantly, and now Milly's emergent sexuality links her also with process. But the conjunction of thought and body in Bloom is strongly indicated here by Joyce as "a soft qualm regret" steals over Bloom, joining his need to defecate with his sense of fatality about Milly: "Will happen, yes. Prevent. Useless: can't move" (67). Process goes on. The body must metabolize, and Milly must grow into a woman. Bloom is, at this point, reluctant to confront difficulties and transform them into some new form, into something meaningful for himself. Yet the tiniest suggestion of the transformative potential is present now, and he thinks: "girl's sweet light lips. Will happen too. He felt the flowing qualm spread over him. Useless to move now. Lips kissed, kissing kissed. Full gluey woman's lips" (67). Here some mental metabolism has occurred; Milly has become Molly, for the "full gluey woman's lips" are Molly's and will be remembered again in connection with their lovemaking at Howth. In "Lestrygonians" this memory will be transformed into something rich and complex, and it will serve to influence his actions.

The "Calypso" episode ends with Bloom's defecation serving as an important comment on what some critics see as his anal eroticism, as well as his own artisitic leanings, and on Joyce's attitude about the unity of body and mind. On his trip to his "counting house," Bloom carries with him a copy of *Titbits,* containing a review by Phillip Beaufoy entitled, *Matcham's Masterstroke.* Both Beaufoy and his work will remain on Bloom's mind through the day, and their significance relates to Bloom's recurring thoughts about fertility (especially since Bloom continues to confuse Beaufoy with that fertile father Purefoy). Here, however, Bloom's actual creativity is limited because his major wish at this time is to avoid unpleasant unrealities and the sacrifice necessary for meaningful transformation. Therefore, this scene also emphasizes avoidance rather than confrontation: "Hope it's not too big bring on piles again. No, just right. So. Ah! Costive one tabloid of cascara sagrada. Life might be so. It did not move or touch him but it was something quick and neat" (69). Rather like defecation, life could be neat if he reformed it into something pleasant. His stool, in shape, size, and consistency has been the product of his careful and regulated ingestion, a fitting analogue for the balanced and well-written prose he has before him and a parody of Stephen's aesthetic theory postulating the artist's distance from his work.

As the blending of thought and body processes continues, Bloom next creates a sketch out of a past series of events. These involve a time when he jotted down Molly's sayings on his cuff. Thus he creates himself creating. Another part of his sketch is the artifice of mutual authorship. Perhaps reacting to the loss of the coauthorship he feels after the death of Rudy, Bloom imagines another creative act for himself and Molly, namely, the writing of a prize Titbit. But Bloom's act is abortive here because the image of Boylan enters his mind. A reference Molly has made to Boylan again involves the mouth: "Is that Boylan well off? He has money. Why? I noticed he had a good smell off his breath dancing" (69). Bloom carries the scene a bit further before he effects his own "masterstroke." Transforming words (Beaufoy's *Masterstroke*) into a physical act and thereby either degrading or dignifying artistic effort, depending on one's point of view, Bloom establishes the relationship between language and body by wiping himself with Beaufoy's Titbit. His own masterstroke thus becomes the physical recognition of the origin of words in body, a recognition of the analogue of digestive processes to creation. For Bloom, as we shall see on a number of other occasions, the organic will always invade both his artistic endeavors and his understanding and response to art. This scene is funny, a parody on the Freudian view of art as sublimation of the anal stage; but there is also, behind Joyce's humor, a serious comment on the relationship of art to body, the interdependence of both.

If "Calypso" seems to be characterized by an attention to the alimentary functions on their more elemental level, "Lotus Eaters" is a more psychological episode in which the body plays a central role as a symbol, and the alimentary process is likewise viewed symbolically. There are several key ingredients in this episode—the lotus and related flower imagery, the psychological state of narcissism, with its focus on the genitalia, and the Eucharist. All these elements have a relationship to one another and point to a level of consciousness that is advanced over that illustrated in "Calypso."

The lotus fruit, apparently a "sweet, sticky fruit growing in grapelike clusters,"[9] seemed to objectify a death experience of sorts for Odysseus because it had the effect of inducing forgetfulness in those who tasted it.[10] Forgetfulness, or oblivion, certainly suggests a loss of consciousness, a loss of self-awareness, that must figure importantly here because memory is so vital to Bloom's creativity. The lotus, therefore, would seem to present a threat to consciousness and creativity.

At first glance it might seem that self-forgetfulness and a loss of consciousness, induced by the eating of the lotus, would contradict the technique of narcissism that Joyce imposed on the chapter. Nevertheless, the two are connected. For Freudians, narcissism is a state of excessive self-love, a state of ego development that is linked to what they designate as a genital rather than oral or alimentary stage. Here the ego, emerging into awareness of itself as a separate entity, begins to create oppositions in its world, that is, to sexualize everything. But this is still an early stage of consciousness that can be seen by the association of Bloom with flowers and vegetative symbolism. Because plants are a lower order than animals, plant symbolism, as opposed to animal symbolism, suggests passivity rather than aggression, subordination rather than dominance. It is no accident that Bloom becomes Henry Flower in this episode and has his strongest identification with plant life here as well. Neumann has interesting comments to make about vegetative symbolism. He says that its presence "denotes, psychologically, the predominance of those processes of growth which go forward without the assistance of the ego. But for all their seeming independence, ego and consciousness are nevertheless characterized at this stage by their reliance upon the determining substrate of the unconscious in which they are rooted, and also upon the sustenance provided by this substrate."[11]

Another important feature of narcissism is the dominance of the phallus. Neumann goes on to say: "The youth has at this stage no masculinity, no consciousness, no higher spiritual ego. He is narcissistically identified with his own male body and its distinguishing mark, the phallus."[12]

To return to "Lotus Eaters," then, we are early made aware of the dominance of flower imagery. As Bloom dreamily contemplates the legends of the tea packets at the window of the Oriental Tea Company, his thoughts move back to the Orient, to a special garden noted for its abundance of flowers, and he thinks of "Flowers of idleness. The air feeds most" (71). The fact that the air feeds flowers suggests that consciousness, even immature consciousness, is being fed by an emergent spiritual principle that is still only partially awakened. That the mind is still predominantly nourished by the unconscious can be seen in the floating flower references. For example, Bloom's vision of the garden includes an image of "big lazy leaves to float about on" (71). He thinks of waterlilies, and he recalls a story or a picture of a man "in the dead sea, floating on his back" (72). We also have, in this chapter, McCoy's mention of the "drowning case at Sandycove" (75). Then Bloom envisions the porter barrels breaking open and their contents flowing together: "winding through mudflats all over the level of land, a lazy pooling swirl of liquor bearing along wideleaved flowers of its broth" (79).

But of course, most important is the final passage where Bloom forsees himself floating in his bath, in the "gentle tepid stream" with his penis the "limp father of thousands, a languid floating flower" (86). This image seems to reinforce Neumann's point that for the narcissistic male, the phallus is only an instrument, important to the collective fertilization of the community. This vision shows Bloom's fathering only in terms of his penis; yet the kind of father he will become during the day requires a religious and artistic imagination, and involves both mind and body in the transformation of body functions into a symbolic act.

Bloom's role as Henry flowe also emphasizes his diminished male role. His relationship with Martha is characterized by a lack of aggression on his part and by an excess of maternal dominance on hers. Neumann seems to describe Bloom's condition when he says: "Those flower-like boys are not sufficiently strong to resist and break the power of the Great Mother. They are more pets than lovers. The goddess, full of desire, chooses the boys for herself and rouses their sexuality. . . . They have no individual existence, only a ritual one. Nor is the Mother Goddess related to an individual one, but only to the youth as an archetypal figure."[13] Thus the images present in this chapter are not really suggestive of a higher order of masculine conscioussness, fathering, or creativity, but are closely tied to passivity and even castration.

One exception might be the rather important phallic image suggested by the ad, which Bloom reads, for Plumtree's Potted Meat:

> *What is home without*
> *Plumtree's Potted Meat?*
> *Incomplete*
> *With it an abode of bliss (75).*

This "meat" image undergoes a number of transformations in Bloom's mind during the day, but it serves essentially to connect food and ingestion with fertility. Beyond these initial meanings, it becomes associated with Boylan and Molly and is thus also a negative image of Bloom's own masculinity.

Another recurring phrase with phallic connotations is McCoy's question to Bloom, "Who's getting it up?" (75). McCoy is asking Bloom about Molly's concert and the organization of it. Bloom will be asked this question again, and it will continue to be disturbing because it is always Boylan, of course, who is "getting it up."

But these phallic images hardly confirm Bloom's own fertility, and a number of other images suggest castration. For example, Bloom watches the horses eating and, as is customary with him, he associates food and urine with sexuality. But the image is negative:

> He came nearer and heard a crunching of gilded oats, the gently clamping teeth. Their full buck eyes regarded him as he went by, amid the sweet oaten reek of horsepiss. Their Eldorado. Poor jugginses! Damn all they know or care about anything with their long noses stuck in nosebags. Too full for words. Still they get their feed all right and their doss. Gelded too: a stump of black guttapercha wagging limp between their haunches. Might be happy all the same that way. (77)

Here Bloom seems to indicate a desire to escape into nourishment, to the alimentary level of consciousness, which would not move him toward any kind of creation, but rather away from it.

Even when he thinks about music his thoughts return to the eunuchs: "What kind of voice is it? Must be curious to hear after their own strong basses. Connoisseurs. Suppose they wouldn't feel anything after. Kind of a placid. No worry. Fall into flesh don't they? Gluttons, tall, long legs. Who knows? Eunuch. One way out of it" (82). His desire to escape his maleness and exist in a nonthinking state where he can merely feed appears even more clearly in this excerpt, and the abortive creations he does attempt reflect his gelded condition.

It is interesting that his creative efforts in this chapter are inspired by women—Martha and the two whores—but not Molly. For example, after he reads Martha's letter, he creates a Bloomian kind of literature. "Angry tulips with you darling manflower punish your cactus if you don't please poor forgetmenot how I long violets to dear roses when we soon anemone meet all naughty nightstalk wife Martha's perfume"(78). His "language of flowers" seems more of an evocation of castration, a verbal rendering of the true state of his relationship with Martha on an associative level. Also important in his relationship with

Martha is that it is based on letters, that is on words, rather than on act and physicality. And, not too surprisingly, it is sterile.

A second attempt at creativity involves Bloom's efforts to regain some masculine self-image. He recalls the song of two whores as he removes the pin from Martha's letter. The pin becomes metamorphosed into a thorn, about which he concludes, "no roses without thorns" (78). The pin then reappears in the jingle in a new context:

> *O Mary lost the pin of her drawers.*
> *She didn't know what to do*
> *To keep it up*
> *To keep it up* (78).

Again, Bloom, creating out of another's "art," has performed an interesting transformation on it. The pin of Martha's letter, which has become a thorn and a source of wounding to him, now becomes a danger to Mary, a source of wounding to her. "To keep it up" is removed from its context indicating male potency and is now used to create an image of female vulnerability.

But these creations, which are inspired not by Molly but by lesser females, are not particularly significant. Perhaps Bloom's most important experience of transformation in this episode in his entry into All Hallows and his thoughts on the Eucharist. Tindall has pointed out the importance of the Eucharist as a means of suggesting communality to Bloom, and, most important, its role in helping Bloom to identify with Christ. Bloom's question, "Are the wafers in water?" and his association of *"Corpus.* Body. Corpse" (80) lead inevitably to the identification of himself in his tub (the chalice) as Host, observing, "This is my Body" (86). Tindall finds the identification ironic because of Bloom's negative attitude toward the mass.[14] Robert Boyle, however, sees Bloom's tub consecration as the "most humanly attractive eucharistic image that Joyce presents" and says that although Bloom as priest cannot give everliving life, he can give "real human life to others."[15] There may be irony in Bloom's lack of understanding about the mass—the wafer is never in the water—but Bloom does assimilate some of the meaning of the rite.

For example, when Bloom first enters the church and sees the women taking communion he only thinks of the experience in sexual terms: "Nice discreet place to be next to some girl. . . . That woman at midnight mass. Seventh heaven" (80). Even the priest becomes part of Bloom's erotic fantasy, and the giving of the wafer takes on the suggestion of oral sex: "The priest went along by them, murmuring, holding the thing in his hands" (80). The idea of eating of the phallus is also suggested, albeit in rather uncomfortable terms.

Bloom concludes that the mass is manipulating the people: "Good idea the Latin. Stupifies them first" (80) but at the same time he is interested in the ingesting aspects of it: "They don't seem to chew it; only swallow it down. Rum idea: eating bits of corpse why the cannibals cotton to it"(80). The mention of cannibals introduces another important motif that will be much more in evidence in "Lestrygonians." But still, cannibalism is the essence of the mass, and Bloom has, on some level, understood the connection. He continues to focus on food: "Waiting for it to melt in their stomachs. Something like those mazzoth: it's that sort of bread: unleavened shewbread. Look at them. Now I bet it makes them feel happy. Lollipop. It does. Yes, bread of angels it's called" (81). Just as the ingested food has its effect on the minds of the suppliants, so Bloom's assimilation of the scene of the mass has its effect on him and he realizes: "There's a big idea behind it, kind of kingdom of God is within you feel. First communicants. Hoky-poky penny a lump. Then feel all one family party, same in the theatre, all in the same swim. They do. I'm sure of that. Not so lonely"(81). Bloom has apparently grasped something of the "big idea"—the meaning of the ingestion of the divine. In "Calypso" he has fed himself, Molly, and the cat. There was no recognition of ritual involved. Here, however, Bloom has recognized the act of ingesting as having a larger meaning, as being keyed to man's participation in process and the need for reciprocity and sacrifice.

Lying in his tub, his "womb of warmth," Bloom seems mainly cognizant of his phallus, and his ideas about sacrifice seem as embryonic as his floating position in the bath. Nevertheless, it is significant that, just as Odysseus did not eat the lotus, Bloom fails to eat it also. Instead of eating the lotus, Bloom begins to "conceive" of his role as sacrifice, and a birth of some higher order of consciousness seems to have transpired.

"Hades" is an episode that seems to suggest mortification. It depicts man as emptied of his life and hence his fertility, and even the ritual of the Church seems empty. On the other hand, "Hades" is also a chapter about filling. What is filled, however, is the earth; nature itself is the grand consumer. The very scale of the process at work in nature seems to overwhelm Bloom, and the Church offers little comfort. For him the phrase "the resurrection and the life" is empty; he thinks instead, "once you are dead you are dead" (105). He also has pondered on the futility of death on a larger scale: "Funerals all over the world everywhere every minute. Shovelling them under by the cartload doublequick" (101).

We get a sense of the earth as one huge devouring orifice through the number of references to "open drains" and "mounds of ripped up roadway" (88). On the drive to the cemetery, Bloom thinks of the Our Lady Hospice for the dying and the dead house that opens below it. The mourners stand over a hole that is "black open space" (110), and Bloom envisions people as "dropping into a hole one after the other" (111). Also, the cattle that pass the carriage on the way to the slaughterhouse are to provide "Roast beef for old England. They buy up all the juicy ones" (97-98). The thought extends the devouring image to England and makes of Ireland the supplier of food.[16] The slaughterhouse and the cemetery are near each other, and both seem to be consumers, one of people, the other of animals.

There are a number of references in "Hades" to objects that are disgorged in some manner or other. The most vivid example is Bloom's horrific vision of Paddy's coffin opening and disgorging its contents: "Red face: grey now. Mouth fallen open. Asking what's up now. Quite right to close it. Looks horrid open. Then the insides decompose quickly. Much better to close up all the orifices. Yes, also. With wax. The sphincter loose. Seal up all" (98). Bloom thinks again of exhuming bodies as they pass "murderer's ground" (100). These consuming and disorging orifices are not associated at all in Bloom's mind with rebirth, and his wish to seal up all, to stop this destruction by nature, is strong. However, although Bloom will become depressed with the cyclical nature of life many times throughout the day, he is most disturbed in "Hades."

"Hades" also contains a number of references to water, but these references suggest little in the way of rebirth or insemination. Of course, Joyce's use of the Liffey reinforces the Homeric parallels, but in "Hades," water seems to assume mainly a destructive quality and is associated with drowning and rotting. Thus the "slow weedy waterway" of the bargeman is imagined by Bloom to be floating "past beds of reeds, over slime, mud-choked bottles, carrion dogs" (99).

Bloom 59

There are other consumers in the chapter, however, that are not of earth but are nonetheless associated with it—flies, maggots, cells, a grey rat, and even a priest. All seem to be types of scavengers, feeding off the flesh of the dead in one way or another. For instance, the cells "or whatever they are go on living. Changing about. Live for ever practically. Nothing to feed on feed on themselves" (108-9). The maggots—"soil must be simply swirling with them" (109)—are also consumers, as are the flies that feed on Dignam: "Come before he's well dead. Got wind of Dignam. They wouldn't care about the smell of it. Saltwhite crumbling mush of corpse: smell, taste like raw white turnips" (114). Again Bloom shows his penchant for imagining an astonishing variety of food and eaters of it. Another important consumer is the "obese grey rat, the "grey alive" as Bloom calls him and about which Bloom thinks: "One of those chaps would make short work of a fellow. Pick the bones clean, no matter who it was. Ordinary meat for them" (114). This rat will reappear in Bloom's thoughts, especially when he thinks of food. The priest is another consumer in "Hades." Father Coffey ("his name was like a coffin") has a "toad's belly" and a "belly on him like a poisoned pup" (103). The animal imagery used to describe him seems to place him more in the class of the animal than the human.

Another interesting feature about these eaters is the fact that they are either fat or swollen. the rat is obese; Father Coffey is bloated. Some stoppage or malfunction that seems to indicate improper assimilation is evident. The substance that fills man, beast, and tomb is gas. Death, therefore, seems less process than a kind of stasis, at least for Bloom. He has a number of thoughts about gas during his underworld journey. The air, poisoned by death, is viewed with special revulsion by Bloom. Besides wanting to seal up all the orifices of decaying corpses, Bloom worries about the "bad gas" of the priest and even Molly's attack of gas after eating cabbage. He also considers "bad gas" in larger terms. Of the cemetery he thinks: "Must be an infernal lot of bad gas round the place. Butchers for instance: they get like raw beefsteaks. Who was telling me? Mervyn Brown. Down in the vaults of saint Werburgh's lovely old organ hundred and fifty they have to bore a hole in the coffins sometimes to let out the bad gas and burn it. Out it rushes: blue. One whiff of that and you're a goner" (104-4). It would appear that the air in this world is as deadly as the water and earth are. Indeed, "Hades" seems to be an episode where all the elements—air, earth, fire, and water—are seen in their destructive forms. Fire, for example, is mentioned in connection with purgatory ("Out of the fryingpan of life into the fire of purgatory" [111]), the "Blazing face: Redhot" (95) of Dignam who has died from symptoms suggested by this kind of fire.

To be sure, there is some suggestion of creativity and fertility in this episode, but it is less prominent than critics tend to think and occurs mostly on the ride to the cemetery. For example, on the trip out, Bloom listens to the bluster of Simon Dedalus and thinks of him as "full of his son" (89). Then he himself becomes full of his own son Rudy, as he creates images of him in a childhood he never lived to have: "If little Rudy had lived. See him grow up. Hear his voice in the house. Walking beside Molly in an Eton suit. My son. Me in his eyes" (89). It is interesting that Bloom first conceives of his son and then has his son conceive of him, "me in his eyes." This atonement of father and son in terms of past time will have ramifications later. Now Bloom has only Rudy and Simon has only Stephen, but on a symbolic level both men are fatherless. Bloom's attempt to make himself a father is seen in his next reminiscence about Rudy's time of conception: "Must have been that morning in Raymond terrace she was at the window, watching the two dogs at it by the wall of the cease to do evil" (89). This evocation of Bloom's time of fathering is only brief here, but will become fuller and more complex, even artistically rendered in "Lestrygonians."

There are other suggestions of fertility, too. Martin Cunningham, for example, notices crustcrumbs on the carriage seat, and these remnants seem to hint at life continuing and people consuming, just as the hawker that sells simnel cakes and fruit on the outskirts of the cemetery seems to be affirming life: Bloom thinks: "Simnel cakes those are, stuck together: cakes for the dead. Dogbiscuits. Who ate them? Mourners coming out" (100). Still, human consumption seems at a minimum within the cemetery, and this absence reinforces the sense of mortification and emptying that accompanies a funeral as well as an underworld experience. Bloom even tries to image the caretaker making love to his wife within the bounds of the cemetery, but seems doubtful about it all: "Gas of graves. Want to keep her mind off it to conceive at all. Women especially are so touchy. Tell her a ghost story in bed to make her sleep. . . . Still they'd kiss all right if properly keyed up" (108).

What Bloom does not do, however, is reject the series of graphic images of death and decay that occur to him. After musing on ritual murder he concludes, "It's the blood sinking in the earth gives new life" (108). It is this sense of the cyclical nature of things that both depresses yet heartens Bloom, and although he is, in "Hades," consumed by images of death, he is imaginatively energized as he leaves the cemetery.

One important source of creative awareness involves the story of the abortive drowning of Reuben J's son. Bloom attempts to tell this story to Dedalus, Power, and Cunningham in the carriage, but as Robert M. Adams helpfully notes, the story is "rudely taken out of the mouth of Bloom," that is, Bloom is emptied of the story.[17] The story is about a boy whose unfortunate love affair is ended by his father's decision to send him away to the Isle of Man, whereupon he throws himself into the Liffey, but is saved by a boatman who is then given a florin for saving the boy's life. (It is Dedalus who quips, "one and eightpence too much," [95]). When Bloom recalls the story later in "Lestrygonians," he will incorporate into it a number of alimentary symbols involving sacrifice, and he will include his ride to the cemetery as well as the quip of Dedalus, thereby re-forming the story.

Another transformation that will emerge from Bloom's cemetery visit involves the meaning of Paddy Dignam's death. Paddy is seen as food for the earth; he is associated with the ad for Plumtree's Potted Meat; he will become backward print in "Aeolus" and be re-formed again from a dog in "Circe."

Bloom, however, will also create a new ad. This particular creation is apropos of time and place and involves the earth itself as consumer/reader. His ad says: "Well preserved fat corpse gentleman, epicure, invaluable for fruit garden. A bargain. By carcass of William Wilkinson, auditor and accountant, lately deceased, three pounds thirteen and six. With thanks" (108). This image of earth as consumer and reader will become repeated in different ways, especially in later episodes as Joyce concerns himself with the relationship between the organic and the linguistic.

Thus in "Hades" everything seems fragmented, in a state of awaiting a new assembly. In some ways it provides a necessary experience for Bloom and one that will help him to encompass the death-aspects of life so that he may learn to use them for new growth and creation.

"Lestrygonians" is, of course a chapter in which a preoccupation with food dominates form and content. Envisioned by Joyce as peristaltic in movement, as imitating the muscular contractions of the digestive system, the chapter abounds in food images that critics are inclined to see as being almost superfluous and used to reinforce Homeric parallels. Nevertheless, the true importance of food images and alimentary symbolism can be inferred by the presence of three other features, cannibalism, sacrifice, and creativity.

Homeric parallels are important in this episode, and it is because of the connection the Greeks saw (a connection very much in evidence in the *Odyssey* itself, as Stuart Gilbert has noted[18]) between the food a nation ate and the type of culture it produced. Like his Odyssean counterpart, Bloom believes "you are what you eat." For example, as he feeds the gulls, he thinks, "If you cram a turkey, say, on chestnut meal it tastes like that. Eat pig like pig" (153). Even his literary theory is based on food: observing Lizzie Twigg and her rumpled stockings he thinks: "These literary etherial people they are all. Dreamy, cloudy, symbolistic. Esthetes they are. I wouldn't be surprised if it was that kind of food you see produces the like waves of the brain the poetical. For example one of those policemen sweating Irish stew into their shirts; you couldn't squeeze a line of poetry out of him" (166). Not only does Bloom assume the relation between diet and ideas, but unconsciously or otherwise, he uses gastronomic images when thinking of creation, so that "waves of the brain" become mirrors of peristalsis, and creativity is imaged in anal terms as "squeezing out a line."

References to cannibalism in the episode are extremely important because cannibalism relates to Bloom's ideas about eating, sacrifice, and fertility and replicates the development of the earlier chapters where Bloom's counsciousness and actions relate to body functions, first on a physiological level in "Calypso," and then on a symbolic level in "Lotus Eaters." Bloom's understanding of the significance of the Eucharist, and its relation to himself, implies his search for a ritual or objectified expression of eating and sacrifice as the means of reaffirming life and achieving a higher order of creativity. Because of his underworld visit to "Hades," Bloom seems more awakened to the cyclical nature of life. Hence many of the images from these earlier chapters come together in "Lestrygonians" and are here richly developed.

The fact that cannibalism in certain cultures is not a primitive or savage manifestation of eating is essential to our understanding of its presence in the chapter. It is, rather, evidence of a sophisticated religious consciousness, for it is by means of ritual killing and blood sacrifice that fertility is guaranteed. Studies by Adolph Jensen and Mircea Eliade have provided interesting insights into this kind of behavior, of which Joyce also would have been aware.[19] Jensen is one of the earliest scholars to argue that so-called archaic societies do not have blood sacrifices such as cannibalism, which is, instead, evidence of a more advanced culture. Furthermore, he argues, it is not the hunting societies that initiate these practices but the cultivator ones. These practices, says Jensen, are religiously founded "ethical" actions and involve the concept of a a primal killing that preceded man's life on earth[20]; the murder of a deity brought man his mortality as well as his propagating powers, and henceforth the deity lived in a land of the dead where his body provided vegetative growth and animal life for man to eat. But by that eating, man partook of the deity himself and thus consumed the god over and over again. This act of ingestion became the basis for all future propagation and fertility, and thus it was of essential importance that the primal murder be remembered and reenacted. As Jensen puts it, "Cannibalism is the *festive remembrance* of the realization that the eating of crop plants in reality is an eating of the deity *in its transmutation.*"[21] The connection of this myth to the mass is apparent, but what is also important is the essential relationship of memory, sacrifice, and fertility to the role that food plays in Bloom's transformations of consciousness.

As previously mentioned, sacrifice is one of the dominant, if only partially understood, concerns of Bloom, and as "Lestrygonians" begins, it is the first motif we are made aware of. Bloom has been handed a throwaway that triggers a string of sacrificial images. He first reads "Blood of the Lamb" as "Bloo . . . Me? No" (151). Whether his inclination to read his name instead of the word "blood" is a bit of egotism or an identification with Elijah and Christ, there is, nonetheless, a connection established between Bloom and blood, and he carries this identification with the sacrificial victim still further: "God wants blood victim. Birth, hymen, martyr, war, foundation of a building, sacrifice, kidney burntoffering, druid's altars" (151). This string of images, moving across categories of single and multiple, animate and inanimate, part and whole, encompasses most of human mythico-religious activity involving the survival of the community and connects the role of Bloom with the creative act. As sacrifice and as artist, he, like Elijah, will forge in the smithy of his soul the uncreated conscience of his race.

But Bloom's view of himself as sacrifice must change from that of mere victim to that of elected sacrifice. Sometimes he views himself primarily as victim. The most memorable example of this attitude occurs at his low point of the day, just before lunch: "This is the very worst hour of the day. Vitality. Dull, gloomy: hate this hour. Feel as if I had been eaten and spewed" (164). His own inadequacy and sense of being victim comes to the fore again as he muses on the limerick of MacTrigger, the ill-fated missionary whose genitals were eaten by the chieftain whose five hundred wives subsequently *"had the time of their lives"* (172). And when Nosey Flynn asks about Molly's forthcoming concert in painfully sexual terms, "Who's getting it up?" (172), Bloom's response is physical, a combination of food imagery and sacrifice: "A warm shock of air heat of mustard hauched on Mr. Bloom's heart" (172-73), and Bloom's heart thus becomes the sacrificial meal.

At one point during his rest by the river, he considers throwing himself into the stream: "If I threw myself down? Reuben J's son must have swallowed a good bellyful of that sewage" (152).

In addition to being sacrificial victim, Bloom considers himself part of a larger process, and in "Lestrygonians" he seems preoccupied with the idea that all life is eating or being eaten; therefore, he increasingly tends to view himself as one of many involved in a vast system of alimentation. "Eat or be eaten. Kill! Kill!" (170), he says, watching the eaters in the Burton.

Again, as Bloom notes the export of Ireland's basic staple—porter—going to England to be consumed, he thinks of the rats on board the brewery barge also consuming the porter. Then he muses on the eating habits of the voracious but picky gulls, the microbes that feed on the droppings of the diners in the Burton, the flea on Nosey Flynn, and finally the terrier that vomits and eats his own cud. And of course one of the more significant feasts in the book is the corpse of Paddy

Dignam whose image blends with Plumtree's potted meat to become Dignam's potted meat.

In this world of process, where everything eats everything else, Bloom feels overwhelmed and sometimes depressed. One reason for these feelings, besides his total proccupation with Molly and Blazes, is to be found in his own reverence for life, for its requirement of service and reciprocity. Bloom's lack of belief in institutionalized religion does not cancel a reverence he has for the relatedness of all things; instead, he needs to create order, to create a cosmos for himself by means of some ritual, in order to render the stream of life meaningful. But what has haunted Bloom throughout his noontime meanderings can be described as a sense of process *not* ordered by ritual, a sense of life that has become desacralized. There are many instances when Bloom ponders rites of passage that seem to have lost their sacredness. For example: "Things go on same; day after day: squads of police marching out, back: trams in, out. Those two loonies mooching about. Dignam carted off. Mina Purefoy swollen belly on a bed groaning to have a child tugged out of her" (164). Here rites of passage lack meaning. Institutions and commerce function mindlessly; surface movement dominates. Madness (which can be divine or associated with ritual sacrifice or dismemberment) is reduced to two pathetic figures "mooching about." A baby is "tugged" into the world, and a dead man is "carted off."

Bloom views the church as responsible for the desacralizing of rites of passage. In the fertility of the Dedalus family, who are so poor that the children are nourished on "marge and potatoes" (152), Bloom sees fertility not as creating life but as destroying it. He blames the priests for encouraging the begetting of children while the priests themselves exist as parasites: "That's in their theology or the priest won't give the poor woman the confession, the absolution. Increase and multiply. Did you ever hear such an idea? Eat you out of house and home" (151). Of course the last line refers not to the children but to the priest. Even the excesses of the porter-drinking rats, who "drink till they puke again like christians" (152) are associated with institutional excess. Also, HELY'S men, "walking along the gutters, street after street. Just keep skin and bone together, bread and skilly" (154), seem to merely exist, imitating process that has no meaning. The constables too, with "Foodheated faces," are described in liturgical imagery as

66    *Stephen and Bloom at Life's Feast*

"Bound for their troughs. Prepare to receive calvary. Prepare to receive soup" (162). Bloom's transformation of their acts into these terms emphasizes not a sacral quality of life but the reverse.

Bloom's most important encounter with desacralized process takes place upon his entry into the Burton for lunch. Again, men become animals ("see the animals feed"), and he watches with disgust men

> swilling, wolfing gobfuls of sloppy food, their eyes bulging, wiping wetted moustaches. A pallid suetfaced young man polished his tumbler knife fork and spoon with his napkin. New set of microbes. A man with an infant's saucestained napkin tucked round him shovelled gurgling soup down his gullet. A man spitting back on his plate: halfmasticated gristle: no teeth to chewchewchew it. Chump chop from the grill. Bolting to get it over. Sad booser's eyes. Bitten off more than he can chew. Am I like that?. (169)

But Bloom is not like these eaters, and before he leaves for Davy Byrne's "moral pub" (171), he thinks: "Couldn't get a morsel here. Fellow sharpening knife and fork, to eat all before him, old chap picking his tootles. Slight spasm, full, chewing the cud. Before and after. Grace after meals. . . . Get out this" (169). He adds, "Out. I hate dirty eaters" (170).

Communal feasting, which once had an important and sacred function, especially to those of Jewish background, is projected by Bloom onto the future. He envisions a community kitchen where people will be "all trotting down porringers and tommycans to be filled. Devour contents in the street" (170). In fact, for the moment, all feeling or relatedness seems absent. Communal sharing is viewed as potentially a disease-spreading behavior: "My plate's empty. After you with our incorporated drinkingcup. Like sir Philip Crampton's fountain. Rub off the microbes with your handerchief. Next chap rubs on a new batch with his. . . . All for number one" (170).

In fact, for Bloom the most negative aspect of this lack of relatedness is everyone's absorbing self-interest. "All for number one" becomes Bloom's comment on the human condition. At the Burton he observes: "every fellow for his own, tooth and nail. Gulp. Grub. Gulp. Gobstuff" (170). And in speaking of the priests' irresponsible encouragement of reproduction and their own greed he notes: "I'd like to see them do the black fast Yom Kippur. Crossbuns. One meal and a collation for fear he'd collapse on the altar. . . . Does himself well. No guests. All for number one" (152). Thornton tells us that

Joyce has blended the Jewish holiest day of Yom Kippur with the Catholic black fast of Ash Wednesday,[22] but the important connection here seems to be that both days involve fasting exercises of rites of mortification, and their purpose is not only to atone for sins but to remember them.[23] Remembering must precede atonement and integration, and remembering also becomes Bloom's means of creation. But it is not his only means.

As Schutte has rightly observed, Bloom is "an incurable tinkerer with language,"[24] and it is in terms of word play, punning, rhyming, and ad-making that we also see Bloom's creative nature at work. For example, a number of puns created by Bloom relate to food. In the phrase "Feast of our Lady of Mount Carmel," *Carmel* becomes "caramel" (155). The Reverend Salmon becomes "tinned salmon" (164).

Bloom also seems to view people in terms of food. For example, Mrs. Breen is described in this manner: "Flakes of pastry on the gusset of her dress: daub of sugary flour stuck to her cheek. Rhubarb tart with liberal fillings, rich fruit interior" (158). As he watches the squad of constables, he thinks of them as having been "let out to graze. Best moment to attack one in pudding time. A punch in his dinner" (162).

In fact, Bloom's entire universe is imaged in terms of food. "Gas, then solid, then world, then cold, then dead shell drifting around, frozen rock like that pineapple rock" (167). Cities and pyramids are "built on bread and onions" (164). "Peace and war depend on some fellow's digestion. Religions. Christmas turkeys and geese. Slaughter of innocents. Eat, drink and be merry. Then casual wards full after. Heads bandaged" (172). Thus the human condition itself is viewed in terms of food imagery.

Of course, a number of Bloom's puns and word formations are associated with fertility. For example, his couplet: "*The hungry famished gull/Flaps o'er the waters dull* " (152) is inspired by his viewing of the rapacious birds. Yet the "flow of the language" (152) leads him to consider Shakespeare, another sacrificial figure, and also a fertile one, and to paraphrase from *Hamlet*: "*Hamlet, I am thy father's spirit/Doomed for a certain time to walk the earth*" (152). The association with Hamlet's father emphasizes Bloom's preoccupation with betrayal and cuckoldry, and the hungry bird becomes Bloom himself as the word *gull* takes on an Elizabethan meaning of trickery and deception. "Doomed for a certain time to walk the earth" is Bloom's paraphrasing—unconscious or not—of the original line which is "to walk the night." Yet for Bloom, the association with earth does seem more appropriate.

Bloom's second transformation of his couplet produces, "*The dreamy cloudy gull/Waves o'er the waters dull*" (166), resulting from his thoughts about Lizzie Twigg and about literacy types who are "dreamers, cloudy," and whose creativity is attributed to the foods they consume. The policeman, on the other hand, could not have a line of poetry squeezed out of him. The alimentary nature of these images forms a logical train of associations that precedes Bloom's own "lines."

Another interesting instance of word play and association involves the ad for Plumtree's potted meat, which has lingered in Bloom's thoughts all morning. The placing of the ad under the obituaries seems to occur to Bloom because of its association (at this point only indirectly) with Blazes, and more directly with Paddy Dignam. By placing the ad in the "cold meat department" (154), Bloom seems to be attempting to render Blazes cold, or perhaps also to be commenting on his own cold state. The association comes up again in Davy Byrne's and is again triggered by food. Note the sequence of associations as Bloom first views the shelves of food, especially the sardines—which will reappear as an important image in "Sirens"—then thinks of having a sandwich: "Sandwich? Ham and his descendants mustered and bred there" (171). Puns on food only accentuate his preoccupation with fertility, however, and he immediately continues: "Potted meats. What is home without Plumtree's potted meat? Incomplete. What a stupid ad! Under the obituary notices they stuck it. All up a plumtree. Dignam's potted meat" (171). The phrase "up a plumtree" seems to be another association related to potency, and Mr. Breen's postcard "U.P.: up" is probably also on his mind. "Cannibals would with lemon and rice," Bloom continues as his thoughts return to his sense of being sacrificed, even dismembered like the missionary MacTrigger whose genitals are eaten (172).

Even Bloom's recollection of Molly's pun on Ben Dollard is inspired by Ben's sexuality, and he takes Molly's pun and develops it further: "A base barreltone voice. He has legs like barrels and you'd think he was singing into a barrel. Now, isn't that wit? They used to call him big Ben. Not half as witty as calling him base barreltone. Appetite like an albatross. Get outside of a baron of beef. Powerful man he was at storing away number one Bass. Barrel of bass. See? it all works out" (154).

Bloom's substitution of B for P on the urinal sign suggests still another way that Blazes influences his creative bent. He reads "POST NO BILLS" though the sign, with letters partially erased, actually reads: "POST 110 PILLS" (153). This visual/conceptual cleverness seems to relate to his preoccupation with ads, but I wonder if the erasure of B (for Blazes and the replacement P for Poldy) isn't behind his interest in the visual transformation.

This kind of B/P substitution occurs a second time—during his conversation with Mrs. Breen. In their discussion of Mina Purefoy's difficult labor, Bloom says "Beaufoy" instead of "Purefoy" mixing up two kinds of creativity. Then he transforms his mistake into a comment on fertility and the creative process: "Phillip Beaufoy I was thinking. Playgoers' club. Matcham often thinks of the masterstroke. Did I pull the chain? Yes. The last act" (158). Here again Beaufoy becomes a spur to his own creativity and Beaufoy's masterstroke becomes his own.

There are a number of word plays involving the alimentary process too. Many deal with water and flowing streams. Bloom is much preoccupied with the idea of life as a stream (153, 155) and also puns about the urinal under the statue of the artistic Thomas Moore. Bloom thinks of Moore's song, "The Meeting of the Waters," thus linking Beaufoy, Moore, and their respective works with alimentary functions as he translates everything back into body and into the flux of life.[25]

Connected with Bloom's associations and word plays is, of course, his great interest in ads. This interest stems naturally from his job, but the comment that most of these advertisements seem to make about Bloom's own creative processes is a negative one. The ads Bloom encounters or thinks about during his lunchtime journey in "Lestrygonians" seem fragmentary and incomplete and also suggest sterility. For example, the first ad he thinks of is:

> Kino's
> 11/–
> Trousers. (153)

This ad on a rowboat elicits from Bloom some thoughts on the renting of water. Water, as a primal element, becomes in turn the stream of life, and he concludes that any attempt to possess water, to stop flux in other words, is futile.

HELY's men with their lettered hats become letters incarnate and metamorphose into a kind of negative emblem of suffering and subsistence living. The ad for Plumtree's potted meat is transformed into Dignam's potted meat (154), which is a potentially fertile image. Yet when coupled with his concept of the meaninglessness of Dignam's death (he is "carted off"), this ad too seems to carry a more negative meaning. The postcard "U.P.: up" operates somewhat like an ad in that it is fragmented and connected with Breen's madness and his fragmented nature.

Most important is Bloom's own "ad": "Wanted smart lady typist to aid gentleman in literary work" (160), which brings him Martha's sterile association, transacted, of course, by *letters*. For Bloom, the only aid to literary work will be, not Martha, but Molly, and his truly creative acts will not be literary at all.

In fact, for Bloom, words ultimately tend to become associated with other types of random elements characterizing process, and he finally thinks: "Useless words. Things go on the same; day after day" (164).

Revolted by the seemingly chaotic manifestation of life's energies, Bloom needs to create order through the reestablishment of ritual. He in effect institutes certain kinds of rites here, for Bloom's hunger, which is really a hunger for meaning, is accompanied by a sense of the sacredness of life. We can see this inclination in the way he combines food imagery with thoughts of Molly: "A warm human plumpness settled down on his brain. His brain yielded. Perfume of embraces all him assailed. With hungered flesh obscurely, he mutely craved to adore" (168). Note that he craves to adore mutely—without words. His hunger up to now has been accompanied by a sense of being sacrificed, eaten, and spewed. Thus he must leave the eaters at the Burton for Davy Byrne's "moral pub" (171).

First he thinks of kosher food: "Kosher. No meat and milk together. Hygiene that was what they call now. Yom Kippur fast spring cleaning of inside. . . . Cheese digests all by itself. Mighty cheese" (171-72).

His thoughts about Yom Kippur may indicate an unsophisticated, perhaps even deficient, understanding of ritual, but another notable if less obvious, aspect of Yom Kippur is that, more than a day of atonement, it is a day of purgation. The cleansing that characterizes purgation has the deeper purpose of restoring men "to that state of wholeness and holiness which is the condition of their fulfilling their function in the world."[26] Since regeneration is the ultimate aim of Yom Kippur, it would seem to be relevant for Bloom, who needs to find a measure of wholeness, a measure of manhood, and a sense of fatherhood that he does not possess in the early morning hours of the day.

Bloom's selection of cheese perhaps seems odd. Of course it is most apparently chosen in reaction to the brutal eating, the animality expressed by the eaters at the Burton. It seems a neutral kind of food because it does not seem to be involved in slaughter or sacrifice. Roy Arthur Swanson, recognizing the eucharistic nature of Bloom's meal, allows that although eating may be cannibalistic it need not be "animalistic," and that Bloom transforms eating into a "pastoral-scale repast."[27] The selection of cheese does seem to suggest Bloom's unwillingness to participate in any "sacrifice" of the kind seen at the Burton. Bloom, like "mighty cheese," would like to digest everything but himself. However, Bloom's thoughts on Dignam's death in "Hades" suggest some additional insights on his preference for cheese at this time. That morning, meditating on the funeral and on the earth as a consuming body, Bloom has thought: "I daresay the soil would be quite fat with corpse manure, bones, flesh, nails, charnelhouses. Dreadful. Turning green and pink, decomposing. Rot quick in damp earth. The lean old ones tougher. Then a kind of a tallowy kind of a cheesy" (108). Here Bloom seems to associate cheese with the process of decay. But he continues a bit later: "A corpse is meat gone bad. Well and what's cheese? Corpse of milk" (114). Beyond decay, there is the suggestion of regeneration. Milk, as one of the primary liquids of life, is still connected here with the nourishing process.

It may be worthwhile to note here, however, that cheese and dairy products are regarded in a number of cultures as charms to assure fertility.[28] In any case, Bloom's rather sparse, even Lenten meal, does seem to revive him: "Mild fire of wine kindled his veins. I wanted that badly" (174), he says.

Immediately after eating, however, Bloom's thoughts return to food again, this time to the dangers in them. Oysters, which as an aphrodisiac are associated with fertility and Boylan, disturb him. An oyster is thought of as a "clot of phlegm" that feeds on garbage: "Effect on the sexual. Aphrodis" (174-75). His inability to finish these thoughts seems to indicate how deeply they disturb him. But he solaces himself with the thought that Boylan could not have had oysters this day since they are out of season. Then he thinks of tainted game, of fifty-year-old eggs, of poisons, of the Hapsburg duke who ate "the scruff off his own head" (175). Next he associates ostentatious social customs and the pretentious preparation of foods with gluttony: *"The élite. Créme de la créme.* They want special dishes to pretend they're" (175). He goes on to associate gluttony with women and seduction: "Wouldn't mind being a waiter in a swell hotel. Tips, evening dress, halfnaked ladies. May I tempt you to a little more filleted lemon sole, Miss Dubedat? Yes, do bedad. And she did bedad" (175). But these thoughts seem to reinforce Bloom's sense of his own sterility and perhaps indicate an unconscious awareness that eating is not a matter of social amenities only, or a tool of seduction, but is associated ultimately with survival, with a biorythmic reciprocity recognized in ritual and religion.

As I have suggested, ritual involves an act of remembering as an essential prelude to renewal and fertility. Memory in its most creative aspects makes a new form as consciousness, as it changes its relation to the event. The result is a new or altered content. Mircea Eliade, in discussing the relationship of memory to ritual, says "The important thing is to memorize the mythical event, which alone is worthy of interest because it alone is creative."[29] For Bloom, the experience of Molly as archetypal female is the mythical event, and the key to the re-creation of his sense of wholeness, i.e. fertility, is his union with her.

An early instance of memory both creating new forms and associating itself with sacrifice can be found in the beginning of "Lestrygonians" where Bloom, standing on O'Connell bridge, looks down at the river and thinks momentarily of sacrificing himself to it. "If I threw myself down?" he asks (152). Then he recalls the story of Reuben's J's son, but with a difference, for his own story has undergone a transformation through time and memory. It now includes the quip of Dedalus in it as well as his awareness of story-making as an art, his art too: "Reuben J's son must have swallowed a good bellyful of that sewage. One and eightpence too much. Hhhhm. It's droll the way he comes out with the things. Knows how to tell a story too" (152).

Reuben's J's son, sacrificing himself for love, ingests a "bellyfull of sewage" and is revived. This mock sacrifice and resurrection, involving digestive processes, also becomes art, that is, a story told by Bloom and retold by Bloom with an added character who is also a storyteller or artist. As he retells the story to himself, Bloom throws the Elijah throwaway into the river, recalls the stale cake he fed to the gulls on another day and, by this mock or analogic sacrifice, creates his lines of poetry about the *"hungry famished gull."* The lines remind him of Hamlet's father's lines, as all the elements—death, digestion, sacrifice, and the artist (Shakespeare) as sacrifice (Hamlet Sr.) and cockold blend with Bloom's experience and his creative processes.

But essentially Bloom's creative processes, although involving food and memory, ultimately involve Molly. And throughout his morning, Bloom has been haunted by memories of Molly and their early days. However, these memories have been degenerating and their content has become increasingly invaded by death, usurper figures, and sterility.[30] It is after a string of sacrificial images that Bloom's first memory of Molly comes. He recalls her love of raisins during her preganancy "Before Rudy was born" (151). His associations at this point begin with the image of the luminous crucifix and move on to the subject of phosphorescence. He remembers the phosphorescence of the codfish, viewed in his pantry as he goes to procure food for pregnant Molly. After this fertile and happy time, memory conveys less happy pictures.

After watching HELY's letter men shuffle down the street, he recalls his job at HELY's the year he married Molly. But this memory triggers yet another meal—the Glencree dinner where Molly wore a dress that she had worn prior to the "choir picnic at the Sugarloaf"—a picnic visited by those all-important flies.

A third memory cluster involves an evening with Professor Goodwin: "Remember her laughing in the wind, her blizzard collar up. Corner of Harcourt road remember that gust? Brrfoo! Blew up all her skirts" (156). The sense of cold, exclusion, and mild pain that always accompanies Bloom's thoughts of Molly's sexuality with other men is followed by a memory of food and warmth that always characterizes his own relationship with her: "Remember when we got home raking up the fire and frying up those pieces of lap of mutton for her supper with the Chutney sauce she liked. And the mulled rum" (156).

Another memory of Molly and Blazes is triggered by Bloom's thoughts of the world evolving via process: "Then world, then cold, then dead shell drifting around, frozen rock like that pineapple rock. The moon. Must be a new moon she said" (167). Gradually Boylan has taken Bloom's place both in relation to Molly and in terms of memory too. Now Bloom recalls a scene where Molly, humming "the young May moon she's beaming, love. He other side of her. Elbow, arm. He. Glowworm's la-amp is gleaming, love. Touch. Fingers. Asking. Answer. Yes" (167). This song of seduction, acted out by Molly and Blazes with Bloom's full awareness, forces Bloom to try to halt the images, stop process: "Stop. Stop. If it was it was. Must" (167).

A still later memory, one that occurs just before he has lunch and one that is even more depressing, indicates how truly low in spirit he is at this time, for he thinks, "I was happier then. Or was that I?" (168). Acknowledging the passage of time and the changes wrought in their sex life, he continues to muse, "Could never like it again after Rudy. Can't bring back time. Like holding water in your hand. Would you go back then? Just beginning then. Would you? Are you not happy in your home, you poor little naughty boy?" (168) This very significant passage brings together at this time of mortification a number of crucial elements that relate to sacrifice, fertility, and memory. Here Bloom feels used up creatively. Rudy has died and so has his sex life with Molly, for although we can't be sure who it is that "could never like it again after Rudy," this statement is one of Bloom's clearest about the absence of a vital sex life. Besides a sense of his own sterility, Bloom also views the unrelenting rush of process as "holding water in your hand" and he thinks, "You can't bring back time." As his depression deepens, his thoughts move back to the present, and we lose sight of Molly. Instead, we hear Martha—that figure imaging present sterility—reducing Bloom to a child.

But Bloom can hold water in his hand, and he can bring back time. He can remember and thereby establish fertility on an imaginative level. After his Lenten meal of burgundy and cheese, he seems to undergo a kind of invigoration: "Glowing wine on his plate lingered swallowed. Crushing in the winepress grapes of Burgundy. Sun's heat it is. Seems to a secret touch telling me memory. Touched his sense moistened remembered" (175-76). Now the warmth of the sun's heat" has become associated, not with Boylan but with Molly. Touch and taste, the only manner in which Bloom really experiences art, dominate. Now Bloom's senses begin to awaken, and instead of viewing water as flux, as destroyer and drowner, he views water as seminal. His senses, moistened into remembering, have been given new life. It is at this point that his major creation of memory begins, and he recalls Molly and himself "hidden under wild ferns on Howth" (176).

His senses seem in command, and it is through them that he creates, among other things, colored and vivid images: "Green by Drumleck. Yellowgreen towards Sutton. Fields of undersea, the lines faint brown in grass, buried cities." Touch is of course a major sense for Bloom: "Scrub my hand under her nape . . . Coolsoft with ointments her hand touched me, caressed." But the most impassioned moment in his memory involves Molly and food: "Ravished over her I lay, full lips full open, kissed her mouth. Yum. Softly she gave me in my mouth the seedcake warmed and chewed. Mawkish pulp her mouth had mumbled sweet and sour with spittle. Joy: I ate it: joy. Young life, her lips that gave me pouting. Soft, warm, sticky gumjelly lips" (176). During his lunch, Blooom has spoken of the meal as "wine soaked and softened rolled pith of bread mustard a moment of mawkish cheese" (174). This ingestion image is transformed into Molly's "mawkish pulp" which is *mumbled*—not spoken, much less written— and is "sweet and sour with spittle."

The scene on Howth has been the subject of a number of discussions and interpretations. Brivic views the scene as evocative of infantile orality where woman becomes a deity who rules the world. He places emphasis on the word *ravished,* sees Bloom as in a nursing situation; "The Molly of Howth Hill," he says, "now reappears as a phallic mother goddess."[31] Although I would agree that the suggestion of Molly as goddess is certainly implicit in this memory, I think that Brivic sees the goddess function in far more destructive terms than the passage calls for. Part of the problem is the Freudian assumption that so-called infantile orality is pregenital, presexual, and therefore should, in the normal course of events be outgrown and replaced by other psychosexual experiences. Jungians, however, tend to view oral (as well as anal) and genital stages as coexistent, interrelated. Neumann explains it this way: "In its beginnings the truly sexual and genital development is also assimilated to this alimentary symbolism. . . . Sexuality is not a later differentiation of the alimentary drive, nor is the alimentary drive a preliminary stage of sexuality. It is characteristic of transitional states that the later, here the sexual phase, is at first apprehended through the symbolism of the former, in this case the alimentary phase."[32]

Rather than strictly imaging the mother-child relationship, this scene suggests other dimensions in Bloom's and Molly's relationship. It is true that the mother world order is associated most closely with body/alimentary stages of consciousness, but this fact does not mean that consciousness is therefore passive and childlike. It should be remembered that the alimentary drive not only poses comfort and security, but also forces growth. As hunger stimulates consciousness and forces its enlargement, so Bloom's hunger does not lead him to satiety and pleasure alone but to growth and transformation. Passivity, which seems best to describe Bloom's role with Molly here, is not necessarily a negative trait. It suggests his ability to surrender himself to what Neumann calls "the intervention of a superior power," an ability that is essential to ego development.[33]

In "Aeolus," the virgins climb Nelson's pillar to "spout their seed," as J. C. Keogh puts it, in an inverted image of insemination that is a statement on sterility.[34] In "Lestrygonians," Molly spouts her seed into Bloom, and her chewed seedcake does not fall on the sterile streets of Dublin. It is instead received by Bloom, indicating his participation in a reciprocity with life's fecundating energies, suggesting also that the fecundating powers of the goddess are neither duplications of male fertility nor threatening replacements of it. Rather they render a wholeness, a complementation to the creative process.

Joyce apparently discussed this scene with Frank Budgen who quotes him as saying, "Fermented drink must have a sexual origin. . . . In a woman's mouth probably. I have made Bloom eat Molly's chewed seed cake."[35]

This memory, a truly creative encomium to love and life, does not signify the removal of all Bloom's problems, but it does signal an important change in his view of and response to the world. By reestablishing or creating Molly in symbolic as well as personal terms he has opened the way for an understanding of his own symbolic function; he has recognized an archetype, a superior power, from which energy, new life, and a more complex consciousness can come.

When Bloom views the terrier vomiting and re-eating his cud on the sidewalk, the meaning of his memory of Molly on Howth becomes clearer to him and to us. As he looks at the terrier he observes:

"Surfeit. Returned with thanks having fully digested the contents. First sweet, then savoury" (179). This scene enacts the transformation that memory has accomplished; for Molly's gift is both sweet and savoury. Like her "soft, warm, sticky gumjelly lips," the instant is sweet. Bloom's full digestion of the contents re-creates the incident as savoury, that is, agreeable, even spicy and aromatic like the seedcake itself, but above all, changed.

As I have suggested, this creation of a new form does not resolve the situation for Bloom. Bloom, like Stephen, would like to hold life in suspension, stop process, especially at those moments when the pain of Boylan's presence becomes acute ("Stop. Stop. If it was it was"). So, after his memory of Molly on Howth, he turns his thoughts to aesthetics—that is, to the "shapely goddesses" "never speaking," whose "lovely forms" are "Immortal lovely. And we stuffing food in one hole and out our behind: food, chyle, blood, dung, earth, food: have to feed it like stoking an engine. They have no. Never looked. I'll look today" (176). Although Bloom can hope that the goddesses are not enslaved by an alimentary system, do not eat or defecate, he can also escape for a moment from the disturbing aspect of process. As he is about to enter the museum, he again sees Blazes and again responds by attempting to stop process. "Quick. Cold statues: quiet there. Safe in a minute." And still later he thinks:

> Where did I. Ah, yes. Trousers. Purse. Potato.
> Where did I?
> Hurry. Walk quietly. Moment more. My heart.
> His hand looking for where did I put found in his
> hip pocket soap lotion have to call tepid paper stuck.
> Ah, soap there! Yes. Gate.
> Safe. (183)

Again relying on his talismanic potato, an organic substance that has now been rendered inanimate, preserved, and his soap, another organic substance produced from animal matter and rendered inanimate, hygienic Bloom again retreats momentarily from the pervading sense of life going on, only to take up his struggle again in "Sirens."

Although Bloom has perhaps acquired some new vision about his role as husband, father, even hero, in "Lestrygonians," his ordeal does not reach its climax until 'Sirens." Whether this climax results in positive or negative changes in Bloom, whether Bloom emerges in despair or regains hope, is open to debate. Stanley Sultan argues that "Sirens" contains Bloom's first conscious "realization . . . of the extent of Molly's importance to him," and that this realization changes his attitude and conduct and transforms him into a man who acts rather than one who is acted upon.[36] Jackson Cope says of "Sirens" that it is "the chapter in which the possibility of renewed communion is recognized and . . . the movement toward that renewal is begun."[37]

To see how this crisis, and the possible renewal that grows out of it, operate in relation to the alimentary process, we may best begin with the Sirens themselves. Robert Graves says that not only were the Sirens "singing daughters of earth," but also priestesses who mourned and bird figures that haunted the land of the dead. Their name, *seirazein*, had two meanings—"to bind with a cord" and "to dry up."[38] Sultan observes that the man in the Ormond—Dedalus the widower, Dollard the bachelor, and Father Cowley the priest— "embody . . . aging male camaraderie, without the impingement of wife, family, or home, the example of the kind of life that is an easily achieved escape from his [Bloom's] predicament."[39] This remark is suggestive because Dedalus, Dollard, and Cowley *do* inhabit a land of the dead and have themselves been rendered dead by the emasculating nature of Ireland as she involves woman and the Church. Thus there is present in the Ormond, not only the lament of Bloom, but the lament for a loss of fertility that is larger than his. And the inverted goddess images of Douce and Kennedy coexist with this emasculated image of Irish fatherhood, Irish artistry, and Irish religion.

Bloom, who, like Simon Dedalus, "must be abstemious to sing" is not abstemious either, not a singer at all, but instead sings "dumb" (276). Interestingly, after hearing Simon, Bloom concludes, "Words? Music? No: it's what's behind" (274). What is behind is the larger meaning that Bloom always intuits, and that intuition is the reason for his ultimate unity with Molly.

In "Sirens," Bloom creates a number of important associations that converge in three major image clusters. One relates to sweets. A second involves his many thoughts about fluids—water, body secretions, flowing language. Out of this cluster comes the third, flowers, which are worn by Sirens, by Boylan and by Bloom as a name. Out of fluids there appear forms of life, vegetative and human; out of sweetness comes both fidelity and betrayal; out of the alimentary metaphor of ingestion of sweetness comes the higher meaning of Bloom's day sea journey.

Bloom's almost "consuming" interest in the image of sweetness involves a complex association of sensation and memory coupled with appetite. It begins most obviously in "Lestrygonians" with his memory of Molly, Howth, and the ingesting of the sweet seedcake. It is picked up again in an interesting way in "Wandering Rocks." Not a haphazard selection, Bloom's choice of the cheap novel, *Sweets of Sin*, is not only based on Molly's taste, but on his own identification of sweets with Molly on Howth. Bloom's chance reading of "*All the dollarbills her husband gave her were spent in the stores on wondrous gowns and costliest frillies. For him! For Raoul!*" mirrors his own situation and causes him to read on to the clincher: "*Her mouth glued on his in a luscious voluptuous kiss.*" This is too close a re-creation of Molly's kiss on Howth to be ignored (236). Bloom continues until stopped by the words, "*The beautiful woman,*" a phrase that he re-reads and which triggers his own fantasy: "Warmth showered gently over him, cowing his flesh. Flesh yielded amid rumpled clothes. White of eyes swooning up. His nostrils arched themselves for prey. Melting breast ointments (*for him! For Raoul!*) Armpits' oniony sweat. Fishgluey slime (*her heaving embonpoint!*) Feel! Press! Crushed! Sulphur dung of lions!" (236). Bloom's fantasy seems to contain most noticeably the image of fluids in words like *melting, showered, oniony sweat, fishgluey slime*, coupled with food; and also there are references to a number of smells like *sulphur dung of lions*.

His interest in, and fondness for, smells is perhaps worth commenting on here. This interest seems neither perverted nor pathological, despite Freudian arguments to the contrary. Although smells of earth and body secretions, which are positive experiences for animals and young children, are replaced by the acquisition of erect posture and increased visual orientation, they also tend to be repressed by Judeo/Christian cultures which emphasize a division between a spirit-oriented, intellectual world, and the world of lower body functions. Such chthonian orientation as remains is usually found in myth and superstition where it operates autonomously (here, for example, smells connect with spirit and air as well as with sweat, blood, and excrement). The presence of this orientation is not a perversion or a regressive tendency, but suggests instead a psychic wholeness that can be the foundation of creative processes, since, under this premise, creativity is not a sublimation of the anal stage but a continuation of it.[40] Such an approach to the question of orality and anality allows us to see Bloom as retaining a wholeness, the very quality that keeps him attached to Molly and one that Stephen lacks.

Bloom's thoughts about sweetness appear especially during the early portion of the chapter, but they become associated with "sweets of sin." This phrase, once just a book title, becomes transformed from an image of nourishment into a concept, a phrase, and thus some deadened words. In Bloom's mind words seem to be associated basically with sterility, and when the organic becomes subsumed in the verbal, it loses its effect on him.

We first find Bloom passing "Moulang's pipes," remaining "in memory" and "bearing in his breast the sweets of sin," which have now been changed into "sweet sinful words" (258). Here, what is contained in memory is not Howth and the gumjelly lips of Molly. Sweets have instead become associated with Molly as betrayer, as the reader of cheap novels (a lover of words), and Bloom now associates her sexuality with the mistress of Raoul, a male upsurper and a sterile literary type. These "sweets" are not ingested like Molly's seedcake; they are borne in his breast as an emblem of sacrifice, becoming "sweet sinful words" (258). "Words" also describe Raoul, a false romantic hero and a false literary creation who can never really replace Bloom.

The next mention of "sweets of sin" occurs as Bloom, on his way to the Ormond, now reads Aaron Figatner's name on a store window: "Why do I always think Figather? Gathering figs I think," he concludes, transforming the word into an organic substance. Then the passage continues:

> And Prosper Loré's huguenot name. By Basis's blessed virgins Bloom's dark eyes went by. Bluerobed, white under, come to me. God they believe she is: or goddess. Those today. I could not see. That fellow spoke. A student. After Dedalus' son. He might be Mulligan. All comely virgins. That brings those rakes of fellows in: her white.
> By went his eyes. The sweets of sin. Sweet are the sweets.
> Of sin. (259-60)

Bloom's train of associations seems clear. The Magna Mater is a goddess; he has gone to look at the goddesses that afternoon and Mulligan caught him attempting to examine the divine orifices. Mulligan is a rake; rakes seek out virgins. The virgin was a goddess; Molly is a goddess though hardly a virgin. She is, furthermore, an adulteress. Sweets carry both positive and negative meanings for him and cause him to conclude this reverie with "sweets of sin."

This refrain occurs again as Bloom passes Cantwell's office. The same elements—time, food, words, fertility, and sexuality—occur in this passage: "By Ceppi's virgins, bright of their oils. Nannetti's father hawked those things about, wheedling at doors as I. Religion pays. Must see him about Keyes par. Eat first. I want. Not yet. At four she said" (260). As usual, food is not far from Bloom's mind, but, nonetheless, he postpones eating as if he has somehow keyed his meal to their meeting time. He is helpless to stop time, to stop Molly and Blazes, to stop eating and says: "Time ever passing. Clockhands turning. On. Where eat? The Clarence, Dolphin. On. For Raoul. Eat" (260).

When at last he finds himself seated in the Ormond with Richie Goulding, he turns the scene with Boylan and Miss Douce into a kind of inversion of himself and Molly on Howth. Miss Douce, as a parody of a goddess figure and symbol of nourishment, "reached high to take a flagon, stretching her satin arm, her bust, that all but burst, so high" gives to Boylan from her jar "thick syrupy liquor for his lips" and "poured slowsyrupy sloe" (265). Boylan tosses "to fat lips his chalice, drankoff his tiny chalice, sucking the last fat syrupy drops" (267), before he leaves. The recurrence of sweetness and liquids, women's breasts, lips, and chalices, demonstrates the important presence of female alimentary symbols, emphasizes the role of woman as container and nourisher, in an inverted way, of course.

Coupled with images of sweetness, and almost always appearing with them, are references to fluids and flowing that metamorphose into flowers (the flow of language, the language of flowers). For example, Bloom has purchased "two sheets cream vellum paper on reserve two envelopes when I was in Wisdom Hely's wise Bloom in Daly's Henry Flower bought" (263). These associations are followed by Martha's remembered "refrain," "Are you not happy in your home," which causes Bloom to think, "Flower to console me and a pin cuts lo. Means something, language of flow" (263). As Bloom's identity flows into that of Henry Flower, he is consoled. But even Martha's flower has contained a pin. She, like all women, is both consoling and threatening. He can avoid being hurt by Martha, but he has also rendered her neutral and thus not very interesting: "Yet too much happy bores," (277) he concludes. His relationship with her is, after all, based solely on language. It would seem that here again, flowers and organic substances are positive for Bloom; when, however, he becomes Henry Flower, he creates for himself a literary identity, and flowers are transformed into language too.

Although he attempts to write to Martha as he sits with Richie Goulding, his efforts are at best half-hearted. "Got your lett and flow. Hell did I put? Some pock or oth. It is utterl imposs. Underline *imposs.* To write today" (279). The staccato effect of Bloom's thoughts may be natural but there is also a suggestion that language fails him and does not flow here. Bloom seems to understand the futility of this effort as he blots the address and conjures a "new prize titbit": something detective read off blottingpad.... Matcham often thinks the laughing witch. Poor Mrs. Purefoy. U.P.:up" (280). Here older images of creative efforts rise to haunt him, and although it may seem that he is summoning his creative efforts to deal with the coming situation, it is not in literary efforts that Bloom proves particularly creative.

Another flower image that seems important to him involves Boylan. As he watches Miss Douce pour the drink for Boylan, he imagines the syrupy liquor flowing: "Looked as if it flowed (flower in his coat: who gave him?)" (265).

However, Bloom, "Bloom by ryebloom flowered tables," becomes part of the flow of language himself and sits with Richie Goulding to have dinner. The fact that so much of the chapter focuses on Bloom having dinner suggests that his meal is in some way associated with his anxiety about Molly. Suzette A. Henke sees the meal as Bloom's "recourse to oral gratification. "He forfeits," she says, "his noontime vegetarian diet and primes himself for battle by consuming a carnivorous meal of the 'inner organs of beasts.' Food offers sensual compensation for sexual loss."[41] Perhaps there is some inconsistency here, however, between the idea of oral gratification and the idea of attempting to invigorate oneself with a meal of meat. If it is true that Bloom takes on a more active role after this scene, it may be less true that the meal is compensatory.

There is also a question about how the meal relates to the four o'clock rendezvous. Sultan says that Bloom "does not want to eat his dinner with Molly's rendezvous in prospect."[42] What we do get of Bloom's thoughts at this point is confusing. The sequence of images that passes through his mind as he passes Cantwell's offices supports different interpretations. The phrase, "Not yet. At four, she said," seems to support the assumption that he wants to put off eating since he associates it with "sweets of sin" and the Boylan/Raoul seducer figures. Yet he actively follows Boylan into the Ormond. This behavior, so different from his earlier encounters with Boylan, may signal that he has changed his mind about eating too, may have perhaps unconsciously decided to "ingest" the fact of Boylan and Molly and the impending meeting. Thus the meal may be an indication of this new way of dealing with the situation.

In any case, Bloom orders a liver and bacon dinner. Liver is an interesting selection for him; of course it is one of those "inner organs" he eats "with relish," but in "Wandering Rocks" he has associated liver with images of sacrifice and birth. In the bookstore, leafing through pictures of foetuses, he thinks: "Infants cuddled in a ball of bloodred wombs like livers of slaughtered cows. Lots of them like that at this moment all over the world. All butting their skulls to get out of it. Child born every minute somewhere. Mrs. Purefoy" (235). With this passage in mind, we may see his selection of liver as an attempt to assimilate the experience of birth, sacrifice, and death, the loss of Rudy, the loss of Molly. Perhaps the eating is, after all, a kind of invigorating rite.

In any event, Bloom's silent eating seems to serve as a kind of counterpoint or correlative to the singing of the men in the Ormond: "Bite by bite of pie he ate Bloom ate they ate. Bloom with Goulding, married in silence, ate" (269). Meanwhile, a number of songs are being sung. The selection from the opera *Martha* is of special importance. It is "*M'appari,*" which Simon does not sing until he has been urged several times to do so by Ben and Father Cowley. Finally, Cowley moves to accompany Simon, and we are also made aware of Bloom's role in the piece. For he has his own kind of overture to contribute: "By Graham Lemon's pineapple rock, by Elvery's elephant jingle jogged. Steak, kidney, liver, mashed at meat fit for princes sat princes Bloom and Goulding. Princes at meat they raised and drank Power and cider" (272).

Bloom next looks at Goulding and is struck by Goulding's state of ill health. Images of disease and death now create this train of associations: "Tenderly Bloom over liverless bacon saw the tightened features strain. Backache he. Bright's bright eye. Next item on the programme. Paying the piper. Pills, pounded bread, worth a guinea a box. Stave it off awhile. Sings too: *Down among the dead men.* Appropriate. Kidney pie. Sweets to the"(272). The old English drinking song, "Down among the Dead Men" seems appropriate indeed, since the land presided over by the Sirens is that of the dead. Besides Richie Goulding and Bloom, we can also count Simon, Ben, and Father Cowley as among them.

As Simon sings, Bloom's sense of loss grows, and he seems totally aware of what is happening at 7 Eccles Street. As he finishes his liver to the tune of "All is Lost Now," he makes an interesting observation: "Touch water. Jungle jaunty. Too late. She longed to go. That's why. Woman. As easy to stop the sea. Yes: all is lost" (273). Here Bloom has realized Molly's archetypal nature, the fluid character of her being. If he cannot hold her, neither will Boylan. However, equating woman with the sea, with primal energy, Bloom feels a keen sense of loss because this knowledge has not yet brought any comfort or hope to him.

Meanwhile, however, Cowley and Bob have persuaded Simon to sing the key piece in the episode: "*When first I saw that form endearing,*" Jeffrey's translation of *M'appari.*" It is truly a lament, but it is also a song of memory, memory that celebrates not form but loss of form. Molly's form is now the form of the song, and Bloom's awareness of the presence of death is intense: "Love that is singing: love's old sweet song. Bloom unwound slowly the elastic band of his packet. Love's old sweet *sonnez la gold*" (274). Here sweetness is associated with the old song, not the new song of Boylan. But Bloom at the same time realizes that it is important, and one thing that is behind the music is the commonality of suffering, the commonality of the sense of loss and death.

Thus Bloom observes his link with everyone present at the Ormond: "Braintipped, cheek touched with flame, they listened feeling that flow endearing flow over skin limbs human heart soul spine" (273). Besides the strong identification he feels with the protagonist of the opera *Martha,* he recognizes a communal loss of substance or form.[43] But lamentation is not an end in itself. It has the ritual function of serving as a prelude to regeneration. Thus it is that Bloom, at this low point, and after his liver and bacon meal, "creates" his own music, his own lament in the language of love, full of fluidities and alimentary images that nourish the sexuality of the passage: "Bloom.

Flood of warm jimjam lickitup secretness flowed to flow in music out, in desire dark to lick flow, invading. Tipping her tepping her tapping her topping her. Tup. Pores to dialate dilating. Tup. The joy the feel the warm the. Tup. To pour o'er sluices pouring gushes. Flood, gush, flow, joygush, tupthrop. Now! Language of love" (274). Having created his own siren song, Bloom asks that Pat remove the remains of dinner and bring him pen and ink. Waiting for Pat to return, he attempts to reduce music to numbers: "Numbers it is. All music when you come to think. Two multiplied by two divided by half is twice one. Vibrations: chords those are" (278).

But Molly cannot be contained in a song; the power of music cannot be reduced to a mathematical formula, and Martha is not a substitute for Molly anyway; "language of love" cannot be formulated in pen and ink on a pad. Writing to Martha may be therapeutic for Bloom, but the relationship does not seem to go forward with this letter.

Interestingly, having gotten past his mathematical definition of music, Bloom returns to a more organic definition of it. Music is "sea, wind, leaves, thunder, waves, cows lowing, the cattle market, cocks, hens don't crow, snakes hissss. There's music everywhere" (282). Music is not just the lament heard in the Ormond. There is life and invigoration to be found in music too.

And, of course, music is also Molly. Not surprisingly, when Bloom thinks of music now, it is associated not with Molly's voice but with her urinating: "Chamber music. Could make a kind of pun on that. It is a kind of music I often thought when she. Acoustics that is. Tinkling. Empty vessels make most noise" (282). Bloom's observation about empty vessels suggests that he, or at least Joyce, may recognize on some level of consciousness that Simon, Ben, and Father Cowley, who have made the most noise in the Ormond, are also empty vessels.

When Bloom does involve human beings with music now, it is with a difference: "*Cloche. Sonnez la!* Shepherd his pipe, Policeman a whistle. Locks and keys! Sweep! Four o'clock all's well! Sleep! All is lost now. Drum? Pompedy. Wait, I know. Towncrier, bumbailiff. Long John. Waken the dead. Pom. Dignam. Poor little *nominedomine*. Pom. It is music, I mean of course it's all pom pom pom very much what they call *da capo*. Still you can hear. As we march along, march along. Pom" (289). And finally, his music: "I must really. Fff" (290). To these kinds of music, music of the stream of life outside the

Ormond, which includes images of death and body processes, Bloom adds his own music. Although his breaking of wind is also music ("Freer in air. Music" [288]), it is a comment on the siren-songs of the Ormond and on the sterile, nationalistic sentimentalism expressed in "The Croppy Boy." But it is also a sign of Bloom's withdrawal from the spell of the Ormond.

Bloom withdraws before Dollard has finished singing "The Croppy Boy." This kind of sentimental and fruitless patriotism does not seem to appeal to him, and he thinks, "Get out before the end" (286). His thoughts are elsewhere—on the statues, "Three holes all women. Goddess I didn't see" (285), and on Mina Purefoy, "Hope she's over. Because their wombs" (286).

A final important flower image involves the song "The Last Rose of Summer," which, though not sung, is played against Bloom's name: " 'Tis the last rose of summer Dollard left Bloom" (288), and ends in a reference to gas. Bloom "felt wind wound round inside. . . . Gassy thing that cider: binding too" (288). Like the binding of the Sirens, the sterile heroics important to the men at the Ormond bind them to a dead land. Bloom's internalization of this sense of decay is flatulence.

After he has left, Dedalus stares at the headless sardine on the plate as the narrator, reminding us again of the "last rose of summer," intones "Under the sandwichbell lay on the bier of bread one last one lonely last sardine of summer. Bloom alone" (289). The image is certainly one of death and even dismemberment. The lament of the last four lines of the song seems to speak of the men at the Ormond more than Bloom however:

> 'Tis the last rose of summer.
> Left blooming alone;
> All her lovely companions
> Are faded and gone;[44]

Bloom may be "faded and gone" from the Ormond, but he has not faded in any other sense. Although the headless sardine, which is usually associated with Bloom, might suggest itself in Freudian symbolism as a dismembered phallus (and certainly Bloom's psychological castration has been a threat if not a reality), the fish has other associations, too. That other hero, the dying and resurrected god, dismembered for the purposes of helping to bring about regeneration, is at least a mythic reality in terms of Bloom. For he seems, after "Sirens," to have achieved some kind of new energy. Furthermore, he seems willing to recognize process and to participate in it. Process is personified as Molly, who, like the sea, is primal, fluid, nourishing, and containing, the domain of the fish.

The merging of the flower imagery with the fish is another demonstration of Bloom's affinity with flow, with the nondifferentiated energies of the sea. Besides the ideas of Christian martyrdom often associated with the fish, the fish is also an important part of the Jewish diet and has other symbolic significances. It is not considered meat and is thought to be prolific because it is not subject to the evil eye. It is especially eaten by women during pregnancy and is also eaten frequently on Friday before Sabbath.[45] Another interesting feature about the eating of the fish on the Sabbath is related in the *Encylopaedia Judaica*, which explains that the act "is said to be in anticipation of the messianic era which will be inaugurated by the eating of the legendary fish Leviathan."[46]

Nor are we allowed to forget the importance of the digestive process to Bloom's more creative approach to life. For his is the last music of the chapter. Leaving behind the Sirens' song that binds the other men to sterile reminiscences, passivity, and lethargy, Bloom stops at the window of Lionel Mark's antique shop. In the window is a portrait of Robert Emmet, another of Ireland's great and lost heroes, and against Emmet's famous last words, Bloom makes from his body a funny counterpoint:

> *When my country takes her place among.*
>   Prrprr.
>   Must be the bur.
>   Fff. Oo. Rrpr.
> Nations of the earth. No-one behind. She's passed.
> *Then and not till then.* Tram. Kran, kran, kran.
> Good oppor. Coming. Krandlkrankran. I'm sure it's
> the burgund. Yes. One, two. *Let my epitaph be.*
> Karaaaaaaa. *Written. I have*
>   Pprrpffrrppfff.
>   *Done* (291).

In a parody of both Christ's last words and Emmet's last words, Bloom's last word affirms the fact that he has not been enticed by the Sirens' song, which gives him indigestion. Instead he has created his own music out of the body and by grounding art in its functions has provided a needed counterpoint.

# FOUR  *Stephen and Bloom*

The chapters that follow "Aeolus," in which Bloom and Stephen appear together, have a special creative quality about them. That is not to say, of course, that the early episodes that deal only with one or the other lack creativity. But in terms of narrative technique, the later episodes signal radical changes in Joyce's approach to his material.

Thus, although captions that appear in "Aeolus" suggest at least a surface change in format, this change also hints at even greater changes to come. "Aeolus" is the first episode in which the narrator works outside both characters and begins to establish a distance that paradoxically conveys a sense of closer containment but within a larger and more creative consciousness.

In terms of the digestive processes, both Bloom and Stephen remain pretty much in character; that is, Bloom is in bondage to time in the form of his past with Molly, in his sense of being a Jew and sacrificial victim, and in his awareness of process and universal cannibalism, brought home to him by Dignam's funeral. Stephen is still in bondage to his mother, to his fear of being devoured, and to his sense of sterility. This bondage and sense of sterility is here presented as a public and widespread malaise and is also linked with language. Rhetoric and surface communication are countered, however, by a sense of ritual and new language that have their groundings in feasts and in eating.

Creativity and sterility in language are major concerns in "Aeolus" and are commented upon in terms of Bloom's thoughts on Paddy Dignam, his recollection of the Passover ritual, and the Chad Gadya song (a song about one thing eating another). The problem is also commented upon in Stephen's vampire poem and in his "Parable of the Plums."

Bloom and Stephen have been set amidst the sterility of Dublin where, as we have said, language is characterized as empty, high-flown rhetoric uttered by the city's might-have-beens. Because of the flatulent character of much of the style, Bloom's and Stephen's thoughts on feasts, ritual, and images of ingestion suggest that these are important ingredients, perhaps necessary for the reestablishment of their own completeness and for the creation of a viable art that will transcend the economic, historical, and cultural aridity of Ireland.

To begin, we find Bloom, who is still musing on his cemetery visit and the state of Paddy Dignam, transferring eating functions to the machines that are like "obedient reels feeding in huge webs of paper" (120) that can also "smash a man to atoms if they got him caught. Rule the world today" (118). Another consumer, in Bloom's view, is the newspaper that has ingested the fact of Paddy Dignam's death and has transformed it, not into meaningful art, but into the lifeless, euphemistic caption: "WITH UNFEIGNED REGRET IT IS WE ANNOUNCE THE DISSOLUTION OF A MOST RESPECTED DUBLIN BURGESS" (118). What has truly been disolved is Paddy's identity. Rather than transforming the daily bread of experience into the radiant body of ever-living life, the caption has reduced Paddy to particles as effectively as earth, cell, maggot, and rat. Bloom, aware of this uncomfortable fact, uses a machine metaphor to re-create the natural processes of dissolution and decay: "His machineries are pegging away too. Like these, got out of hand: fermenting. Working away, tearing away. And that old grey rat tearing to get in" (118). The truly negative tone and vision of these processes—devouring earth and devouring machine—are emphasized by Bloom's thoughts about fermentation, which are probably intensified because of his Jewish background and the fact that Jewish ritual involving communion meals forbids the consumption of fermented food because such food was thought to be putrescent.[1] Bloom's awareness of so much fermentation suggests that he lacks understanding of the meaning of sacramental meals that if understood, take consciousness beyond the decaying aspects of life and convey a sense of renewal.

Thus for Bloom the news of Paddy's death is "stale" (118). He prefers ads and side features and proceeds to invent a "Dear Mr. Editor" question that asks "What is a good cure for flatulence? I'd like that part" (119). Flatulence, often caused by decay, poor digestion, or the taking in of air, of course characterizes the language of this chapter. If excrement has a creative component and is linked to fertility, then flatulence, the production of mere wind, suggests emptiness and sterility. "Shite and onions!" Mr. Dedalus replies to Ned Lambert's reading of the rhetoric of Dan Dawson (126).

More important in regard to Bloom is the caption that reads: "AND IT WAS THE FEAST OF THE PASSOVER" (122). Thought by some critics to be ironic (Marilyn French considers it a "slap at religious formulations of experience"[2]), the caption is, I think, another signal of Bloom's awareness of his role as sacrificer rather than sacrificed and his perhaps still-unrecognized need for revivifying ritual. The caption is, of course, a quote from Exodus 12 and introduces a number of ingredients that relate to Bloom's creativity—his identification with Moses, the waste land motif, sacrifice, fertility, and fatherhood. Rather than a rejection of religious formulations, it indicates Bloom's need for them.

In any case, the caption is followed by another reference to Dignam. The typesetter is setting the type backwards, and as Bloom watches, he spells out Paddy's name, "mangiD. kcirtaP" (122), which causes Bloom to recall his father's reading (backwards) of the Haggadah. His thoughts go backwards, too, to his father and his childhood, and time becomes no longer historical but liturgical: "Pessach. Next year in Jerusalem. Dear, O dear! All that long business about that brought us out of the land of Egypt and into the house of bondage *alleluia. Shema Israel Adonai Elohenu*. No, that's the other" (122). Bloom has, of course, substituted *into* the house of bondage for *out of,* but his is a substitution we would expect him to make, given his state of mind about Molly and 7 Eccles Street. This passage may indeed indicate Bloom's distance from his boyhood teachings, but the Passover recollection seems important here because it is a festival where certain foods are eaten for the purpose of commemorating the flight from Egypt but also for celebrating a particular kind of freedom. What is stressed in the Passover feast is the idea of "volitional dedication," or elected sacrifice.[3] What seems suggested here is that it is not enough for Bloom to be "free" from the bondage of Eccles Street and the chaos of process. Nor should he resign himself to being simply a victim. He must opt for a particular kind of sacrifice.

Contrasted with the "stale" news happenings in linear Dublin time and the machines that also "tell" ("Sllt. Almost human the way it sllt to call attention. Doing its level best to speak" [121]), the Haggadah, or telling ritual, is a recital of a mythic event still important in liturgical time. That event, the deliverance of the children of Israel from Egyptian bondage, is important because it re-creates that event and becomes a "script of a living drama" that stresses acceptance of a special role both for the race and the individual.[4]

At this point Bloom's thoughts about Passover do not establish either his own sense of mission or his sense of being creative, however. More than anything, the negative manifestations of process seem to remain with him, and what he remembers with the greatest accuracy is the Chad Gadya or "Only One Kid," which he recalls as: "And then the lamb and the cat and the dog and the stick and the water and the butcher and then the angel of death kills the butcher and he kills the ox and the dog kills the cat" (122). Bowen emphasizes the importance of Bloom's accurate recollection of "a relatively little used section of the ritual," because it says something about his attitudes towards Jewish survival and his own role as a Moses figure.[5] The song, as an enumeration of the slaughter and eating of one thing by another, was taken as an illustration of the fate of the Jewish people and their ability to survive their persecutors. Its last lines are: "And the Holy One, blessed is He, came and killed the Angel of Death that slew the slaughterer that slaughtered the ox that drank the water that quenched the fire that burned the stick that beat the dog that bit the cat that ate the kid that father bought for two zuzim. One kid, one kid."[6] Bloom, however, does not accept the other allegorical meaning of a "jus talonis" but concludes: "Sounds a bit silly till you come to look into it well. Justice it means but it's everybody eating everyone else. That's what life is after all" (122). It would seem that Bloom has a lot more cogitation to do on the subject of sacrifice, cannabalism, and his own fertility. In the meantime, it is Stephen whose role in "Aeolus" has more to do with the creative process, and food is for him a dominant metaphor of transformation.

Stephen enters the scene after Bloom has left and in the middle of a discussion between Myles Crawford and John MacHugh, who argues that the corruption of Roman and English empires was due to a "cloacal obsession." While the Romans constructed the water closet, the Jews were looking to the mountain, and the Irish, as Lenahan says, "were partial to the running stream" (131). Although MacHugh can proclaim, "The closetmaker and the cloacamaker will never be lords of our spirit" (133), the rhetoric of this chapter has certain affinities with eliminative functions that Joyce does not want the reader to miss. It is at this point that Stephen enters with O'Madden Burke and first reveals his mysterious writing on the beach at Sandymount. The verse has been written on Deasy's paper on foot and mouth disease (a subject that also comments on the state of the language in Ireland) and is essentially taken from "My Grief on the Sea" by Douglas Hyde, whose lines are:

> And my love came behind me—
> He came from the South:
> His breast to my bosom
> His mouth to my mouth.[7]

Stephen has turned the dead lover into a vampire and his verse reads:

> On swift sail flaming
> From storm and south
> He comes, pale vampire
> Mouth to my mouth. (132)[8]

The poem shows some artistic aptitude but is hardly original; perhaps the most interesting thing about it is Stephen's use of the word *vampire*. The line show again the presence of guilt and his mother's death and their associations with being eaten. Michael Seidel points to Madame Blavatsky's theosophic views of vampires as particularly relevant to Joyce's use of the image. Blavatsky claimed that vampires were beings who, because of their earthly or materialistic natures, remained tied to the body, becoming, in Seidel's words, a "special sort of ghost."[9] But Stephen has certainly turned what was a figure threatening to his mother to one that threatens him. And beyond the connections of ghost, Hamlet senior, and the ghost of Stephen's dead mother with all their Oedipal associations, the vampire image points most strongly to a deeper fear in Stephen that involves less of a sexual and more of an alimental threat. For, as Seidel rightly observes, Stephen "has been having a difficult time all day distinguishing between the nourisher and the blood sucker,"[10] Thus, although the poem shows a sensitive and lyrical mind at work, it also shows an obsessed one as well, and it is further evidence of the problem of eating or being eaten and Stephen's attempt to render process in terms of words. But from this world or projection, Stephen does seem to move to a world of more concrete realities.

The most interesting of Stephen's creations is, thus, his "Parable of the Plums," his vision of the two "Dublin vestals" who climb Nelson's pillar to "see the views of Dublin" (145). Having bought "one and fourpenceworth of brawn and four slices of panloaf," as well as "four and twenty ripe plums," they ascend the staircase to the top where they eat their brawn and bread, go to the railings, become giddy from the heights, and finally sit, "peering up at the statue of the onehandled adulterer" (148) until they get cricks in their necks. Too tired to look either up or down, they then eat the twenty-four plums and spit the plumstones down on the city.

Inspired by the discourse of MacHugh (interrupted by a meaningful belch) on Moses and the Egyptian high priest in which the high priest, in colorful rhetoric, argues for the cultural and material dominance of Egypt, the "Parable" offers a countering comment not only on the messianic quest, the promised land, and the problem of bondage, but on the link between cultural sterility and sterility in language.

The meaning of the parable is hard to pin down, however. It is thought to involve ideas about sterility and creativity. William York Tindall sees it as a kind of epiphany where the vestals, named Kearns and McCabe, the latter being the name Stephen has earlier assigned to one of his "midwife figures" in "Proteus," should assist at some birth. The plumstones are the seeds that fall on sterile ground; the pillar is sexual and a symbol of British power; the vision of the city involves signs of Roman dominance.[11] M. J. C. Hodgart argues that the plumstones are seeds that "will die on the stoney ground, unless fertilized by some urine of Bloom's humanity and Stephen's art."[12] J. C. Keogh says that the "city of Dublin is fertilized in vain by the virgin onanism of her citizenry, whose towering symbol is the statue of the great onehandled adulterer."[13]

"The Parable of the Plums," this *"Pisgah Sight of Palestine,"* which implies a vision that is not experienced (since Moses never entered the promised land), needs to be related to Stephen's response to process, to his ingestion or assimilation of the world of experience. James Maddox argues that Stephen here clearly "seeks to overcome his own aversion toward experience," and it is this effort that evokes such clear prose and realistic details,[14] But again, on the most basic level, experience means an awareness of physicality and implies a dynamic of physical giving and taking. Thus, it is not surprising that Stephen again chooses a subject where eating is a major component. Also, his subject matter seems be derived from earlier associations with eating as well as with women and creativity, which are also linked to ingestion. Stephen's breakfast encounter with the milkwoman, who, with her shrunken breasts, serves English dominance and symbolizes the sterility of Ireland, is not disassociated from Stephen's mother or from the "midwives" on the beach. The women figures that both feed Stephen's imagination and threaten to absorb him are, in the early hours of the day, faded, ghostly images—the mother actually a ghost, the milkwoman almost one. Both nourishing and devouring figures are, in one sense at least, pale and receding. They are more palpable to Stephen's disturbed psyche and less real as art.

To encounter life is to make these images less ghostly. As Stephen begins to create his parable, he gives his vestals ages and a place of residence, a concrete identity. Yet as he sets his stage, his mind is filled with a disturbing image of a "damp night reeking of hungry dough"(145). Here again, Stephen uses food (as well as dampness) to create the disturbing aspects of "real life" for himself. He envisions against a wall, a couple: "Face glistening tallow under her fustian shawl. Frantic hearts." Then he thinks, "On now. Dare it. Let there be life"(145). Whether this response is aimed at the couple's consummation of their sexual act or at Stephen's own emergent story is not important since the act of fertilization is there in either case. By uniting his mind with the "damp night" and the "hungry dough" (an interesting and telling inversion that may give us another glimpse of the cause of Stephen's usual aversion for food), Stephen has, at least momentarily, mated with experience. Thus the Dublin vestals are logical developments of the female images he has been thinking about that morning. Like the vestals, May Dedalus has lived under the shadow of an Ireland dominated by the patriarchal values of England and Rome. She, like them, has given up her seed to barren Irish earth. Is Stephen, after all, a seed that will flourish or die? And she seems to be causing his death by keeping him in bondage to the fallow world of church, country, and motherhood. She, like the vestals, has cast her seed upon the concrete heart of Dublin.

The important orifice here is the mouth, the mouth that gives birth to words, that also spits out seed, that eats bread and brawn (perhaps the masculinity of Ireland). But these mouths are futile ingesters: the seed spit by the vestals does not yield fruit. These images are contradicted by another oral giver of seed, namely, Molly.

Stephen's *"Pisgah"* vision is expressly that at this point because it does not contain Molly yet—or rather, the writer of *Ulysses* has more incorporating to do. But Stephen's vision of a sterile planting, a non-transformative eating, contains some seed of artistic creation because, like the old milkwoman, the vestal/midwives have connections with the new and fertile as well as with the old and sterile. Stephen will give them life by encountering and assimilating them. He does this with moderate success.[15]

One final notable fact about Stephen's "Parable" is that it is oral. Not only does an oral tale suggest a return to the beginnings of fiction-making, but also the oral creation has significance for Stephen. He has ingested negative images about life and has expressed some truth about experience, his truth. Even though he remains threatened by the spectre of devouring and sterility, he will use threatening elements to create his art.

In "Aeolus" Stephen's problems coexist with Bloom's. Their bondage to the past is all-persuasive. Bloom seeks ritual practices or insights to free him from the negative implications of process and help him to see a sacred rather than a linear time. This freedom will enable him to understand volitional sacrifice and symbolic fatherhood, both of which figure in his coming relationship to Stephen. Stephen finds the ingestion of food an analogue for the creative processes and establishes a vital language to replace empty rhetoric as he grounds his art in body processes.

Because we are already familiar with the ways in which Joyce associates food with fertility, it is not surprising to find that "Oxen of the Sun," an episode dealing primarily with fertility, has as its setting a meal presided over by Stephen and attended by Bloom. Throughout this episode we have a sense of both real and symbolic communal meals being celebrated with suggestions of a number of religious festivals—the Shabout, Jesus' feeding of the multitudes, the Last Supper, the Feast of the Blessed Virgin Mary of the Rosary, and, of course, the Pentecost. These references to sacramental meals are not mere dressing but are a part of the dynamic of birth and creativity with which the chapter is concerned.

The communal feast, celebrated by the irreverent medical students, occurs in the lower floor, the common room of the maternity hospital—at night—at a time near the vernal equinox (when many festivals take place). The land is experiencing a severe drought, Mrs. Purefoy a fruitless labor, and Bloom an equally fruitless dream of fatherhood. These conditions give evidence of a time of suspended animation, a time of stasis, and suggest a prelude to renewal and the promise of creativity.

Joyce's famous remark about "Oxen" in one of his letters is worth quoting again here, especially the portion where he says that "Bloom is the spermatazoon, the hospital, the womb, the nurse, the ovum, and Stephen the embryo."[16] This probably facetious remark suggests, nevertheless, that Joyce may have had in mind Bloom's emergence, on some level, as a father, a fertilizer/creator, possibly of a new Stephen, who in turn can become the creator of the Word.

The episode opens with an invocation that calls for "quickening and wombfruit" (383), a particularly meaningful invocation because Joyce's cosmos in *Ulysses* is in need of quickening. "Wombfruit" refers not only to Mrs. Purefoy's hard labor, nor to labor and birth in general, but to the birth of artistic powers, the Word, even the birth of the artist in whom the Word is contained.

One method of quickening in this episode involves the imagery itself, which blends food and organic substances with human, intellectual, and religious levels of consciousness and thereby transforms and quickens the language. The womb of earth brings forth fruit in the fertile season; the womb of the archetypal female gives birth; the vessel of the unconscious creates language.

As the chapter opens, Stephen, drunkest of them all, sits "at meat" with the other medical students, presiding over a table on which "there was a vat of silver that was moved by craft to open in the which lay strange fishes withouten heads . . . And these fishes lie in an oily water brought there from Portugal land because of the fatness that therein is like to the juices of the olive press" (387). Again the headless sardine appears, here contained in oil from a plant. The description goes on: "And also it was marvel to see in the castle how by magic they make a compost out of fecund wheat kidneys out of Chaldee that by aid of certain angry spirits that they do into it swells up wondrously like to a vast mountain" (387). Beyond the presence of a table full of bread and sardines is the suggestion of magical transformation that the archaic language especially conveys. The "swelling" of the wheat, succeeded by the leavening process of decay, and the production of gas iterates the whole life and death cycle. The blending of vegetable and animal imagery in the passage, like the sardines in oil delivered from the olive press, also suggests the metabolic process whereby a new substance is combined by way of the destruction of the older, sometimes disparate ones. This is, in other words, an embryonic sacrifice.

The phrase "wheat kidneys," also mentioned by Stephen in "Proteus," alludes to the Song of Moses (Deut. 32:13-14), where Moses celebrates God's blessing to Jacob: "And he made him to suck honey out of the rock, and oil out of the flinty rock; Butter of kine, and milk of sheep, with fat of lambs and rams of the breed of Bashan, and goats with the fat of kidneys of wheat."[17] The numerous references to fluids—honey, oil, butter, fat, milk, and even the reference to sucking and sweetness—make it appear a truly Bloomian passage, for Bloom, like Moses, celebrates the beneficence of these substances because of his 'open" or "alimental" character.[18]

This passage continues (in fourteenth-century style) with a reference to the other, second most important food transformation for the human race, the making of wine: "And they teach the serpents there to entwine themselves upon long sticks out of the ground and of the scales of these serpents they brew out a brewage like to mead" (387). Frank Budgen says, in his discussion of "Oxen," that Joyce has brought together two phases of life, "men drinking ale and women bearing children," and he argues that drink is creative and considered divine because of its contribution to the civilizing of the race.[19] What Budgen seems to be getting at is the fact that the making of bread and wine from the wheat and the grape is the first process of transformation of which man became conscious. Thus, not only does "Oxen" describe the development of English, the evolution of fauna, the growth of the human foetus, but the development of ritual. The transformation of the two staple foods is itself the source of the metaphor of the mass and the artistic process *in embryo*. Out of it comes the metaphor of the eating of the god, the alchemical concept of transmuting *materia prima* into gold; the notion of the refinement of soul out of the body. It is this basic transformation that *inspires,* infuses with life, and quickens. Indeed, we are dealing with one of the most complex metaphors of religious and artistic consciousness and one upon which Stephen will draw to create art out of the daily bread of experience.

Stephen seems to dominate the scene (sometimes more as a master of ceremonies than a priest), and we feel he is the most intelligent and articulate of the students, probably destined to be apart from them. Although he has not yet proved himself to be an artist, or at least a fertile one, he will not remain sterile like the students.

As the scene opens, we see quickly the nature of this sterility. A discussion goes on as to whether in difficult cases of birth the mother should be sacrificed to save the child or the child to save the mother. A discussion about the sins of contraception follows. Joyce's famous remark to Frank Budgen, that the killing of the sacred oxen had signified to him "the crime committed against fecundity by sterilizing the act of coition" is usually brought up at this point and is given serious attention by many critics.[20] J. S. Atherton, however, suggests that the "tone of the passage . . . leaves one in doubt as to its seriousness,"[21] and I would agree. At least one can be certain that the medical students are partially the target of Joyce's attack, and Henke is right to point out that the crime against fecundity deals with "emotional, rather than with physical, prophylaxis."[22] The male bonding presented to us here is indeed sterile, and Stephen's association must ultimately be "fruitless" because it cannot make him physically whole.

At this point, Stephen fills all the cups and proposes a toast: "Now drink we, quod he, of this mazer and quaff ye this mead which is not indeed parcel of my body but my soul's bodiment. Leave ye fraction of bread to them that live by bread alone" (391). Stephen's unmistakable imitation of Christ at the Last Supper has been noted by critics. He is, for one thing, paraphrasing Jesus's words (Matthew 4:4) that "man shall not live by bread alone but by every word that proceedeth out of the mouth of God." But Father Boyle makes the point that in Catholic communion practice, those who live "by bread alone" are the laity who in former times received only the bread during communion. He notes that Bloom, in "Lotus Eaters," is aware of this because he observes that the priest "doesn't give them any of it" (81), that is, the wine. Stephen has set himself over the laity, Boyle argues, and as priest can drink from the chalice.[23] It may also be true that the wine, a divine substance, as opposed to water, a component of the female principle, would naturally be preferred by Stephen whose need to transcend the elemental is obsessive. For example, his making the mead his soul's bodiment is explained in an interesting way by Boyle. He argues that Stephen's mead is his soul's bodiment because, "Unlike Christ, who undergoes no change at all, the artist acquires a new 'body' in which his soul will operate, namely his ink, which is now informed with the disembodied substance of the artist. His new body is the letters of the alphabet."[24]

The suggestions of the Last Supper further reinforce Joyce's conscientious use of food as a structuring dynamic for creativity. In the Last Supper, the sacramental nature of the meal connects food to a higher order of consciousness and adds to that sacrament the idea of priest as sacrifice. Alan Watts notes the "collossal cannibalism" of life that continues "only at the cost of death" and observes that because of this state of things, sacrifice is an ever-present necessity. The mass represents a true sacrifice because it is volitional. Watts says: "The performer of a self-sacrifice is at once Priest and Offering."[25] Stephen's awareness of this role and the nourishing aspects of the mass have led him to associate the role of the artist with that of the priest. This divine nourishment creates, in Boyle's words "a new conscience—a *knowing-with* Christ" which, when associated with the artistic process, allows Stephen to create a new form, "a new conscience, a *knowing-with* the artist."[26]

Another sacramental meal suggested by this scene, however, is Jesus' feeding of the multitudes. (Mulligan testifies to this analogue when, arriving late and raindrenched, he asks "for whom were those loaves and fishes" [403].) This meal also occurs in the waste land, according to most New Testament versions, in the wilderness to which Jesus has retreated and into which the multitudes have followed him. Rather than send the people back into the villages to obtain food, Jesus takes up the seven loaves and the few fishes, blesses them, and distributes them to the thousands. Mark 8:8 concludes, "So they did eat, and were filled: and they took up of the broken meat that was left seven baskets." The significance of this transformation seems to lie not so much in the fact that seven loaves fed so many people but that the spiritually hungering multitudes were fed by the Word. That is, the food here is more than food; it is "transaccidentated" into spiritual sustenance. Stephen, like Jesus, knows that "bread alone" is insufficient, but the multitudes and the medical students are unaware of this.

Nevertheless, these allusions, as important as they are, do not turn Stephen into an artist. He is more characterized by sterility at this point. His boast about being the "giver of life" to the "ghosts" who will "troop to my call" is rebuffed by Lynch who says, "That answer . . . will adorn you more fitly when something more, and greatly more, than a capful of light odes can call your genius father" (415). Moreover, he is still trying to grapple with the image of the female as creator, and the nature of his struggle can be clearly seen in the speech on creativity that follows his toast: "Mark me now. In woman's womb word is made flesh but in the spirit of the maker all flesh that passes becomes the word that shall not pass away. This is postcreation" (391). Stephen's discussion of "postcreation," where he separates female creation, "the word made flesh," from the masculine, hence spiritual and immortal creation where "all flesh that passes becomes the word that shall not pass away," indicates, as Maddox puts it, that Stephen is trying "like the fetus struggling to be born, to establish independence from his mother."[27] Stephen's words to the medical students are significant also because they are filled with the references to two feasts involving the Virgin, the Feast of the Blessed Virgin Mary of the Rosary, and the Feast of the Motherhood of the Blessed Virgin Mary.[28]

Stephen's struggle to assert "the artist's superiority over Mary as producer of the Word," to use Boyle's words,[29] is due to his inability to accept, to be made fruitful, to be open to the idea of the virgin—virgin matter, unploughed soil. Frank Zingrone, in his discussion of Joyce's use of the alchemical images of D'Annunzio's *Marriage of Fire and Water,* says, "It is through the woman that the poet must learn how to reconcile these primordial elements, the agents of all change, to 'marry' them in order to connect with higher powers."[30] Later Stephen again comments on this bondage to the female: "The aged sisters draw us into life: we wail, batten, sport, clip, clasp, sunder, dwindle, die: over us dead they bend. First saved from the water of Old Nile, among bulrushes, a bed of fasciated wattles: at last the cavity of a mountain, an occulted sepulchre" (394). Stephen never escapes containment by the female, even when he chooses Moses and Jesus as paradigmatic heroes. Moses is contained in a basket and floated on water and is saved by a woman. Jesus is contained by the tomb of earth. Both Moses and Jesus form a beginning and an end of sorts, creating a linear historical time frame that is no less depressing for Stephen than the cycles of nature. The fact that his pronouncements are next interupted by a devastating clap of thunder—Nobodaddy "in his cups" (395) and another alimental image—is not so much a sign of God's disapproval as a sign of Stephen's captivity in nature, for in this episode, nature and its cylical processes haunt Stephen almost as much as they do Bloom. His image of God as a devouring being seems an intellectualized or literary version of Bloom's thoughts on process. For Stephen, God is "an omnivorous being which can masticate, deglute, digest and apparently pass through the ordinary channel with pluterperfect imperturbability such multifarious aliments as cancrenous females emaciated by parturition, corpulent professional gentlemen, not to speak of jaundiced politicians and chlorotic nuns" (420). This passage, like Stephen's sardonic references to the Virgin, suggests again his aversion to types of creation grounded in the body or in the female. One way he works toward his concept of "postcreation" is by depicting such types of creation as related to devouring.

And yet Stephen's preoccupation with the Virgin and the Advent is essential to his development as an artist, not just because of the creative images associated with it, but because of the relation of the Advent to the captivity of the children of Israel. It is interesting that feasts that celebrate the Advent and the freedon from captivity in Egypt also celebrate a break with the past and the forgiveness of sin. Stephen, at one point in this chapter says, "There are sins or (let us call them as the world call them) evil memories which are hidden away by man in the darkest places of the heart" (421). These evil memories do indeed haunt Stephen to the extent that only when he is free from bondage to the past will he be able to be a truly creative artist. Therefore, his interest in the Advent involves first, the problem of bondage and only second, the problem of creativity. Bondage to the past becomes then the major subject here and a complement to the issues of creation and birth.

Memory is a source of bondage to both Stephen and Bloom. We know that Stephen's bondage is to Ireland, church, and mother, and he expresses this state of things in biblical terms as he tries to erase the curse of memory: "Remember, Erin, thy generations and thy days of old, how thou settedst little by me and by my word and broughtest in a stranger to my gates to commit fornication in my sight and to wax fat and kick like Jeshurum. Therefore has thou sinned against the light and has made me, thy lord, to be the slave of servants" (393). His invocation for Ireland to remember is countered ironically by his own inability to forget, and rather than call Ireland to remember, he is called to remembering the one thing he most wants to forget: his mother. First, however, in one of those "retrogressive metamorphoses" that dominate the chapter, Ireland becomes merged with the lands of the Israelites as Stephen continues: "Look forth now, my people, upon the land of behest, even from Horeb and from Nebo and from Pisgah and from the Horns of Hatten unto a land flowing with milk and money" (393). In an echo of "Proteus" and "Aeolus" and paraphrasing God's words to Moses, Stephen changes the Old Testament mountains—sources of inspiration, revelation and of the law, the word—into a sterile inversion that is Ireland. He very pointedly concludes: "But thou has suckled me with a bitter milk: my moon and my sun thou has quenched for ever. And thou has left me alone for ever in the dark ways of my bitterness: and with a kiss of ashes hast thou kissed my mouth" (393). All the foregoing images, the "kiss of ashes" that refers to Stephen's mother, the references to, and punning on, the lands of milk and honey, and to the mountains which are symbolically sources of inspiration, involve nourishment and sustenance that is celebrated and ritualized in feasts.[31] We recall also that kissing is associated with ingestion, especially for Stephen, and that for him to be kissed by his mother, or anyone else, is to be devoured. Breath is usually associated with the Holy Ghost, but for Stephen it is also associated with death and with his mother. When she appeared to him in a dream, he recalls "her breath bent over him with mute secret words, a faint odour of wetted ashes" (10) Also, his mother's words are characterized by mystery; they are mute and secret and have no relation to light, inspiration, immortality as Stephen's words will have.

The feasts that give the digestive processes cosmic significance becomes more abstract, more spiritual as human consciousness develops. That is, food comes to stand for the law, for the word, which in turn becomes the true nourishment. Stephen, presiding over his irreverent friends' meal, a mock Last Supper, laments his and Ireland's bondage and sterility. And yet the reference to biblical promises, to feasts that celebrate God's covenant with the children of Israel, as well as the Incarnation itself, suggest that Stephen is working toward a tentative kind of creativity. These feasts are used to suggest this creativity and to suggest also the reestablishment of the fatherhood of Bloom on a spiritual or symbolic basis. But before discussing the key feast of the chapter—the Pentecost—it is necessary to examine Bloom's role in "Oxen."

Bloom does not really partake of the revelry or of the eating in the common room and seems to be there because he is concerned about Mrs. Purefoy. He appears as a sorrowful overseer, feeling both for Mrs. Purefoy and for Stephen. But Bloom, like Stephen, is in bondage. The land flowing with milk and honey, which is promised to Moses when he has led the children of Israel out of Egypt,[32] is only to be achieved after they are free. Bloom, like Moses, is there to lead Stephen out of bondage in some manner, but he must first free himself. Alan Watts, in discussing the problem of deliverance from the past, says: "So long as the mind is captivated by memory, and really feels itself to be that past image . . . it can do nothing to save itself; its sacrifices are of no avail, and its Law gives no life . . . it remains hopelessly and helplessly captive, just so long as this dead image continues to give any illusion of life."[33] Bloom's bondage to process and memory has been especially pointed up in "Lestrygonians" and "Hades," and we are aware here too of the continuation of this state of mind—but perhaps with a difference that is suggested by Stephen's phrase "retrogressive metamorphoses" (394). After experiencing an understanding of Mrs. Purefoy's pain, and pity for Stephen's fear of thunder, as well as distress for the poor diseased cattle who are to be slaughtered ("What . . . will they slaughter all" [399]), Bloom begins to share certain images of sterility, betrayal, and death with Stephen. After the mystical disappearance of Haines, the narrator seems to blend the minds of both men: "The mystery was unveiled. Haines was the third brother. His real name was Childs. The black panther was himself the ghost of his own father. He drank drugs to obliterate. For this relief much thanks. The lonely house by the graveyard is uninhabited. No soul would live there. The spider pitches her web in solitude. The nocturnal rat peers from his hole. A curse is on it. It is haunted. Murderer's ground" (412).

After this unveiling of Haines, Bloom has his first vision. It seems to be something more than memory because we are told that Bloom is no longer "ruminating, chewing the cud of reminiscence" (413). This phrase is important not only because it suggests Bloom's alimental nature, but because the "cud of reminiscence" picks up on two images from "Lestrygonians." The first involves Bloom's own eating on Howth and the second the terrier who has vomited his cud: "Returned with thanks having fully digested the contents. First sweet, then savoury" (179). But memory seems to be of a different sort here. Bloom envisions himself as "young Leopold, as in a retrospective arrangement, a mirror within a mirror," carrying his wheaten loaf." He next becomes the "fullfledged traveller for the family firm." Then, however, "the mirror is breathed on and the young knighterrant recedes, shrivels," (413). Here breath, inspiration, destroys vision, but creates Bloom next as a father of a different sort. Now he finds himself "paternal and these about him might be his sons. Who can say? The wise father knows his own child" (413). Here, on a comic level, the spirit has moved on the mirror, erasing the dead images Watts speaks of, and allowing a more fruitful present image to be born. Bloom seems, at least for the moment, less "helplessly captive," and the dead image has receded, allowing Bloom's sacrifices for Stephen to become meaningful and active. His assumption of symbolic paternity, the end product of his vision, seems positive enough, although doubtless impermanent.

Bloom's next vision of his first sexual encounter with Bridie seems sterile, and it is true that his encounter with this "bride of darkness" is followed by the narrator's taunt, "No Leopold! Name and memory solace thee not. That youthful illusion of thy strength was taken from thee and in vain. No son of thy loins is by thee. There is none now to be for Leopold what Leopold was for Rudolph" (413-14). But what the narrator might also be pointing out is that since memory will no longer solace him, Bloom will now live in some better, more creative present. Bloom's "illusion" of strength is perhaps taken from him "in vain." Does this then mean that Bloom's illusion of strength is gone and that his loss is in vain, or is the deprivation in vain because Bloom's strength *will* go on? The fact that "there is none now to be for Leopold what Leopold was for Rudolph" does not mean that symbolically or consubstantially there is no father-son relationship for Bloom, only that biologically there is none. There is no son of his loins. Stanley Sultan argues that Bloom's vision is a "reiteration of the idea of the familial line, the 'proliferant continuance' which is presented . . . in Bloom's thoughts about Rudy's coffin and his father's deathbed."[34] Sultan goes on to say that Bloom does not reassert his claim on Molly but instead gives up any hope of having a son and seeks a substitute in Stephen.[35] But I think Stephen is more than a substitution. He is a son to Bloom because of Bloom's developing understanding of consubstantiality, due in part to his earlier "ingestion" of the meaning of the mass in "Lotus Eaters."

The ensuing vision of the waste land does not seem to offer hope either: "Swiftly, silently the soul is wafted over regions of cycles of cycles of generations that have lived. A region where grey twilight ever descends, never falls on wide sagegreen pasturefields, shedding her dusk, scattering a perennial dew of stars" (414). And after the vision of a "mare leading her fillyfoal"—perhaps symbols of Molly and Milly—the vision concludes: "They fade, sad phantoms: all is gone. Agandath is a waste land, a home of screechowls. . . . Netaim, the golden, is no more '(414)."

Mulligan, aware of Bloom's reverie, makes a facetious but interesting comment. Cautioning the students against breaking into Bloom's reverie, he says, "It is as painful perhaps to be awakened from a vision as to be born" (416). This comment suggests the change in Bloom as well as the connection between awakening, vision, and birth.

These actions bring us to the subject of the Pentecost. Harry Blamires has pointed to the important Pentecostal images that he suggests are "hinted at" but are "neither precise nor predominant" at first but become more definite as the chapter progresses.[36] He also observes that the increasingly chaotic discussion and the obscurity of language corresponds to the apostles' speaking in many tongues. I think that not only are the Pentecostal elements present, but also that they are essential correlatives to creativity and the birth of the Word. What is also important, however, is the fact that the Pentecost is a feast, that the ingestion of food was involved in the transformation process that led to the creation of the Word.

For one thing, the Pentecostal feast was born out of an earlier one—the Jewish Festival of Weeks, or the Shabout, and is an evolutional development itself. It was celebrated in honor of the grain harvest when the first fruits, the new bread, were offered to the deity in return for which God gave the Israelites the law. The two loaves of the offering came to symbolize the tablets of the law, derived from the mountain, the source of inspiration.[37] Thus the Shabout celebrates a birthday—the birth of the Torah, the birth of the Israelites' covenant with the God who delivered them out of bondage.

As the Shabout celebrates the birth of the covenant between God and the Israelites, it becomes in the Pentecost the birth of the church and celebrates yet another deliverance out of the bondage to the past. The transformations involved in both feasts are alimental in their origins, and the alimentary process evolves so that nourishment is seen as a spiritual as well as a physical event. The first fruits become bread which become tables of law and the Word; the Word, in turn, becomes food. The connection between bread and the mountain is established earlier in the chapter where bread is even described as a "vast mountain" (387). Gaster also notes that the eating of dairy dishes, especially cheeses, is associated with the Pentecost. One argument for the basis of this custom is that cheese (Hebrew *gebinah*) is orthographically close to the Hebrew word for mountain (*gabnunim*). To eat of the cheese/mountain is therefore to ingest the meaning of the law.[38] The eating of cheese in honor of the law is, in any case, an established custom. The *Jewish Encyclopedia* points out that the law is also likened to honey and milk.[39] What these customs and food metaphors suggest then is the close identification of food with spiritual forms of sustenance.

In the Pentecost, the apostles, like the medical students, are gathered in one body to eat and drink, to celebrate a birth—one of the Torah, the other of Mina Purefoy's baby. Rites of *plerosis,* or filling—enacted in communal feasts—are here transformed and spiritualized. The apostles are filled with the Holy Spirit. First there is the "rushing mighty wind" and the "cloven tongues as of fire, and it sat on them" (Acts 2:2–3). The apostles, now gifted with many tongues, can spread the Word. The people, however, take them to be merely drunk, but Peter tells them of God's promise: "To pour out of my Spirit upon all flesh; and your sons and your daughters shall prophesy, and your young men shall see visions and your old men shall dream dreams" (Acts 2:17). The alimentary basis of the feast is never obscured either. The flames are like tongues; the spirit is "poured" into the apostles, and they are fed a new kind of food.

According to the *Catholic Encyclopedia,* the Pentecost is a "feast of Messianic blessing."[40] Indeed, the feast of the medical students, with Stephen presiding and Bloom attending, has its messianic overlay. The many references to both Moses and Jesus suggest that Bloom and Stephen are both associated with the role of messiah.

The question of how much creativity really is present in this chapter will, perhaps, never be answered. In the Bible, the disciples are empowered with the word; Jesus is that word, and Pentecost is, in effect, the birth of the true meaning of the Incarnation, the "word made flesh." Maddox describes the Incarnation as "the perfected expression of the Word. In the perfected Incarnation, the distinction between substance and expression, between intention and act, would disappear."[41] But Stephen cannot realize this achievement. He tries to become the creator, the giver of life, however, and says: "You have spoken of the past and its phantoms. . . . Why think of them? If I call them into life across the waters of Lethe will not the poor ghosts troop to my call? Who supposes it? I, Bous Stephanoumenos, bullockbefriending bard, am Lord and giver of their life" (415). *Bous Stephanoumenos* means ox–or bull-soul. *Noumena* is breath, but also in Kantian terms it is that which is apprehended by thought, which is known to exist but cannot be experienced, and to which no properties can be intelligibly ascribed. But Stephen cannot yet quicken into life because he is still bound to dead images of the past, and Lynch's unpleasant reminder of his artistic failure and memory of his mother almost cause him to leave at one point.

Still, something has happened in "Oxen." It has rained in Dublin; Mrs. Purefoy has given birth; Bloom has dreamed dreams that have perhaps freed him from bondage to the past, bondage to the dead and the living. Stephen has uttered the Word, even if it is only "Burke's!" (423). By becoming the consubstantial father of Stephen, Bloom has become a kind of incarnation of an aspect of the Shabout. The purpose of offering the firstfruits to the deity involved belief that the new was dangerous until brought into contact with the old. By this offering, the limits of temporal existence were transcended. Instead of being a source of bondage, the past became a source of freedom from mortality. Bloom, overseeing Stephen, oversees also his incipient creativity.

Incarnation blurs distinctions between old and new, time and space. Bloom and Stephen have long been seen as complements. Bloom incarnates—perhaps imperfectly— process, natural cycles, and rhythms; he is at peace with the alimental and elemental. Stephen cannot become the word until he has married within himself the oppositions that fragment him. Bloom seems to function as a promise of that psychic marriage. Stephen attempts to deny the presence of food, earth, and lower body functions in particular; Bloom affirms them.

Bondage to the past must be replaced by an understanding, not a repudiation, of the eternity of process. Then the old becomes the generator of the new; out of old language the new is born; out of the Shabout came the Pentecost; out of the fruits of the earth comes the fruit of understanding, the Word; out of the Mosaic messiahship comes the ministry of Jesus; out of these sacramental events is born the artist—the greatest ingester and metabolizer of them all.

Turning to "Circe," perhaps the most experimental and provocative chapter in its use of fantasy, psychodrama, dream, and confession, we are confronted with a set of problems in regard to the alimentary function and the creative process. 'Circe" seems dominated by images of anality, and the vision, contrary to popular criticism, seems more excremental than sexual, although the two are not unrelated. Also, a sense of shame, projected through the episode's confessional aspects and the accusing figures that appear throughout, suggests a courageous exploration of what Mark Shechner refers to as "the most anxiety-producing aspects of Joyce's psychosexual nature."[42]

The dissolution of boundaries between unconscious and conscious, male and female, illusion and reality, subject and object, animate and inanimate, tempts us to read Joyce's personal experience into this episode. Consequently, "Circe" has also been the object of much psychoanalytic criticism. Because we are not dealing specifically with Bloom's thoughts about food and the creative process or with Stephen's problems about guilt and his fear of being devoured, we must ultimately regard the episode as a large *vas mirabili* where ingestion, digestion and excretion are process, existing beyond individual characters, a metamorphic representation in itself of the formation of a work of art. "Circe" is then, the culmination of the food metaphor that begins with Stephen's fears about the world of instinct and his guilt about his mother and also with Bloom's defecation and his "outrage" to Phillip Beaufoy in the outhouse. Excrement becomes the dominant element in "Circe" because excrement is both the first and last product, the source of all new growth, the *materia prima*—the end product of Stephen's bread of daily experience. That is why, despite its confessional and nightmarish aspects and its paranoid quality, "Circe" is also, as some critics acknowledge, sometimes with puzzlement, a celebration.[43]

That "Circe" can be a celebration while concomitantly revealing the darker, unconscious workings of the mind and the more unpleasant aspects of human existence is linked to the fact that it depicts process becoming art. The elements of the chapter are essentially familiar, previous events of the novel, ingested and metabolized into a new form. The fact that excrement and an attention to the lower body pole is so evident in so creative a chapter implies a major Joycean insight about the creative process, a revelation that will become more explicit in *Finnegans Wake* when Shem creates ink from his own excrement.

It is important to get beyond the notion that the content of "Circe" is simply grotesque, and it is also important to avoid the tags of "sin" and "evil" although both are concepts that have important influences over the body's oral, anal, and genital responses to the world, especially in the case of Stephen. For the present, I would like to discuss the emphasis on the lower body pole with regard to its functions in the episode and to suggest that this emphasis was not due solely to Joyce's enjoyment of cloacal detail, nor to his attempt to battle literary repression, but rather to the fact that such detail points to the sources of energy that appear to be initiated only on so-called higher levels of consciousness. We must remember that for primitive people—and hence for the primitive consciousness in us all—all body secretions are endowed with mana, and all parts of the body are considered alive and sacred. Neumann reminds us, furthermore, that in terms of body symbolism the dominant creative substance is not semen at all: "In creation mythology, urine, dung, spit, sweat, and breath (and later words) are all elementary symbols of the creative principle."[44]

When using the phrase *lower body pole* in relation to "Circe," we must speak mostly of the anus, but there are also a number of vessel or container references that suggest at first womb or female genitalia. For example, the general descriptive movement in the early pages is inward, into nighttown, into the brothel, into the women, suggesting, as the bawd says, "maidenhead inside" (431). The street is described as filled with "drains, clefts, cesspools" (433). Bridie Kelly, Bloom's first sexual partner, stands "in the gap of her den furtive" (441), and in one of the gaping doors, a crone "rams the last bottle in the maw of his sack" (430).

There are ingestive processes operating, too. Bloom is about his usual custom of acquiring food. Here he is first seen "cramming bread and chocolate" into his pocket (433), and he next proceeds to buy *"a lukewarm pig's crubeen"* and a *"cold sheep's trotter"* (434). Molly is imagined by Bloom being fed a mango by a camel and is also remembered by Bloom and Mrs. Breen eating a spiced beef sandwich (447). Richie Goulding carries a bag full of *"polonies, kippered herrings, Findon haddies and tightpacked pills"* (447). Pat, the waiter of the Ormond, carries a dish of *"spillspilling gravy"* (447). Bloom's feeding of the protean dog recalls his feeding of Banbury cakes to the gulls at lunchtime. Bloom, in turn, is fed by Zoe in the brothel. Foods such as oysters are mentioned a number of times as aphrodisiacs (461, 516), and we are told of serpents that feed on the milk of women and cows.

However, as one might expect in a chapter like "Circe," food is also put to some rather strange uses and takes on the inverted character of the episode. Most often it is placed in containers—Bloom's pockets, Richie's bag. That is, it appears already to have been ingested, to have been already assimilated, and some items have the suggestion of excrement about them. For example, Bloom, as messianic figure, has *"hambones, condensed milk tins, unsaleable cabbage, stale bread, sheeps' tails, odd pieces of fat"* dumped on him (492). Paddy's spilling of gravy and even Bloom's chocolate are suggestive of excrementa. (It is after Bloom is fed the chocolate by Zoe that he undergoes his most strenuous trial with Bella.) Bloom is also called "dungdevourer" by Bella (530). Even Bloom's feeding of the dog has an excremental quality about it, and the feeding seems more like an elimination. In "a dark stalestunk corner" Bloom *"unrolls one parcel and goes to dump the crubeen softly but holds back and feels the trotter. . . . With regret he lets unrolled crubeen and trotter slide"* (453).

As mentioned above, food is very often contained, and a number of sack, pouch, pocket, and bucket images that often contain secret things besides food and organic matter are used. Bloom's pockets become metaphors of ingestion as he crams them with his bread and chocolate. After emerging from Olhousen's he pats his pockets "with parcelled *hands watch, fobpocket, bookpocket, pursepocket, sweets of sin, potato soap"* (437). He continues to worry about his pockets as he envisions Molly beside her date palm tree, and although he tries literally to ingest this vision *"in deep agitation, swallowing gulps of air, questions, hopes, crubeens for her supper,"* he "bestows" parcels in his pockets (439). When he reaches the brothel, Zoe takes his potato from his pocket and places it "greedily" into her own (476). Later, the

Babes and Sucklings sing in an inversion of the Howth scene: "Clap clap hands till Poldy comes home,/Cakes in his pocket for Leo alone"(486). Bloom's most important "pocket" is his scrotum which gets a thorough handling by Zoe. Doubtless the shrivelled black potato removed from his pocket is a correlative for his own sack and its contents, which seem symbolically lacking in these scenes.

Other characters also possess containers that are associated with secret things and excrement. Ellen Bloom, described as wearing a *"blouse with muttonleg sleeves buttoned behind,"* a phrase that characteristically includes food and anal references, is upset with Bloom (in his vision) and ransacks *"the pouch of her striped blay petticoat. A phial, and Agnus Dei, a shriveled potato and a celluloid doll fall out"* (438). These dessicated religious artificats seem more suggestive of defecation than birth. Philip Beaufoy, in another of Bloom's visions, appears as Bloom's accuser carrying a large portfolio labeled "Matcham's Masterstrokes" (458). Given the connection between Beaufoy and the outhouse, we are inclined to associate the contents of this container with excrement also. Gerty McDowell accuses Bloom of seeing "all the secrets of my bottom drawer" (442).

A number of buckets make their appearance in "Circe," too. One is Mary Driscoll's. Another is the subject of the Gaffer's story. This particular bucket, albeit a possible figment of Bloom's imagination, is supposedly the salvation of Bloom who, undergoing a severe intestinal attack, made use of it—with embarrassing consequences. The Gaffer tells of Bloom "doing it into the bucket of porter that was there waiting on the shavings for Derwan's plasterers" (450). Bloom himself is forced to recall, or reinvent, this incident later. Much later, during Stephen's confrontation with Privates Carr and Compton, Edward VII appears sucking his red jujube and carrying the same plasterer's bucket, on which is now inscribed, "Defense d'uriner," a prohibition that seems to associate the English king with British fastidiousness that is ultimately a repression and an indication of sterility. Stephen must, of course, kill the priest and king, and Edward is finally seen rattling an empty bucket. Thus in "Circe" a full and overflowing bucket seems a positive image.

The teapot, first mentioned in connection with Mother Grogan, also becomes an important container. In his sexually coded conversation with Mrs. Breen, Bloom says, "I'm teapot with curiosity to find out whether some person's something is a little teapot at present," to which Mrs. Breen replies, "Tremendously teapot!" (445). Bella also refers to Bloom's penis as a teapot, taunting, "Where's your curly teapot gone to or who docked it on you, cockyally?" (541).

And of course there is a different kind of pot—Molly's chamberpot. Without belaboring Tindall's comments about containers,[45] we can see that they do seem to have a great importance for Joyce, and in "Circe" it would appear that disparate elements, seemingly random, are carried in containers and are transformed because they now have become symbols and therefore carry associations. "Circe" itself is also an apparently random collection of contents—speeches, actions, even objects—that, in being so contained, have become a new form. The fundamental analogue that operates here is digestive. The objects excreted into the mind of the reader, after undergoing transformations, create out of Bloom's and Stephen's experiences the emergent work of art.

Another interesting feature of "Circe" is that because of the inverted nature of the episode, where everything is upended, mouths and vessel imagery suggesting the mouth become more suggestive instead of the anus. For example, Privates Carr and Compton, early in the chapter "burst together from their mouths a volleyed fart" (430). Paddy Dignam's "coalhole" is both mouth and anus, and Tom Rochford, who *"fixes the manhole with a resolute stare"* before executing *"a daredevil salmon leap in the air"* is *engulfed in the coalhole,"* too. (474).

Some vessel images seem sexual but still have an anal quality about them, and they deal in some way with food. An example is Stephen's play on Omar Khayyam's "loaf and jug of bread and wine" (433). Stephen merges male and female symbols, here effecting a double transformation. Using gesture to replace language (Stephen has also surrendered his ashplant), he tries to best Omar by turning words into body. Besides being keyed to the idea of "movement back from rationality to animality," as Blamires puts it,[46] the scene seems to suggest that Stephen, having been given the gift of tongues in "Oxen," still has need of the body to inform a viable art. Lynch's question, "Which is the jug of bread?" is both sexual and androgynous (433). Later, Bloom, using a similar image, will say, "Man and woman, love, what is it? A cork and bottle" (499). Thus the normal world, in which ingestion also signifies assimilation, is overturned in "Circe" and various inversions are carried to uncomfortable extremes in order to express natural, cyclical rhythms and to affirm the dynamic of ingestion and elimination.

The many references to kissing in "Circe" reinforce the argument that it is closely associated with eating and assimilation. Early in the episode, Mrs. Breen makes much of kissing. She asks Bloom to "kiss the spot to make it well," but she also offers him a *"pigeon kiss . . . her pulpy tongue between her lips"* (446). Bloom immediately associates the kiss with Molly, thinking, "Kosher. A snack for supper. The home without potted meat is incomplete" (446). Kissing, sweetness, stickiness recall Molly and the ingesting of the seedcake on Howth and counter the thought of the potted meat. When the kisses become dramatis personae and fly about Bloom, they repeat a number of images of sweetness: "(*Warbling.*) Leo! (*Twittering.*) Icky licky micky sticky for Leo! (*Cooing.*) Coo Coocoo! Yummyumm Womwom! (Warbling.) Big comebig! Pirouette! Leopopold! (*Twittering.*) Leeolee! (*Warbling.*) O Leo!" (475). Zoe's lips also remind Bloom of Molly and sweetness. He is first aware of "dumb moist lips," but later they become "*odalisk lips lusciously smeared with salve of swinefat and rosewater*" (477). Later, kissing the nymph will become an important source of conflict for Bloom.

It is not surprising to find, in an episode where lower body poles play such an important role, that the sense of smell is important as well. Smell is more basic than sight and is more characteristic of animals who are, of course, earth-oriented. Smell dominates early human consciousness, too, before the child learns to sit and finally stand. Then sight and speech, the more spiritualized functions, take over. But in "Circe," where the world is essential, olfactory images are numerous. Zoe possesses "*cloying breath of stale garlic*" (477) that is not unpleasant to Bloom. In fact, he is drawn to her by smell: "*He hesitates amid scents, music, temptations,*" and then Zoe "*leads him toward the steps, drawing him by the odour of her armpits*" (501). Bloom is also aroused by the smell of her slip "*in whose sinuous folds lurks the lion reek of all the male brutes that have possessed her*" (501). Later, Virag will also discourse on the attraction of male insects to the "smell of the inferiorly pulchritudinous female possessing extendified pudendal verve in dorsal region" (515). When Bella Cohen arrives, she describes herself as "all of a mucksweat" (527), and the Hoof demands that Bloom "smell my hot goathide" (529).

That Bloom enjoys posterior odors we know already, but his bent is confirmed by the sins of the Past who accuse him of "gloating over a nauseous fragment of wellused toilet paper presented to him by a nasty harlot" (537). And Bella further elaborates on Bloom's predilection when, in punishing him, she forces him to do what he really likes to do best: "By day you will souse and bat our smelling underclothes also when we ladies are unwell, and swab out our latrines with dress pinned up and a dishclout tied to your tail" (538). Bloom also smells "onions. Stale. Sulphur. Grease" (554) on Bella. His early sensuous experiences have been titillated, as he confesses, by "the mingling odours of the ladies' cloakroom and lavatory, the throng penned tight on the old Royal stairs" and "the dark sexsmelling theatre" (548). The importance of odor to Bloom is perhaps most clearly delineated in his encounter with the nymph, whose metamorphosis also involves smells.

Bloom's fondness for smells has its origins in his interest in anal matters, an interest that we have seen manifested many times before. In "Circe" however, this interest receives its most extensive attention. In the beginning of the episode, the motorman of the sandstrewer, who nearly runs Bloom down, calls him "shitbreeches" and accuses him of doing the hattrick (which, according to Tindall, means covering "a turd on the curb with his hat . . . telling the policeman it is a bird"[47]). Bella calls him "adorer of the adulterous rump" and "dung-devourer" (530). Bloom's inclinations have been variously interpreted. Brivic sees Bloom's devotion to matter and excrement as a kind of religion which sets him amidst a "modern world of industrialism and capitalism."[48] Many critics tend to view him as a masochist for whom fantasy is a positive purge. I think the questions raised about Bloom's interest in matters excremental, especially in this episode, can be best answered by a consideration of Joyce's use of purgation. For him, purgation would seem to exist not only in terms of religion and ritual, but also in alchemy and art. Purgation in "Circe" cannot refer only to Bloom's peculiar and personal psychic makeup or to Joyce's need to work through repression and his own psychosexual fantasies. What we see in "Circe" is the manifestation of Joyce's larger artistic concerns about the creative process. To explore this process, he had need of excremental images.

To this end, it is important not only that Bloom's fantasies involve excremental images and grow out of his day's experiences, but also that Bloom be associated with excrement itself. There are numerous examples of the former. Many of Bloom's sexual fantasies seem tinged with anality. He has surprised Mary Driscoll "in the rere of the premises" (461). To Mrs. Bellingham he has given "a blossom of the homegrown potato plant" (446). He has also lauded her "nether extremities." He has urged Mrs. Talboys to "soil his letter in an unspeakable manner, to chastise him as he richly deserves" (467). Bloom's encounter with Virag also emphasizes his perhaps excessive interest in bottoms. Virag's observations of "backview" and "intimate garments of which you are a particular devotee" (512) depict another instance where a relative reproaches Bloom for his anality. Virag also points out to Bloom Zoe's "rere lower down" and adds, for Bloom's enjoyment, a further elaboration of the "two additional protuberances, suggestive of potent rectum and tumescent for palpation which leave nothing to be desired save compactness" (513). As already mentioned, the Sins of the Past also focus most particularly on Bloom's anal preoccupations. Their accusation is, "By word and deed he encouraged a nocturnal strumpet to deposit fecal and other matter in an unsanitary outhouse. . . . Did he not lie in bed, the gross boar, gloating over a nauseous fragment of wellused toilet paper presented to him by a nasty harlot, stimulated by gingerbread and a postal order" (537).

Sometimes excremental images reflect on his own body functions. The Gaffer's story of Bloom's defecation into what he takes to be a bucket of plaster but is in reality a bucket of porter, is a source of shame for Bloom. Whether the story is an actual happening or not, it serves the purpose of connecting logically in Bloom's mind with Philip Beaufoy and the morning outhouse incident. Bloom rehearses the experience as follows: "*Bowel trouble. In Beaver street. Gripe, yes. Quite bad. A plasterer's bucket. By walking stifflegged. Suffered untold misery. Deadly agony. About noon. Love or burgundy. Yes, some spinach. Crucial moment. He did not look in the bucket. Nobody. Rather a mess. Not completely. A* Titbits *back number*" (462). Apparently Bloom has lacked recourse to Beaufoy's *Titbits,* but it is also evident that Bloom's waste products have a way of combining with other materials associated with transformation—first the bucket of porter ("wine" is here turned into excrement) and then the printed page. The Gaffer has made a story out of Bloom's personal act of defecation. In "Circe," the story is one of many random elements that make the chapter an artistic whole. Beaufoy's story is also related to Bloom's "bottom" and is linked to the Gaffer's story, thereby making a comment on the creative process and linking it with body processes again. Beaufoy argues that his mature work has been "disfugured by the hallmark of the beast" (459). This accusation is reiterated in the art of "Circe," the chapter that is also "disfigured" by the same hallmark. It is no accident that Beaufoy is summoned by Myles Crawford, who in "Circe" is editor of the "*Freeman's Urinal*" and "*Weekly Arsewiper*" (458), another comic yet serious insistence that the written word has some relation to the hindparts. The jump from these associations to Shem's fecal ink is not great.

Bloom is also, however, associated even more directly with excrement as his role takes on archetypal dimensions. Even in the beginning of the chapter we get hints of his role as scapegoat. He emerges out of a fog amid "middens," or dung heaps, and "stagnant fumes" (433). He is almost immediately reproached by his father, mother, and wife for being soiled in some way. Rudolph recalls a night when he returns home drunk with "mud head to foot," and we also have a vision of Bloom in "youth's smart blue Oxford suit . . . coated with stiffening mud" (438). A distressed Ellen Bloom seems to look for Bloom amid her petticoats, not quite as if he were being born, and says "sacred Heart of Mary, where were you at all, at all?" (438). Molly, beside her date palm in Bloom's next vision, calls him a "poor old stick in the mud" (440). Later in the chapter, after his resurrection, Bloom is "rolled in a mummy" and falls "into the purple waiting waters" (550).

If we link Bloom to scapegoat ritual, the identification with excrement becomes more logical. Vickery, pointing to certain motifs such as the singling out of the scapegoat, the heaping of ridicule upon him, his trial and punishment, and the atmosphere of Walpurgisnacht and the Saturnalia, argues for Bloom as cast in this pattern.[49] Gose also emphasizes the use of scapegoat ritual, but sees Bloom's role as that of a comic actor. He says, "Joyce's handling of ritual motifs suggests that his interest is much more in comic regression than in the mystery of archetypal patterns."[50]

It is also helpful, however, to focus on the scapegoat ritual as it relates to food and the digestive process. First, on a psychosexual level, the scapegoat is directly associated with excrement because in many cultures, particularly the Judeo-Christian one, the deemphasis of the lower body pole, and the elevation of the spirit and intellect, gave birth to scapegoat psychology. Neumann says:

Whereas a child identifies the ingestion of food with the pleasure of growing consciousness, the anal order becomes its first association with evil. At the first the giving-off of feces was an approved creative process; now gradually the principle of adaption to an order of consciousness becomes incarnated in it. Just as meal time becomes a ritual of positive assimilation, so the anal time becomes ritual devoted to the rejection of the negative element, an unconscious rite by which evil is removed. . . . This specifically human development of anal rejection provides one of the foundations of scapegoat psychology, of the notion of expelling one's own evil as something alien.[51]

This view of part of oneself as being disgusting, smelly or evil becomes shared by a community, wherein each person's evil can be projected onto a single external object. Then the scapegoat becomes one of the functions of the rites of purgation. Bloom becomes the personification of that which is expelled by society.

This role has been set up for him from the beginning. Not only is he an outsider in terms of religion, ethnic background, and his remove from Eccles street, but like his talismanic potato, which is a "killer of pestilence by absorption" (478), Bloom is also an absorber of evil. This absorbing function of the scapegoat is explicit in Jewish ritual. Here the scapegoat is associated with Yom Kippur, the Day of Atonement, a day of fasting and purgation (the ritual has occupied Bloom's thoughts during his luncheon in "Lestrygonians"), where the children of Israel confessed their sins before a live goat that then bore their sins into the wilderness. The ritual is described in Leviticus 16:21: "And Aaron shall lay both his hands upon the head of the live goat, and confess over him the iniquities of the children of Israel, and all their transgressions and all their sins, putting them upon the head of the goat, and shall send him away by the hand of a fit man into the wilderness."

Bloom has been associated with a number of sacrificial animals throughout "Circe," but the most interesting is the "stinking goat of Mendes" (492), an opprobrium applied to Bloom by Alexander J. Dowie. Vickery describes this animal as "an Egyptian beast-god worshipped as the productive force in nature."[52] Thornton points out, however, that the goat is associated with Osiris, the major dying/resurrecting god in Egypt,[53] whose dismemberment is particularly characterized by the loss of his penis, later restored by Isis. Certainly Bloom's loss of potato, his humiliation, and his resurrection connect him to such figures as this.

The Bloom/goat/excrement connection is also reinforced by the presence of the nanny goat, which is seemingly an attribute of Molly. She is associated with Bloom's memory of Molly on Howth and appears, "walking surefooted dropping currants" (176). She reappears again in "Circe," resurrected by the language of the waterfall, which also has its urinary aspect, and we hear repeated: *"High on Ben Howth through rhododendrons a nannygoat passes, plumpuddered, buttytailed, dropping currants"* (550). Coming after the waterfall, and in contradistinction to the sphincterless nymph, the nannygoat, with appropriate linguistic word play on the part of the narrator, drops her fertilizing currants the way Molly had dropped her seedcake into Bloom's mouth. The merging of mouth to anus, eating and excreting, again underlines the importance of excrement in connection with the coming of new life.

Another animal of importance is the pig. The pig figures especially in the fantasy that involves Bella, but in ancient ritual the pig, because of its reproductive abilities and its uterine shape, was a symbol of female genitalia and an attribute of the goddess, especially Aphrodite. There is more than a Homeric parallel involved in the presence of the pig in "Circe." The older mythology involves the festivals of Aphrodite where priestesses (like Bella) appeared as men dressed as women.[54] Thus, although the scene with Bella is certainly a fantasy that, on a psychological level, involves elements of masochism,[55] there is, on a larger transpersonal level, a ritual and archetypal component that elevates the action beyond the merely personal. Bloom's encounter with Bella involves his ingestion into an earlier, nondifferentiated consciousness and is an experience of devouring. Bella makes this point clearly: "I shall have you slaughtered and skewered in my stables and enjoy a slice of you with crisp crackling from the baking tin basted and baked like the sucking pig with rice and lemon or currant sauce. It will hurt you" (532-33).

Indeed, all of Bloom's trials seem to be manifestations in some form of this archetypal act of devouring. Even the vision Bloom has of himself as Messiah illustrates the sacrifice and the new creation. Shechner has argued that Bloom's messianic tendencies are associated with masochism, with "castration and futility."[56] Nevertheless, on a ritual level, Bloom as a reformer lives out in his vision a key transformation. Just as the alchemical vessel changes base metals into gold, matter into a divine substance, Bloom, in his New Bloomusalem, erects a magnificent building in the shape of a pork kidney. His act of creation obviously is grounded on the organic. His elevation is described, not surprisingly, in terms of many food images that have passed through his mind on that day, while he continues to eat a raw turnip throughout the vision. On a more spiritual level, his compassionate nature "ingests" a blind boy, an old couple, some ragged children, and a veteran. His "obesity" here also points him up as a saturnalian fertility figure. Yet when Crofton notes, "This is indeed a festivity," Bloom replies. "You call it a festivity, I call it a sacrament" (489). We never lose touch with the body when creativity is involved, although all Bloom's acts of creation carry his own peculiar Bloomian stamp.

However, as scapegoat figure, Bloom must be sacrificed, and Bella tells him: "We'll bury you in our shrubbery jakes where you'll be dead and dirty with old Cuck Cohen. . . . We'll manure you Mr. Flower!" (544). The language here again is particularly excremental. The association of uncleanness with death and burial returns, as Bloom's earliest visions of himself as mud-coated are recalled. Yet the image of a flower in manure combines the two linked, if seemingly disparate, processes and suggests on one level that Bloom's creative flower identity is not killed by his immersion in manure, but is revived by it. As Bloom (and Stephen) will be immersed in "manure"/earth of the unconscious and become revived psychologically, so also will Joyce revive the artist's work by an inclusion of all so-called lower elements, which in reality function as the soil of his artistic creation.

We can see that Bloom, after being taunted and ridden by Bella, is then "killed": "*Broken, closely veiled for the sacrifice,* [Bloom] *sobs, his face to the earth*" (544). Next, the Circumcised mourn for him and "*cast dead sea fruit upon him*" (544) in an act that will be repeated with the appearance of the nannygoat dropping currants.

Nevertheless, after the funeral pyre is erected, the nymph appears. She seems to be a particularly important figure. Brought down from the picture, "The Bath of the Nymph," which hangs above Bloom's bed, she is accompanied by the yew and waterfall. Blamires thinks that the "yews, the nymph and the waterfall hint at an unmentionable accusation,"[57] but Bloom's confessions do not seem to leave much that is unmentioned. Furthermore, there is more of a suggestion of renewal in these images. The evergreen yews certainly are symbols of renewal, and the waterfall has seminal and urinary qualities.

In any case, Bloom does admit to certain acts or thoughts of which he is ashamed. He discusses his encounter with a girl, the "flow of animal spirits," the "capillary attraction," and his predilection for "girling" and argues for the needs of the body. This all seems harmless enough and is followed by the appearance of the nannygoat. But the nymph enters the scene and reproaches him strongly: "We immortals, as you saw today, have not such a place and no hair there either. We are stonecold and pure. We eat electric light" (551). There are few words here that carry positive meaning for Bloom. "Stonecold," "pure," and the eating of electric light deny anything that is organic, and the nymph cannot represent anything that Bloom really "worships." Nonetheless, he goes on to confess to her some of his sexual and anal-oriented activities: "Enemas too I have administered. One third of a pint of quassia, to which add a tablespoon of rocksalt. Up the fundament" (551). And he adds, "I have paid homage on that living altar where the back changes name" (551). Here begins Bloom's denial of the image of womanhood that the nymph projects. Bloom's actions evidence feeding, and even administering an enema is a kind of feeding, and to create of the buttocks an altar is to return to the source of creation.

The episode continues with images that suggest the female hindparts of which Bloom is so enamored. Bloom extols "the warm impress of her warm form. Even to sit where a woman has sat, especially with divaricated thighs" (522). Meanwhile the nymph appears as a nun and admonishes Bloom, "No more desire. . . . only the ethereal. Where dreamy creamy gull waves o'er the waters dull" (552). This passage brings us back to Bloom's earlier disdain for AE (Russell) and Lizzie Twigg, all of whom are "literary ethereal people" (166) who eat the wrong food and produce weak insipid poetry. Bloom's rejection of the nymph and the kind of art she stands for seems to begin forcefully at this point, for it is here that the button of his trousers snaps. Despite the song of the sluts, Bloom does challenge both them and the nymph/nun. Soundly rebutted, the nymph cries "Sacrilege!" and, as a "moist stain" appears on her robe it would seem that Bloom has "sullied" her. But this stain is a major transformation effected by Bloom on his image of woman. Likening him to "Satan," another cloven-hoofed figure, the nymph then "strikes at his loins" (553). But Bloom is not to be emasculated by a nymph. He seizes her hand, parrying her attack and, "*with a cry . . . unveiled, her plaster cast cracking, a cloud of stench escaping from the cracks,*" she flees from him.

The nymph's role is variously interpreted. Vickery sees her as a "creature ridden with fear, hatred, and the desire to destroy."[58] But she also seems to function here as a personification of Bloom's problem with art as well as with women. Certain kinds of art, like certain kinds of virginity, stop process, and the stopping of process seems to go against Bloom's sense of things. It is important here also that the nymph is sphincterless. Her removal from process is thus illustrated on a more basic level than simply a sexual one. Bloom needs to worship the adulterous rump, not a sphincterless one. It is especially comical here that Bloom, always unable to respond aesthetically to art, has kissed the nymph in "four places," and also "shaded" her parts (546). In other words, he responds kinetically to her portrait. For Bloom, woman remains organic and fluid, demanding a response from him, even if his methods of participation seem odd or at least funny to us.

Stephen's role in "Circe" seems less important that Bloom's, but as Stephen's fantasies and guilts, his obsession with being eaten become intensified, we can see the ingestive and excretory aspects emerge even more clearly.

We have already discussed Stephen's need to create language to counter the perceived threat of engulfment by process. In "Circe," language—Stephen's kind of language—fails, and the boundaries usually created by it are dissoved. Stephen too must deal more directly here with instinct, the unconscious, and process. This change in language can partially be explained by the Viconian view, cherished by Joyce, that chaos is a prelude to new beginnings and that language must have these new beginnings in myth and gesture.

In "Circe," inanimate objects or usually mute things take on the power of speech, but Stephen's language loses power. Walking with Lynch, Stephen is seen reciting a passage that Thornton says is translated, "I saw a stream of water welling forth from the right of the temple, Alleluia: bringing salvation to all those who stood in its course."[59] This utterance at this point seems ironic; the water welling forth here seems more likely to be associated with cesspools and the urinating prostitute. But the waters of creativity well up too, and the content of "Circe" deals partially with Stephen's linguistic paralysis and his emotional awakening. In any case, the ritual recited here gives way to Stephen's speech to Lynch about gesture as universal language: "So that gesture, not music, not odours, would be a universal language, the gift of tongues rendering visible, not the lay sense but the first entelechy, the structual rhythm" (432). To render visible by means of gesture and mime is a characteristic means of expression in "Circe." Its action does accomplish that "first entelechy," and the structural rhythm is alimentary. The gift of tongues is an apt metaphor here for the process of emptying and filling that have been freed from the linguistic boundaries that limit understanding.

Subsequently, we find Stephen's speeches to be rather selfcontained, usually unintelligible. His conversation with Lynch's cap, for instance, suggests his remoteness and his sterility. With the cap he discusses a musical problem and evolves his own musical theory where the dominant and tonic form an ellipsis and create a journey and return.[60] The cap, which mocks him, is not only more easily understood, but seems to verbalize the meaning we are supposed to glean from Stephen's eleborate metaphor, even while the cap mocks that meaning: "Jewgreek is greekjaw. Extremes meet. Death is the highest form of life. Bah!" (504).

In "Circe" Stephen acts more than he talks, and his body functions and emotional problems associated with them come to the fore. One of Stephen's more important references to food involves seeing himself (not for the first time) as the prodigal son: "Imitate pa. Filling my belly with husks of swine. Too much of this. I will arise and go to my . . . " (517). Here language fails him; his problem is that he cannot imitate pa and return to pa. Also, as in many other instances, Stephen resists assimilation that involves body functions. Filling is therefore associated with uncleanness, sinning, and femaleness. As in the rest of the novel, Stephen would attempt to use literary constructs, parables, and riddles to establish his artistic self as masculine and transcendent. But this tactic fails in "Circe."

Besides having his belly filled, Stephen also plays the piano and dances. The language of his "dance of Death" is interesting because it is energetic, depending more on sound than on meaning and describes the physical: "*Stephen with hat ashplant frogsplits in middle highkicks with skykicking mouth shut hand clasp part under thigh, with clang tinkle boomhammer tallyho hornblower blue green yellow flashes*" (578). This is truly a "dance of death" because it lacks any cerebral quality and contains instead the auditory, the visual, and the physical. Significantly, when he stops, his mother arises before him. She, like Paddy Dignam, has been eaten and is "noseless, green with grave mold" (579). Her appearance only pictures in dramatic form Stephen's deepest fears that he has, in fact, been guilty of her death. His killing of the mother is translated into an act of eating, since for Stephen, devouring seems to be the dominant form of killing.

It is not surprising to find Mulligan on the scene now since he has all along functioned as a kind of meditating figure between Stephen's masculine/intellectual/verbal side and the female/unconscious/voiceless world of the mother. Here he appears in his trickster's garb "in particoloured jester's dress," (580) which reinforces these associations. "She is beastly dead," he tells Stephen, stating what is bound most deeply to disturb him. He then goes on to accuse Stephen of killing her "dogsbody bitchbody" (580). Here Mulligan's association with food is also repeated. He carries in this vision a "smoking buttered split scone" into which he weeps *tears of molten butter* (580).

Stephen urges his mother to speak "the word known to all men" (581). It may be, as many critics have argued, that the word Stephen craves to hear is *love* or some word carrying his absolution, but it also seems true that this objectification of Stephen's deepest anxieties, the core of his neurosis, is also the place where words—the one word or the many—do not suffice. Utterance of words creates, in Viconian terms, a cosmos and constrains chaos, but chaos is what Stephen needs to confront on its own, not on his, terms.

The primal, fundamental experience depicted here is reflected in the alimentary imagery. The mother is of course not May Dedalus at all, but The Mother, the Terrible Mother even, who is the devourer, the destroyer of ego consciousness. Dark and mute, she is the "corpsechewer! Raw head and bloody bones! (581) to Stephen. Her hand, which becomes "*a green crab with malignant red eyes*" (582) clawing at his heart, represents eating too. Here are merged the images of Mother, the "snotgreen sea," death and cancer—too much for Stephen, who utters "Shite!" (582). More than an expression of anger, his epithet is a definition. His desperate dictum, "the intellectual imagination! With me all or not at all. *Non serviam!*" (582) expresses his rigid dualism and his uncompromising, if futile, stand. His subsequent smashing of the chandelier and the ensuing darkness, "ruin of all space" (583), leaves him in the darkened world of the mother so that his loss of consciousness, in his collapse in the street, is inevitable.

Before his collapse, one last important vision takes place. This vision, the black mass, that occurs outside the brothel, emerges from a Dublin on fire—with its dead, in "white sheepskin overcoats and black goatfill cloaks" (598) rising amid a clamor of witches, a rain of dragon's teeth, and an opening chasm into which Rochford and others fall or leap. An altar is seen in the midst of this bedlam and on it lies Mina Purefoy, apotheosized as *"goddess of unreason . . . naked, fettered, a chalice resting on her swollen belly"* (599). "Father Malachi" of course presides. The chalice with its *"bloodripping host"* is consecrated by Mulligan to *"Corpus Meum."* Then the Reverend Mr. Hugh C. Haines Love reveals his *"grey bare hairy buttocks, between which a carrot is stuck."* The worship of dog—*"dooooooooog"* (600) is established. All these images represent Stephen's phobias, especially the chasm, the teeth, the dog, his suspicions about the homosexuality of Mulligan (and his own self-doubts). Perhaps the most disturbing aspect of the black mass is Mina Purefoy herself. It is she who is creative and who retains the chalice. The chalice itself, with its blooddripping contents, foreshadows Molly's menstruation in her chamberpot and is another image of female fertility that Stephen must somehow learn to pay obeisance to.

The black mass seems to be an inevitable feature in a chapter such as this and is particularly the product of a mind that has been trained in religious orthodoxy. Maddox says, "Stephen's mental creation of the Black Mass is demonstrative of his dichtomous nature."[61] Certainly Stephen's interest in the eucharistic image and his fears about his own animal nature projected onto ambigous figures like Buck and the protean dog all come together in this scene. Whether Stephen has been freed in any way through this vision seems doubtful, and his loss of consciousness—metaphorically a necessity—is here more of an escape than a confrontation. Part of his salvation involves Bloom and, with Bloom, the figure of that protean dog.

The dog, Stephen's nemesis in "Proteus," plays a major role in "Circe" too. For one thing he is the single most important ingester, and he aids in establishing a connection between ingesting and transformation. Indeed, his transformations are many. As he slinks after Bloom, he becomes a spaniel, a retriever with a "sniffling" nose to the ground (437), a terrier that whines "piteously" (448), a retriever again who places his muzzle in Bloom's hand. He is garryowen, a "wolfdog" that lies on his back wriggling "obscenely" (453), the mastiff that finally eats the crubeen and trotter, the bulldog that growls through "*rabid scumspittle*" (454) and a "gorging" boarhound. He is mentioned again in conjunction with Paddy Dignam's funeral where he becomes a beagle that gnaws on Dignam's face (452). And after "*he has gnawed all . . . he grows to human size and shape. His dashschund coat becomes a brown mortuary habit*" (472). As the dog becomes finally a "ghouleater," Dignam in turn takes on the dog's characteristics and "*bays lugubriously*"(472). Paddy, who, like the dog, was eaten, now excretes: "I must satisfy an animal need. That buttermilk didn't agree with me," he says (473). All these transformations link animal and human, eating and excretion, and establish the eating of life by life and the resultant transformations.

The dog follows Bloom; however, we tend to see it as associated with Stephen. Certainly it seems a kind of attribute or totem animal, although its functions are complex. We have seen its relationship to the metaphor of Christ/fox and the fox that buries its grandmother. It is also associated with the underworld dog Cerebus and has connections to *Faust*. But beyond these associations, the dog seems to represent animal needs. The merging of the dog with Paddy unites animal with human. Because Stephen still fears all process, hunger, ingestion, and assimilation, the dog is dangerous, potentially destructive, and uncontrollable. Yet Stephen must assimilate the meaning of the dog, the meaning of his animal nature.

We know of Stephen's fondness for the image of the artist as priest. In *A Portrait* he envisioned himself transmuting the daily bread of experience into the radiant body of everliving life. The radiant body still seems more comfortable to him than the daily bread of experience. Boyle points out that Stephen uses the alchemical word *transmute* instead of *transubstantiate*.[62] This alchemical rather than religious word emphasizes the working with *materia prima* and forces one's attention to the creation of the work from lowly substances. Stephen must become comfortable with these substances, and Bloom is helpful as a meditating figure here.

It is Bloom who has fed the dog throughout the night, and when he sees Stephen's condition at Bella's, he immediately wishes to feed him. But because he has fed the dog, he has nothing for Stephen. He finds Stephen smoking (a sterile oral gratification perhaps), and when Stephen drops his cigarette, Bloom picks it up, deposits it in a grate, and says, "Don't smoke. You ought to eat. Cursed dog I met" (560).

Yet in a sense, Bloom has fed Stephen. He has responded to the side of Stephen that needs nourishment—his animal side—and in this night experience, Stephen's hungry instinctual side has, in effect, both sought out Bloom and been fed by him.

We know from following Bloom through his day that he is an inveterate feeder even more that he is an inveterate eater. During the course of this long day, he had fed the cat, Molly, the gulls, and the dog—or dogs—and now, seated in the cabman's shelter with a thirsty and not-too-sober Stephen, Bloom, hampered by the sometimes stilted, circumloquacious language of the narrator, thinks, "Something substantial he certainly ought to eat, were it only an eggflip made on unadulterated maternal nutriment, or, failing that, the homely Humpty Dumpty boiled" (656). Of course this language is not necessarily Bloom's at all, for we have a narrator telling us in his turgid style what Bloom has apparently been thinking. But what happens to language in this episode offers a clue to what happens to meals and body functions as well. What Bloom has thought of here as substantial is described in anything but substantial terms. The "eggflip" suggests a scrambled egg made with milk, which has itself become "unadulterated maternal nutriment." In place of one clear, monosyllabic noun, we have two latinate adjectives, one judgmental, the other more simply descriptive, and a latinate noun. The boiled egg alternative has become a "homely Humpty Dumpty," a literary allusion.

Bloom's major concern for Stephen, however, involves Stephen's eating habits, and their relationship begins, if not ends, with food. Bloom is sincerely worried about Stephen's poor diet. "Can't you drink that coffee, by the way? Let me stir it and take a piece of that bun. . . . Try a bit" (634). Again, later, he urges, "Have a shot at it now," and Stephen reluctantly tries "the offending beverage" (635). Bloom doesn't let the subject drop, but continues to urge solid food: "I'm a stickler for solid food. . . . You ought to eat more solid food. You would feel like a different man." Stephen's reply, "Liquids I can eat" (635), reinforces Sheldon Brivic's argument that Stephen's rejection of solid foods is associated with his rejection of the material world, "his bitter recoil from the world of matter" that goes back to his mother's death and her association with things mutable.[63] Again, when Stephen does think of food, it is in relation to his family, all of whom are going hungry. Here his "mind's eye" vision of another dismal family meal, couched in the narrator's murky language (less murky when dealing with uglier aspects of the scene), still conveys a realistic picture of their poverty:

> His sister, Dilly, sitting by the ingle, her hair hanging down, waiting for some weak Trinadad shell cocoa that was in the sootcoated kettle to be done so that she and he could drink it with the oatmeal water for milk after the Friday herrings they had eaten at two a penny, with an egg apiece for Maggy, Boody and Katey, the cat meanwhile under the mangle devouring a mess of eggshells and charred fish heads and bones on a square of brown paper in accordance with the third precept of the church to fast and abstain on the days commanded, it being quarter tense or, if not, ember days or something like that (620).

This picture of hungry children admonished by the church to fast and abstain is both an ironic and pathetic picture. It somewhat explains Stephen's need to avoid that real world, the world of experience, of concrete objects, of matter, and of food.

Stephen's unpleasant associations and Bloom's unsuccessful urgings are not only in keeping with their characters, but are important correlated with the language of the chapter. Critics have made a number of negative comments about this langauge. It has been called "flatulent" by Hayman, "diminished" by Bruns, "decrepit" by Gilbert, and "deceptive, using circumlocutions and euphemism" by French.[64]

Marilyn French is perhaps getting closer to the problem of the language when she observes that the "ungrammatical relations" among elements of the sentences as well as the paragraphs points to "wrenched, distorted or inadequate relations among things."[65] What interests us here is one kind of relation, namely the relation between life as process and life as fiction, and the role of language in the creation of that fiction. The fiction itself is not "wrong" because it deceives; the language that separates fiction from its source in process is, however, a language that destroys its own life.

In these final episodes—"Eumaeus," "Ithaca," and "Penelope," we have the "Nostos," or homecoming chapters, and the emergence of the creator of *Ulysses*. But we cannot forget that this creator is still the artist/priest figure who must enter the accidents of his ink and infuse it with life. Turning to Father Boyle's discussion of Joyce's use of the eucharistic image, we recall that the transmutation of the daily bread of experience means, in terms of the mass, that the bread into which

Christ has entered has taken on his substance.[66] As the bread becomes changed, becomes the Christ, so the daily bread of experience becomes the artist. However, "Eumaeus" is a comment on the failure of this "transmution" to take place, or so the creator of *Ulysses* would have us believe, and the creator of *Ulysses,* as opposed to the narrator of "Eumaeus," creates that disparity for us by separating language from process.

When we examine the meal that takes place in the cabman's shelter, we see the problem of language delineated in an interesting way. Language as a function of the upper body pole—of mind and mouth—stands opposed to the lower body pole-expression. Food, expressed in language, becomes something other than food; it becomes words that stand for words.

For example, wine in "Eumaeus" becomes one of the "drinkables" Bloom mentions that are "in the shape of a milk and soda or a mineral" (613). It no longer possesses its sacred transformational qualities. Bloom, it is true, allows as how it is "both nourishing and blood-making and possessing aperient virtues" (615), but the nourishing, transformational, and purgative functions of the wine are lost in a wordy lecture on the evils of drink. Its magical properties have been buried in language that is full of conceptualizing, moralizing, and judgmental phrases and get lost in "the much vexed question of stimulants" (615).

The coffee that Bloom is so intent on getting into Stephen is described as a 'boiling swimming cup of a choice concoction labelled coffee" (622). It is also referred to as "coffee, or whatever you like to call it" (645), or a "cup of what was temporarily supposed to be called coffee" (622).

The roll or bun Stephen is served undergoes the same kind of treatment. We hear of the "socalled roll" (623) and "a roll of some description" (622), an "antediluvian specimen of a bun" (622). It is also "like one of our skipper's bricks disguised" (634).

References to bread show the same tendencies. When Bloom smells the baking bread as he passes the bakery, his sense response is lost as the narrator describes him inhaling "with internal satisfaction . . . the very palatable odour of our daily bread" (614). Not only is the description of a simple act laden with polysyllabic adjectives, but bread has now become "our daily bread." The phrase is biblical and a cliché. Bloom continues to think of bread in literary/musical terms as well as in puns, as he muses, "Of all commodities of the public the primary and most indespensable. Bread, the staff of life, earn your own bread, O tell me where is fancy bread? At Rourke's the baker's, it is said" (614). Although this passage is also witty and more Bloomian than most of the passages in "Eumaeus, "wordiness and a judgmental tone force us to recall that for Joyce, words were things, animated by a life of their own. But here words are denied most connotative and even denotative functions. They tend to be abstract and are not animating. They are merely words. By drawing attention to themselves as words they lose their connection with process, of which we are reminded only euphemistically in "Eumaeus."

And yet, despite the seemingly deadening effects of the language, life and process go on. In the very beginning of the chapter, we are told of the "fetid atmosphere of the livery stables" (613) and are given, in euphemistic phrasing, a slightly excremental image that will be important to the later portion of the chapter when the sweeper's horse (obviously in the employ of the author of *Ulysses*) comes on to clear up his narrator's linguistic waste. The horse seems to share most resoundingly his creator's view when, "having reached the end of his tether so to speak" it halts and, "rearing high a proud feathering tail," adds its own "quota by letting fall on the floor, which the brush would soon brush up and polish, three smoking globes of turds" (665). The final phrase suggests that the pretentious language has also fallen with those turds.[67]

Thus, in "Eumaeus," food and life substances are turned into clichés. Mulligan is thought by Bloom to know "which side his bread is buttered on" (620); Bloom nourishes suspicions about Murphy (626); he refers to "the cream of the joke" (617), of spoiling "the hash" (657), or of being "warm as a toast on a trivet" (658). Finally, and in anticipation of "Ithaca," this meal becomes a written cipher: "coffee 2 d., confectionary do" (660).

However, there is, as I have said, a real world going on despite the artificial language. The ice cream car is adjacent to the urinal; the cabman's shelter, despite its colorful name, is still a place to eat, and within this eating place some interesting artistic events take place. We learn something more about fiction.

The most interesting comment on the separation of language from process, and its relation to the making of real as opposed to false fiction, occurs here in the person of our dubious sailor, W. B.

Murphy. That Murphy is a liar, a sham sailor, a spinner of elaborate fictions cannot be debated. He may even be, as Maddox has suggested, a "witty portrait of the artist as James Joyce" who "combines a pretense of self-revelation with a great deal of shamming."[68]

Whether or not Murphy is Joyce, he is nonetheless a figure of major importance. First, despite the fact that "Eumaeus" has been characterized as a tired chapter, Murphy is anything but a tired character. He abounds with energy in spite of the seemingly devitalizing effects of language. One factor that contributes to the vividness of Murphy is his dialogue. Much of the chapter contains indirect dialogue, but Murphy is allowed direct speech. Another element that enhances Murphy's vividness is the fact that he is an ingester. Beneath the euphemisms of the narrator, we see Murphy first in terms of "a pair of drowsy baggy eyes, rather bunged up from excessive use of boose" (623). He relates his tales while chewing tobacco. At one point we get a picture of him with two flasks of ships' rum "sticking one out of each pocket for the private consumption of his burning interior" and from which he takes "a good old delectable swig . . . with a gurgling noise" (638).

But Murphy not only ingests; he eliminates as well. Directed to the urinal by an unseen person, but "giving it a wide berth," we are told that he has "eased himself close at hand, the noise of his bilgewater some little time subsequently spashing on the ground where it apparently woke a horse of the cabrank" (638-39).

Murphy's tales are obviously suspect, but they are characterized by what might be seen as an excessive attention to eating in various forms and under some strange conditions. As he talks, he uses "his partially chewed plug" to aid him in his narration:

> I seen queer things too, ups and downs. I seen a crocodile bite the fluke of an anchor same as I chew that quid.
> He took out of his mouth the pulpy quid and lodging it between his teeth, bit ferociously (625).

The "pulpy quid," reminscent of Molly's chewed seedcake and the regurgitated cud of the terrier in "Lestrygonians," might cause us to look on Murphy as part of a more fertile and imaginative world than the sterile linguistic one in which he seems trapped.

In any case, Murphy is particularly animated by his tale of the Peruvian maneaters "that eats corpses and the livers of horses" (625). He embellishes on these cannibals in terms of their eating habits:

"Chews cocoa all day long. . . . Stomachs like breadgraters. Cuts off their diddies when they can't bear no more children" (626). His references are supposedly verified by a postcard that only seems to prove the falsity of person and tale. Yet his tale involves a subject that connects with important motifs of the book. Certainly Bloom and Stephen have both concerned themselves with cannibalism—Stephen with a personal, mother-oriented kind, Bloom with a ritualized and more universal version. Murphy, ignorant of the symbolism behind the maneaters' actions and the association of such activities with the establishment of community survival and fertility, would never connect the cannibals' actions with the eating of the god projected in the symbolism of the mass. But Joyce would, and part of his strategy here seems to be to present these ritualized and highly symbolic acts as naked manifestations of energy, as a counterpoint to the conceptualized and deadeningly civilized style of the narrative.

As the narrator's language separates words from things that live, Murphy's language gives animation but lacks conceptualizing ability. Contrasting language that has become literary with language that is basically oral, Joyce can point up the problem of differentiating between fiction that is false and fiction that is real.

Murphy's role has other ramifications. He speaks of the Chinese eating rats in soup and the lice that eat him (he, like Stephen, does not bathe much). Of the lice he says, "Sucks your blood dry they does" (631). The rat that gets plump on graveyard meals, that so appalls and fascinates Bloom, and the vampire images that so appall and fascinate Stephen are played on and given new fictional treatment in the form of Murphy. Each of these threatening eaters of the dead lives off Murphy in some way, but none devitalizes him. The lice are carried on his skin; the rats are carried in his tale. In both cases, the devourer has been ingested, or neutralized, by Murphy and has become part of his sailor-storyteller corporeality. None of Murphy's gruesome tales evokes the slightest horror from his listeners because Murphy has transformed the horror into comedy.

As the final act, Murphy opens his shirt to reveal a tattoo about which there is, of course, a story, a story that involves eating. Murphy's tattoo has been done by one Antonio who just happens to have drawn himself on Murphy's chest and who can be made to curse the mate or laugh at a "yarn" when Murphy pulls the right way on his skin. Antonio is the harbinger of Shem in *Finnegans Wake,* who will write the history of the human race on his skin with his own excremental ink.

Antonio has written himself into the accidents of body and skin much as Christ unites with the accidents of bread and wine. The artist has not simply disappeared into his work; he has been transaccidentated. As Shem is described as "transaccidentated by the slow fires of consciousness," and as Stephen has the "smithy of his soul" in which to effect the work, so Murphy has his "burning interior" (638). The accidents of the ink, or here the tattoo and skin, like Joyce's many styles, will cause him to appear as symbolist, ironist, and realist.

Antonio has his story, too. He has been devoured by sharks: "He's gone too. Ate by sharks after. Ay Ay," Murphy laments (631). Given what we know about Stephen's fear of being devoured or drowned, we must take this denouement as an important element. In the outpouring of trivial and stultifying language, there has emerged a figure who embodies the act of storytelling while he lives comfortably with process. He assimilates his experience in a particularly brilliant way, thanks to Joyce. As a man of the earth (or the sea), he is at home with his body functions, and he carries on his own skin a history that is both picture and tale. He carries on his chest both the form and substance of art, the artist written into his work who, subsequently and inevitably, is devoured by life but remains smiling and cursing through the accidents that are his medium.

In "Eumaeus," the artist and priest is in total control and proves it by encasing himself in a dead language only to transcend it. Should we fail to get his message, Joyce has left it indelibly printed on Murphy's skin. Art and life interplay. False art is stripped away to reveal kinesis, without which art cannot be made.

"Ithaca" is always discussed as the episode where Bloom and Stephen share a secular communion over their cups of Epps's cocoa. This cocoa, described as "Epps's massproduct, the creature cocoa" (677), has long been thought of as a food that Joyce has related to the mass, in which, as Gifford puts it, "Bloom is functioning as priest, Stephen as communicant."[69] Tindall sees Stephen as receiving the body of the host and finds cocoa to be, according to Webster's, botanically called *theobroma,* a Greek word for god-food. Tindall then goes on to say that "receiving Bloom's god food, Stephen, the young dog pretending to be god, becomes a god. Through 'creature' (or created) cocoa he puts on creative power."[70] Whether or not one accepts Tindall's full exegesis, there seems to be little doubt that Joyce is almost forcing his readers to see a relationship between food, god, human and spiritual communion, and creativity. But again, as in "Eumaeus," the style of the chapter suggests a disparity between form and content, which again tends to separate the basic transformational functions of eating from the transformational function of creating art through words.

One of the first things to be noted about the food references in "Ithaca" is that they, like a number of other elements, are subject to cataloguing. One of the first among many lists involves the contents of "the lower middle and upper shelves of the kitchen dresser opened by Bloom" (675). On the middle shelf, among other items, are:

> An empty pot of Plumtree's potted meat, an oval wicker basket bedded with fibre and containing one Jersey pear, a halfempty bottle of William Gibney and Co's white invalid port, half disrobed of its swathe of coral-pink tissue paper, a packet of Epps's soluble cocoa, five ounces of Anne Lynch's choice tea at 2/–per lb. in a crinkled leadpaper bag, a cylindrical canister containing the best crystalised lump sugar, two onions, one the larger, Spanish, entire, the other, smaller, Irish, bisected with augmented surface and more redolent, a jar of Irish Model Dairy's cream, a jug of brown crockery containing a noggin and a quarter of soured adulterated milk, converted by heat into water, acidulous serum and semisolidified curds (675).

Under this rather tedious listing is contained the story of Molly's affair with Boylan that afternoon as well as a number of items associated with Molly herself—the pear, cream, onions, and Spain. We have heard about Plumtree's potted meat throughout the day and have by now endowed the phrase (for it is first an ad) with a number of associative meanings, mostly having to do with fertility, potency, cannabalism, sacrifice, and death. We do not know until later that the "empty pot" of meat and the half-empty bottle of port are the remains of Boylan's and Molly's feast. Nevertheless, Bloom doubtless suspects that they are. But more important is the question of what this listing does for us as readers. It purports to be a straightforward, objective denotative listing of items, but what are we to make of a port bottle that is described as "half disrobed of its swathe of coralpink tissue paper," after which "lump" sugars and the "adulterated milk" creep into consciousness with the connotative potential.

Later on, another list appears, this time in conjunction with

Bloom's account of his day's expenditures. On this list appear the foods he has purchased—his pork kidney, "Banbury cakes," "Lunch," "1 Dinner and Gratification," "1 Pig's Foot," "1 Sheep's Trotter," "1 Cake Fry's plain choclate," "1 Square soda bread," and "1 Coffee and bun" (711). These items appear in an impersonal listing but they are surely highly connotative to the reader. Indeed, as Hugh Kenner has rightly observed, "Though 'objective' is what we generally hear 'Ithaca' called, objective is exactly what it is not."[71]

What then is the relationship between language and content, especially content that relates to the digestive process? As we have seen in "Eumaeus," Joyce's prose style is a disguise thrown off to reveal the all-too-human Murphy who carries his tale of transformation on his transforming skin. Hence, we may suspect Joyce of doing the same thing in a different way in "Ithaca." Whereas Joyce uses the prose style of "Eumaeus" to reveal the falsity of literary language, he seems intent here on demonstrating the limits of scientific or mathematical or technical language to suppress the organic and the human. Of course Joyce may, as critics have always contended, be attempting to diminish the implications of Bloom's meeting with Stephen. But the point may be that relationships continue to exist only in a context of constant change despite attempts to render them meaningful or static through language.

However, Joyce's own discussion of "Ithaca" suggests his emphasis is on the objective, abstract, and scientific quality of the language. He says: "I am writing *Ithaca* in the form of a mathematical catechism. All events are resolved into their cosmic, physical, psychical etc. equivalents . . . so that the reader will know everything and know it in the baldest and coldest way, but Bloom and Stephen thereby become heavenly bodies, wanderers like the stars at which they gaze"[72] Yet despite Joyce's intentions, another feeling about "Ithaca" persists. A. Walton Litz makes the helpful point that the language of "Ithaca" fails to dehumanize Bloom and Stephen, that although it removes them from the personal to the archetypal and establishes stellar reaches in place of terrestrial ones, the result is that those stellar reaches are "supersaturated with Bloom's humanity, a humanity that is enhanced if anything by the impersonality of the prose."[73] It is on the macrocosmic and mythic scale that certain realities are made visible, and it is also here that true relationships are realized.

If this is so, then perhaps even abstract statements and lists of objects also are infused with their originally animate and also symbolic contexts. The presence of a type of communal meal, the mention of Plumtree's potted meat, Stephen's narration of the "Parable of the Plums," and his other "oral" rendering—the ballad of "Little Harry Hughes"—followed by his and Bloom's urination in the garden and Bloom's final rest on Molly's rear, suggest that we are still in the midst of organic life processes. Kenner's observation of "Ithaca" 's style as a "symbiosis" between author and Muse might also be extended to talk about the symbiosis between language and content,[74] a symbiosis enhanced by the fact that the most impersonal language is used to carry the most highly connotative material.

Certainly these wanderers, like the stars, are at this point only sitting in a kitchen which, as Tindall rightly points out, is a place of creation.[75] Bloom is, as usual, a feeder who even has affinities with Mulligan. Like Mulligan, Bloom also functions like an alchemist as he bustles about his kitchen, making fire and boiling water. Like Mulligan, Bloom is both an ingester and a feeder of Stephen. Nevertheless, Mulligan is a mock priest and contrasts with Bloom who is related to the host (673, 688, 692, 695) whose function we are supposed to take seriously within the limits of Joyce's comedy. The food he offers Stephen seems endowed with at least some significance. For example, in "Eumaeus" Bloom has been anxious about Stephen's diet and has urged him to eat solids. Stephen, however, prefers liquids. The fact that cocoa is a solid dissolved in liquid suggests in mundane terms a blend of oppositions. Perhaps the most solid food mentioned here is Molly's cream.

But Joyce is not interested in being solemn about the wrong things. If he has made this meal a kind of celebration akin to a secular mass, he seems also to be interested in undercutting its ritual aspects and does so with stilted, technical language. Thus he describes Bloom's preparations of cocoa in the following way: "He poured into two teacups two level spoonfuls, four in all, of Epps's soluble cocoa and proceeded according to the directions for use printed on the label, to each adding after sufficient time for infusion the prescribed ingredients for diffusion in the manner and in the quantity prescribed" (676). Any sense of ritual seems denied by the language that creates instead a formula in its place. Although to be sure there is some hint of formula in ritual, here formula has gone an evolutionary step forward and has become words on a label.

Another example of Joyce's use of a label involves Plumtree's potted meat. The phrase comes up as an answer to an ambiguous question posed by the narrator:

What is home without Plumtree's Potted Meat?
Incomplete.
With it an abode of bliss (684).

We then hear what sounds like a mixture of label and advertising information: "Manufactured by George Plumtree, 23 Merchants' quay, Dublin, put up in 4 oz. pots, and inserted by Councillor Joseph P. Nannetti, M. P., Rotunda Ward, 19 Hardwicke street, under the obituary notices and anniversaries of deceases" (684). Here it would seem that Plumtree's Potted Meat has moved from being a clever ad in Bloom's mind to an important symbol whose ramifications are even now not yet played out. The ad has, during the day, been transformed as a result of being associated with Paddy Dignam; it is associated with the eating of the genitals of the missionary MacTrigger to insure the fertility of the chief in "Lestrygonians," and it has been the emblem of Boylan's potency. Here it seems to have lost much of its connotative quality and has been returned to a place on a label. As a label, the item has reached an ultimate state, like so much of the data in this chapter. But that is not all that occurs with it.

Returning for a moment to the description of Bloom's making of the cocoa, we infer he is reading a label because of the presence of phrases like "prescribed ingredients for the diffusing in the manner and in the quantity prescribed" (676). This description is followed by key words such as "creature cocoa" and "massproduct," which on the contrary, are loaded with the connotative material and on which interpretations like that of Tindall lean so heavily.

Another similar kind of transformation occurs with regard to Plumtree's potted meat. After the technical data has been given, there appears a different kind of sentence: "A Plumtree is a meatpot." This sentence, laden as it is with associations, begins to work transformations on both words, leading the narrator who may or may not be imitating Bloom to coin "Peatmot. Trumplee. Montpat. Plamtroo" (684). This language seems a good deal more than coldly scientific or precisely technical. Plumtree as meatpot is connotative enough. From it we may be forced to think of male and female imagery, symbols of fertility, Molly, Blazes, and the "Parable of the Plums." Does Plumtree's potted meat become elevated to some linguistic eighth sphere as it leaves, or appears to leave, older associations behind? It would appear not. When Bloom retires to his bed he encounters not a conceptualized potted meat, but actual "flakes of potted meat, recooked"(731). A fairly elaborate cluster of associative images has been transformed into flaky remnants found, to be sure, in his bed. But these are brushed aside by Bloom. Having become actual, the potted meat is eliminated symbolically. This kind of play, this rendering of things in concrete, denotative language, from which they seemingly escape and become living entities, at least in terms of the work's fiction, imitates the mass where the divine substance is infused into the accidents of bread and wine. We are reminded of the comparison to the mass offered in the early part of the chapter and again in the examples of Bloom's kinetic poetry.

This poetry, produced after he has taken his communal meal with Stephen, is presumed to be accurate renderings of poetry Bloom has written in his youth. All of his creations, the newspaper poem, the anagrams, the acrostic he has written to Molly, share one common feature: he has written himself into each of them. For example, the last lines of the poem read:

> *If you so condescend*
> *Then please place at the end*
> *The name of yours truly, L. Bloom* (678).

The anagrams he has made from his name are:

> Ellpodbomool
> Molldopeloob
> Bollopedoom
> Old Ollebo, M. P. (678).

And finally, his acrostic:

> *Poets oft have sung in rhyme*
> *Of music sweet their praise divine.*
> *Let them hymn it nine times nine.*
> *Dearer far than song or wine.*
> *You are mine. The world is mine.*

What we have here seems to be a comic but nonetheless valid example of the poet writing himself into his art. We also have another example of identities being rearranged in terms of letters. Unlike Stephen's

*Stephen and Bloom* 139

dictum that the poet must disappear into his work, Poldy remains a lettered presence.

Another interesting listing that involves food occurs near the end of the chapter where events of Bloom's day are catalogued as types of ritual. It is best to quote it in full: What Bloom "silently" recapitulates is:

> The preparation of breakfast (burnt offering): intestinal congestion and premeditative defecation (holy of holies): the bath (rite of John): the funeral (rite of Samuel): the advertisement of Alexander Keyes (Urim and Thummin): the unsubstantial lunch (rite of Melchizedek): the visit to museum and national library (holy place): the bookhunt along Bedford row, Merchants' Arch, Wellington Quay (Simchath Torah): the music in the Ormond Hotel (Shira Shirim): the altercation with a truculent troglodyte in Bernard Kiernan's premises (holocaust): a blank period of time including a cardrive, a visit to a house of mourning, a leavetaking (wilderness): the eroticism produced by feminine exhibtionism (rite of Onan): the prolonged delivery of Mrs Mina Purefoy (heave offering): the visit to the disorderly house of Mrs Bella Cohen, 82 Tyrone street, lower and subsequent brawl and chance medley in Beaver street (Armageddon): nocturnal perambulation to and from the cabman's shelter. Butt Bridge (atonement) [728-29]

We may be doubtful about the use of these ritual tags as tools of exegesis. Both Gifford and Thornton have elaborated extensively on these references and observed that most are to be found in the Old Testament.[76] Gifford argues that some of the rites are keyed to certain times of the day, but this argument seems tenuous. Furthermore, some "rites" are not really rites at all. The rite of Samuel is vague. Much is made of his death in the Old Testament, but the only rites associated with him involve exorcism. The rite of Onan is misleading, since Onan masturbated and was punished by God. The wilderness suggests a number of rites of purgation and is associated with scapegoat figures, but there are numerous references to the wilderness in both Old and New Testaments. The heave offering has nothing to do with birth and seems to be used in connection with Mina Purefoy for comic effect. If the Urim and Thummin have a ritual basis it has been lost, since the words are highly abstract ones. Standing for two essential parts of the sacred oracle, the words mean "Fire" and "Truth" or "Light" and "Perfection" respectively. Also, holocaust and burnt offering are synonymous. As in many other places in "Ithaca," it would appear that accuracy in expression does not mean accuracy in information.

Whether the ritual tags can tell us anything is doubtful, but if we begin with the premise that all ritual acts are based on the dynamics of emptying (mortification and purgation) and filling (invigoration or feasting), we may be able to focus on the dynamics involved in each reference and the event to which it is supposedly keyed. When we do this with the burnt offering—Bloom's pork kidney—we note that this kind of sacrifice was a special one that involved the consummation of the *entire* animal and was performed only under priestly offices.[77] Essentially it is a rite of purgation. Yet Bloom does not fast or purge himself here but, rather, eats. The same kind of reversal occurs with the tag *holy of holies* which refers to the most sacred and intermost part of the Jewish tabernacle but also, as Gifford notes, to a prayer that specifically mentions the orifices of the body and involves thanks to God for the fact that these orifices exist and are open.[78] However, these orifices are supposedly open to receive; Bloom's orifice is presumably expelling. Here a rite of invigoration has been turned into a purgative one. The rite of John, which refers to his baptism of Jesus, seems apt in a sense, but in "Lotus Eaters" we have more of a sense of Bloom as sacrifice. A truly comic tag is the *holy place* which presumably refers to the museum and library. When we recall that Bloom's real purpose for visiting the museum was to view the sphincters of the goddesses, we have to realize that Joyce's purpose here is less than serious. The rite of Melchizedek, which refers to a special, even ideal priest who was considered a type of Christ and who was remembered for bearing bread and wine, seems fitting for Bloom's lunch. But the tag *Simchath Torah,* which Gifford tells us involves a ritual reading of the Pentateuch on the last day of the Feast of Tabernacles, suggests itself as another rite of filling and seems ironic, in view of the fact that the words Bloom receives come from *Sweets of Sin.* The "Shira Shirim," or Song of Solomon, celebrates a marriage in beautiful and sensual terms, and its application to Bloom's experience at the Ormond also seems ironic. It is true that the Song is also read in the Feast of the Tabernacles and is another rite of filling. Bloom's ingestion at this point of the day means his coming to terms with what is happening at 7 Eccles Street. If Armageddon, the apocalyptic battles between good and evil, is a rite of invigoration, it does seem appropriate for "Circe," if extravagant, as is the tag *atonement* for Bloom's meeting with Stephen in the cabman's shelter. Also, atonement is associated with rites of mortification and involves fasting.

What all of this means is simply that these ritual tags are imprecise, to say the least, but they do suggest Bloom's multiple roles as sacrificial figure (burnt offering, holocaust), as Christ figure (rite of Melchidek, atonement), harbinger of Christ (rite of John, the wilderness), hero (Armageddon), and even suppliant (heave offering). What Joyce seems to have done is to make ritual both immanent, in terms of Bloom's acts, and transcendent. The language of the chapter takes the individual beyond the mundane and into the eternal and transpersonal. Nevertheless, rituals are not ultimately concepts but acts, and as such retain their basic character of ingestion and elimination, taking and giving. This distance between act and the name of an act is amply illustrated in "Ithaca." What is also illustrated is that distance must be bridged by art.

Stephen, as potential artist, seems to remain just that by the end of "Ithaca." He does seem to move toward some contact with the world of experience with the help of his priest/meditating figure Bloom. We see evidence of this movement in the fact that he drinks the cocoa and, having ingested some experience, he is impelled to create. His creations involve a repetition of his "Parable of the Plums," not, of course, understood by Bloom, and a new utterance, the ballad of "Little Harry Hughes."

Again, Stephen is not writing. His only written product has been his vampire poem, composed in "Proteus." He is producing rather, a derivative piece *orally*, and again, as in his "Parable," his meaning is not clear. But the most important fact about the ballad is its alimentary aspect. It tells us that Stephen's creative efforts continue to involve his emotional disturbance and are alimentary in origin. In the ballad, however, his problem is more disguised. The ballad describes the fate of a little Jewish boy who, while playing ball, first hits the ball over the Jew's wall, second, breaks the Jew's windows, and third, is enticed by the Jew's daughter who, having lured him into a room, cuts off his head with her penknife.

On the surface there seems to be little connection between eating and the boy's fate. But Bowen has supplied some additional lyrics that show that food is used as an enticement in the song. The additional verses are as follows:

> The first she offer'd him was a fig,
> The next a finer thing,
> The third a cherry as red as blood,
> And that enticed him in.
>
> She set him up in a gilty chair,
> She gave him sugar sweet.
> She laid him out on a dresser board
> And stabb'd him like a sheep.[79]

Stephen's alteration of the lines is worth noting. The image of the sheep is certainly sacrificial but the loss of head, the loss of his intellectual powers, would be far more fearsome to Stephen, and so the beheading image makes more sense. The use of a penknife as a weapon is also provocative since Stephen has previously thought of his pen (as opposed to Mulligan's lancet) as a weapon. Obviously phallic, the penknife in the hands of a temptress figure would also be extremely threatening for Stephen.

The ritual aspects of the ballad are interesting too. First, Stephen implies a ritual interpretation by his own exegesis of the words: "One of all, the least of all, is the victim predestined. Once by inadvertence, twice by design he challenges his destiny. It comes when he is abandoned and challenges him reluctant and, as an apparition of hope and youth holds him unresisting. It leads him to a strange habitation, to a secret infidel apartment, and there, implacable, immolates him, consenting" (692). These lines suggest Stephen's fears. "Strange habitation" and "secret infidel apartment" are key images for him, going back to Davin's country woman with the batlike soul in *A Portrait*. They also indicate that Stephen dislikes anything secret—a word that he usually associates with his mother, with mystery and ultimately with the female as devourer.

Bloom, as "victim predestined" and also as "secret infidel" is perhaps victim in his own mind and infidel in Stephen's. But he does think of ritual murder as Stephen recites the ballad. Michael Seidel, in his study of Stephen's fondness for the vampire image, observes that Bloom has also thought of ritual murder in "Hades" where he thinks, "It's the blood sinking in the earth gives new life. Same idea those jews they said killed the christian boy" (108), and that ritual murder is a "form of vampirism."[80] Seidel sees Bloom as a devouring figure too, linking him with the panther image, and argues that Stephen fails to stay the night because he regards Bloom not only as a father figure and savior, but also as a vampire, taking new life from Stephen.[81] If Seidel is right, we have both in the figures of Bloom and Molly, as well as in the image of ritual murder, aspects of devouring that must work on deep levels of Stephen's psyche. If Stephen's phobia becomes the reason for rejection of Bloom's hospitality, we have at least one hopeful consequence resulting from the recitation of the ballad. Instead of his strange laugh, Stephen has attempted to explain his song. Nonetheless, it is not Stephen who is the artist here, only the creator of *Ulysses*.

If Bloom and Stephen are wanderers among the stars, they are also urinators in the garden, where, "contemplating the other in both mirrors of the reciprocal flesh of theirhisnothis fellowfaces" (702), they, like both victim and infidel, do blend. But the blending is not in terms of actual existence; it is on the mythic level. We can see this blending of oppositions in their thoughts. Bloom focuses on the actual: "the problems of irritability, tumescence, rigidity, reactivity, dimension, sanitariness, pelosity," and Stephen abstracts process and thinks of "the problem of the sacerdotal integrity of Jesus circumcised" (703), a problem of spiritual wholeness limited by physical dismemberment.

The reconciliation/resolution of the book must mainly involve Bloom, and, of course, Molly. And it is no accident that "Ithaca" ends in the right place—on Molly's rear. The message of the potted meat is life's cyclical repitition of eating and elimination, both of food and of lovers. The narrator tells us not that Bloom smiles but that *had* he smiled, he would have smiled to reflect that: "Each one who enters imagines himself to be the first to enter whereas he is always the last term of a preceding series even if the first term of a succeeding one" (731).

Bloom's settling down on Molly's rump for the night reconciles the opposition of being neither "first, last, only, alone, whereas he is neither first nor last nor only nor alone in a series originating in and repeated to infinity" (731). In this sense Bloom has, in truth, succeeded Boylan. His equanimity is based on the important knowledge that "processes of adaptation to altered conditions of existence" is a reality. Yet this conviction is also the key to "Ithaca" 's style. Language, as it is used as process, adapted "to altered conditions of existence," remains alive and is realized in a "reciprocal equilibrium." That is, just as an equilibrium is realized between "the bodily organism and its attendant circumstances, foods, beverages, acquired habits, indulged inclinations" (733), so "Ithaca" projects a similar equilibrium between energy of language, the body, and notions of plot and character that make up the "attendant circumstances."

Bloom's true atonement involves the merging of the cosmic and the organic, and their merging is explicitly conveyed by the relationship established between the "eastern and western terrestrial hemispheres" and Molly's "adipose posterior female hemispheres." The passage that follows is an encomium to the digestive process and to all bodily, excretory, hence creative, energies, and Molly's rump becomes: "redolent of milk and honey and of excretory sanguine and seminal warmth, reminiscent of secular families of curves of amplitude, insusceptible of moods of impression or of contrarieties of expression, expressive of mute immutable mature animality" (734). This most connotative of passages, associating Molly with the promised land, suggests her as a source of creative liquids—liquids that Stephen fears. Yet Molly's rear, as it is "expressive of mute immutable mature animality" is a contradiction that seems appropriate. It is the muteness of raw energy—Stephen's "vital sea"—that is the enveloping symbol for "Ithaca" and for Bloom. This enveloping symbol encompasses both impression and expression. Bloom's "at-one-ment" with Molly's rump and his understanding of it as symbol even provides him with a "proximate erection" (734).

Finally, language and organic substances combine and bring forth newly created words. As Bloom kisses (ingests) the "plump mellow yellow swellow melons of her rump" (734), touch, sound, smell, and sight are taken up and transformed linguistically, expressing Bloom's final fading thoughts on kissing each "plump melonous hemisphere, in their mellow yellow furrow, with obscure prolonged provocative melonsmellonous osculation" (734-35). Bloom as "manchild in the womb" has not regressed, but is ready to be born into a new day and falls asleep appropriately, under the "square round" of the picture of the auk's egg. The final answer to the final question, "Where?", is self-evident.

# FIVE *Conclusion*

In case we should forget that the creative process is grounded in the body, we are reminded brilliantly of that fact by Joyce in the last episode of *Ulysses*. The questions that still engage critics in regard to "Penelope"—Molly's morality or lack of it, her actual lovers, the meaning of her *yes*—are all fascinating, but I wish to focus this discussion on Molly as body, and I wish to examine the personal and archetypal aspects of her in order to suggest that she is finally a function of the book, that her relation to Bloom and Stephen, although important, is not as important as is her relation to the work *Ulysses* itself. For Molly is a vessel, a kind of transducer, an energizing force, who reestablishes the connection between body and the creation of art. In so doing, she becomes, for the novel, both food and word.

One key to the formation of her character and role can be found in Joyce's interest in the ideas of Giordano Bruno. Both Gose and Voelker have provided insightful explorations into this area of Joycean influences.[1] To summarize briefly, Joyce seems to have been keenly interested in Bruno's dissatisfaction with the Aristotelian categorizing of nature, which he saw to be both fixed and in flux, and therefore difficult to establish with rigid rules, since for Bruno (and also for Joyce), matter was predominant over the form through which it moved. Bruno's doctrine of immanence, his principle of the coincidence of contraries, and his concept of learned ignorance are also of prime importance for the understanding of Joyce's creation of Molly. About Bruno's doctrine of immanence, Voelker has this to say:

> Bruno's doctrine of immanence has sweeping implications for the conclusion of *Ulysses*. Since the senses preceive the real while the intellect manipulates only useful fictions, Molly's sensuality accords with Bruno's irrationalism—especially since she proves herself able to leap from sensory to intuitive modes of perception—it is not surprising to find Bruno attributing a higher intelligence to animals (who possess only the vegetative and sensitive faculties) than to men (who also possess the intellective).[2]

It is these philosophical premises that also allow us to better see that Molly's references to food and the digestive processes are linked to Joyce's ideas about creation.

Thus this final episode opens with a reference to a meal—that important breakfast that Molly has been ordered to serve Bloom on the coming day. Whether she does, in fact, get Bloom's breakfast, and whether this possible change in their early morning behavior patterns reflects a significant change in their relationship is perhaps impossible to establish. Nevertheless, we have begun Bloom's day with a breakfast and have ended his day with another one. Furthermore, there are associations in the opening lines of "Penelope" with the Christmas dinner scene in *A Portrait*. The thoughts of breakfast cause Molly to remember a past breakfast Bloom has eaten in the *City Arms* (the only other time Bloom has ordered breakfast from Molly). That time is connected to Dante Riordan who lived below the Blooms at the *City Arms*, and Molly's comments on Dante—"her soul greatest miser ever. . . . God help the world if all the women were her sort down on bathing suits and lownecks" (738)—link body denial with a deficient soul and underscore Dante's failings and their effects on that Christmas day in Stephen's past.

Furthermore, breakfast, the breaking of the fast, signifies in ritual terms the end of a period of sterility, the reestablishment of rites of *plerosis,* a dynamic that is carried into the artistic realm as well. After the wordiness of "Eumaeus," where language draws attention to itself and disguises things, and after the dessicated, fragmentizing prose of "Ithaca," where language becomes separated from connotative meanings, "Penelope" seems to offer both us and the language new life.

One strong impression we get about Molly is that she is, in her way, as great an ingester/assimilator of life as Bloom is. This is true on both the literal and metaphoric levels. She is, for example, overweight: "My belly is a bit too big Ill have to knock off the stout at dinner" (750). But her love of food is clearly evidenced by the fact that food is almost always recalled in connection with some male encounter or flirtation. Beyond the obvious use of such details and realistic touches as the inevitability of meals and pub life, Molly's association of food and eating with interesting men seems to suggest that the taking in of food is associated with the taking in of love and of life.

Examples are numerous. In her recollections of old Gibraltar days with the Stanhopes, she thinks of "lovely teas" and "scrumptious current scones with raspberry waters I adore" (755). Also, her memories of Mulvey begin with her being served breakfast in bed (Mrs. Rubio brings her coffee). Another meal that foreshadows Bloom's advent involves Molly's kissing of Mulvey. She recalls: "He put his tongue in my mouth his mouth was sweetlike young" (759). The ingestion of sweetness is thus important not only to Bloom but to her. She remembers Val Dillon as "that big heathen I first noticed him at dessert when I was cracking the nuts with my teeth I wished I could have picked every morsel of that chicken out of my fingers it was so tasty and browned and as tender as anything only for I didn't want to eat everything on my plate" (750). Boylan is also recalled in terms of food. She relates an early flirtation where he admired her feet while they "both ordered 2 teas and plain bread and butter" (745). And her most impersonal flirtation associated with food is perhaps with a "man with the curly hair in the Lucan dairy" (745) where she was tasting butter.

But most of her recollections involving food also involve Bloom. The Glencree dinner is particularly mentioned (750, 774) and seems important in view of the fact that Bloom also mentions it in "Lestrygonians." Another dinner is mostly recalled in terms of the coldness of the evening, the warmth of the house, and the "rum in the house to mull" when she is with Bloom. Her memories of Bloom and food range from the cosmic—Bloom carrying his paid-for soup that he is determined to finish before the concert at Mallow recommences, "with the soup splashing about taking spoonfuls of it hadn't he the nerve" (748)—to the half-romantic vision of Molly as pastry-covered grain goddess: "He was on the pop of asking me too the night in the kitchen I was rolling the potato cake theres something I want to say to you only for I put him off letting on I was in a temper and with my hands and arms full of pasty flour" (743).

Molly also seems to share with Bloom the assumption that you are what you eat, but for her this idea is much more strongly related to her own sexuality. As she wonders about Bloom's infidelity, for example, we can see that she views both sex and love as related to food: "He came somewhere Im sure by his appetite anyway love its not or hed be off his feed thinking of her so either its was one of those night women if it was down there" (738-39).

Molly makes similar assumptions about Boylan. They have apparently supped that day on "port and potted meat" (741)—the potted meat being the famous Plumtree's potted meat of Bloom's musings—and she says, "It had a fine salty taste yes because I felt lovely and tired myself and fell asleep as sound as a top" (741). Molly is also convinced that oysters are aphrodisiacs, and says of Boylan's abilities, "He must have come 3 or 4 times," concluding, "He must have eaten oysters I think a few dozen" (742). And, in accordance with her assumptions about appetite and sexual activity, she adds, "He must have eaten a whole sheep after" (742). Plumtree's potted meat would seem to have evolved from being a comment on Bloom's fertility to being a comment on Boylan's. Consumed by Boylan and Molly it suggests fertility, but Molly has not been fertilized and she later notes, "Poldy has more spunk in him" (742). Furthermore, the fertility suggested here is as symbolic as the relationship between Stephen and Bloom is. The meat droppings, like Bloom's plum pits ("He gets the plums and I the plumstones," Bloom has mused on the beach in "Nausikaa," [377]), still suggest seeds of rejuvenation despite Bloom's despairing tone and contrast with Stephen's plum seeds of sterility.

Besides Plumtree's potted meat, two other foods seem to be of significance in "Penelope," and, not surprisingly, they are associated with the female, namely, eggs and milk. Bloom is to get eggs—"a couple of eggs" (738) for breakfast; Stephen, in Molly's Spanish fantasy, is to have "dos Huevos" (779). These references are straightforward enough, but eggs obviously blend fertility with nurturing. They are also vessels, and in some cosmogonies the egg is seen as the earliest container of the world. Gose links up the numerous egg references to the auk's egg from the Sinbad story to the Golden Egg of Madame Blavatsky's theosophic system, to the Great Circle, the "O" that delineates the earth, to Joyce's reference to "Penelope" as a huge earthball."³

Milk is mainly associated with Molly's amplitudinous breasts, which are in turn associated with her sexual attractiveness, and she is constantly thinking of them. "Ill change that lace on my black dress," she thinks, "to show off my bubs" (763). She remembers how her breasts appealed to Mulvey: "They were just beginning to be plump . . . he caressed them outside they love doing that its the roundness there I was leaning over him" (760). When she speaks of Milly's breasts it is only in reference to her own. She thinks of herself as a young girl when her breasts "were shaking and dancing about in my blouse like Milly's little ones now when she runs up the stairs" (761).

But these natural, if rather vain, expressions of pride in her body do not convey everything about her breasts, for her breasts do represent nurturing also, and especially when connected with Boylan or Bloom. About Boylan Molly thinks, "I think he made them a bit firmer sucking them like that so long he made me thirsty" (753), and "Theres the mark of his teeth still where he tried to bite the nipple" (754). Although these references still reflect more sexuality than maternity, Molly does go on to say, "Much an hour he was at them Im sure by the clock like some kind of a big infant" (754). In her memories of Bloom, the connection between nurturing and her own body are even more in evidence. Thinking of her nursing of Milly she says: "I had a great breast of milk with Milly enough for two what was the reason of that he said I could have got a pound a week as wet nurse all swelled out . . . I had to get him to suck them they were so hard he said it was sweeter and thicker than cows then he wanted to milk me into the tea well hes beyond everything" (754). Again we have the reference to sweetness that seems so important to Bloom, too, and is always associated with their relationship.

Also, we cannot avoid being reminded of the old milkwoman with the shrivelled breasts that offers cows' milk to the students in the Martello tower that morning. William P. Fitzpatrick notes: "For Stephen, Ireland is a mother with old shrunken paps, while Molly is frequently associated with cream and her breasts are of legendary proportions. . . . In the sterility of modern Ireland Molly as the principle of creativity and fertility is sorely needed."⁴

Thus Molly is nurturer in a number of ways, although she seems somewhat less than typically maternal. Her feeding is basically positive. However, there is one instance where, as we might expect, given her contradictory nature, she gives us an example of negative nurturing. She is fascinated with the poisoning of a husband by a wife. The incident seems to produce several changing, even contradictory, responses in her. First she is appalled: "Wasn't she a downright villain to go and do a thing like that"; then she qualifies her disapproval: "Of course some men can be dreadfully aggravating drive you mad"; this comment is followed by a calmer reflection: "White Arsenic she put in his tea off flypaper wasn't it." Finally she accepts the whole affair with a typical rationale: "She must have been madly in love with the other fellow to run the chance of being hanged O she didnt care if that was her nature what could she do" (744). For Molly, of course, moral questions based on religious or legal precepts are seen as meaningless when set against the forces of nature. If the figure of the Terrible Mother rises momentarily to the surface here, her ferocious aspect is somewhat mitigated by Molly's acceptance of Her and women's totality. Ironically, Dante Riordan is often likened to the figure of the Terrible Mother, yet she is an embodiment of patriarchal attitudes, an animus-ridden woman, more threatening than Molly at any time.

Although a number of critics have doubted Molly's ability to nurture, and although she may not strike us as typically maternal, she is archetypically so. For example, in spite of her indignity over Bloom's demand for service the next morning, Molly still envisions rather happily a meal for Bloom. First she recalls his demand: "Then he starts giving us his orders for eggs and tea Findon haddy and hot buttered toast I suppose"(764). Then she adds her own embellishments: "I think Ill get a bit of fish tomorrow or today is it Friday yes I will with some blancmange with black currant jam like long ago not those 2 lb pots of mixed plum and apple from the London and Newcastle Williams and Woods . . . I hate those eels cod yes Ill get a nice piece of cod"(764). (Perhaps her preference for currants is associated with the "Circe" vision of Howth where the nanny goat, her totem animal, drops currants.)

In any case, she also envisions serving breakfast to Stephen. Delighted to envision having a "long talk" with this "intelligent well educated person" and thinking also of Stephen's state of exhaustion, Molly allows as how "I could have brought him in his breakfast in bed with a bit of toast. . . . Or if the woman was going her rounds with the watercress and something nice and tasty there are a few olives in the kitchen he might like"(779). And she concludes, perhaps significantly, "I suppose he'd like my nice cream too"(780). This thought comes immediately after a reference to Bloom: "I'll throw him up his eggs and tea in the moustachecup she gave him to make his mouth bigger," and the blending of pronouns suggests that the recipient of the cream might just as easily be Bloom. Nevertheless, the softening of tone suggests that she means the recipient to be Stephen. Then she imagines waking him up in Spain where she will bring him breakfast: "Dos huevos estrellados, señor"(779). Yet as her fantasy develops, her images of Stephen seem to blend with those of Bloom. "Ill just give him one more chance," she thinks, "Ill get up early in the morning. . . . I might go over to the markets to see all the vegetables and cabbages and tomatoes and carrots and all kinds of splendid fruits all coming in lovely and fresh"(780). These words are followed by "who knows whod be the 1st man Id meet"(780). Because of the pronoun confusion generated by her flow of words, we cannot be sure if Stephen or Bloom is the recipient of these "splendid fruits," but surely these references point to Molly as some kind of nourishing figure.

If we have any doubts about this function, they can be resolved by a reminder that the most poetic rendering of a meal occurs in the final pages of the episode, and it is a meal we have had recounted to us before. It is the eating of the seedcake by Bloom. We have seen how, in "Lestrygonians" the memory of Howth, Bloom's "cud of reminiscence"(413), is the image that revives him at his lowest point of the day. Here we see that it is no less important an event for Molly. In this chapter of ends, it appears at the end of her monologue and deserves to be quoted in full: "The sun shines for you he said the day we were lying among the rhododendrons on Howth head in the grey tweed suit and his straw hat the day I got him to propose to me yes first I gave him the bit of seedcake out of my mouth and it was leapyear like now yes 16 years ago my God after that long kiss I near lost my breath yes he said I was a flower of the mountain yes so we are flowers all a womans body yes"(782). Bloom's taking of the seedcake is not a symptom of infantile regression, but indicates instead an acceptance of the archetypal realities. Molly's supposed dominance, evident in the next phrase, "I knew I could always get round him," is countered, as usual, by her very next words, "and I gave him all the pleasure I could"(782). That this final passage involves a conflation of

Bloom's and Molly's Howth experience with her Gibraltar days with Mulvey is not important, because the act itself is timeless and impersonal, or rather, transpersonal. Nor is Bloom's importance diminished, because he understands.

Molly, so hungry for love and life, also makes many references to being filled. Whether she is filled in sexual terms—"to make you feel full up"(742), or in terms of love—"it fills up your whole day and life"(758), or in terms of the female body—"whats the idea of making us like that with a big hole in the middle of us"(742), she is a personification of rites of *plerosis*. While menstruating she speaks of having "too much blood up in us"(769). There is also her rather comical sexual experiment: "After I tried with the Banana but I was afraid it might break and get lost up in me somewhere"(760).

Again, this state of bring filled is not in any way static, for Molly's eliminative functions are also given a lot of attention. One important "eliminative" function is, of course, her menstruation. It has received a variety of readings ranging from the sweeping and associative to the pragmatic and realistic. Richard Ellmann says: "In allowing Molly to menstruate at the end Joyce consecrates the blood in the chamberpot rather than the blood in the chalice, mentioned by Mulligan at the beginning of the book. For this blood is substance. . . . The great human potentiality is substantiation, not transubstantiation. . . . It is this quality which the artist has too."[5] Henke thinks, rather, that "Joyce wants to assure us that Molly is not pregnant."[6] Both interpretations are useful, but I think Ellmann makes an important connection between menstruation and the creative process. Menstrual blood is not only the first female transformation mystery, but is also food, food that nourishes the embryo. Although her passing of blood indicates the absence of a literal, physical embryo, the blood that fills the chamberpot is symbolically the substance that nourishes the the embryonic artist. It is the stuff of life on which the artist must feed. Molly herself seems to elevate the blood to archetypal meaning when she proclaims "Its pouring out of me like the sea" (769).

The chamberpot may make a comical chalice too, but the humorous aspect of it does not undercut the relationship of the pot to the creative process. Ellmann contends that Joyce first establishes Molly as a Gea-Tellus figure only to demythologize her by "bringing her down with a thump onto the orangkeyed chamberpot at 7 Eccles street."[7] But the primal goddesses were often associated with vessels. Neumann tells us

"It is the vessel that preserves and holds fast. But in addition it is the nourishing vessel that provides the unborn as well as the born with food and drink."[8]

Certainly Joyce is having fun with Molly's urination and its association with music. Still perched on her pot, Molly's tuneful flow below is matched by a tuneful flow above. She says, "O Lord what a row youre making like the jersey lily easy O how the waters come down at Lahore" (770). Gifford notes that the Jersey Lily was Mrs. Langtry, the lover of the Prince of Wales, and Molly seems to have transformed her into a kind of anima figure. Gifford also observes that the "waters of Lahore" reference is from a poem of Southey's.[9]

Besides the body functions just discussed, there is the last, and perhaps the most important function, elimination, and especially the part of the body associated with it, the rump. In this regard, Joyce's description of the "Penelope" episode and its function is most revealing. The full passage reads as follows: "*Penelope* is the clou of the book. . . . It begins and ends with the female word *Yes*. It turns like the huge earthball slowly surely and evenly round and round spinning, its four cardinal points being the female breasts, arse, womb and cunt expressed by the words *because, bottom* (in all senses, bottom button, bottom of the class, bottom of the sea, bottom of his heart), *woman, yes*."[10] Although Joyce establishes four points, the dominant one would seem to be the "arse." His emphasis on its importance is, of course, in evidence throughout *Ulysses,* but his letters to Nora are also suggestive. In one, for example, he says, "I prefer your arse, darling, to your bubbies because it does such a dirty thing,"[11] That for Joyce, the female rear is the cardinal point seems suggested by letters to Nora, but when he transfers this devotion to Bloom, he is doing so for artistic reasons.

In "Penelope" Molly has some comments to make on Bloom's near-fixation. She refers to the "last time he came on my bottom" (740) and to the "usual kissing my bottom" (739), both of which hint at Bloom's reverence for those famous "female hemispheres." She also mentions his underwear fetish: "He's mad on the subject of drawers" (746). Although Molly fails to understand his preference for this part of the anatomy ("we haven't 1 atom of any kind of expression in us all of us the same 2 lumps of lard" [777]), it is not her idea of expression, but Bloom's (and Joyce's) that counts.

Certainly "Penelope" is more than the character of Molly Bloom.

The whole area of language seems called into discussion in this episode. Critics have concerned themselves with such elements as Joyce's use of eight sentences as a structuring device, having its origins in Vico's conception of completeness and recurrence; they have also been aware of the importance of the element of contradiction in Molly's monologue, contradiction that seems intentionally placed there by the author.[12] Indeed, it would almost seem that Molly, in her use of language,is intent on undermining it. In any event, what we have in "Penelope" is a language characterized by any absence of beginning , middle, or end (an absence of linear time), a language characterized by fluidity, amplitude, earthiness, song, and contradictions that do not cancel but include, that do not nullify meaning but rather enhance it. For the "form" of the language serves as Joyce's statement about matter, substance, art, beginnings, and endings.

Again, Joyce supplies us with some hints as to his purpose in his letters. He tells Frank Budgen, "I am going to leave the last word with Molly Bloom—the final episode *Penelope* being written through her thoughts and body."[13] Later he elaborates further to Budgen, "The last word (human, all too human) is left to Penelope."[14] In both statements, the word is emphasized. It is grounded in humanity, in body, and Joyce means what he says. Molly Bloom is his word, his last word on language and the creative process.

Going back to Stephen's attitude toward women and language, we recall that in both *A Portrait,* and *Ulysses* Stephen has associated women with nonlanguage or with a mysterious language, a language that they alone seem to possess. For example, the lips of the prostitute he kisses project a "vague speech." The image of the bat woman and the girl on the beach are visual, silent. His dead mother is always envisioned as mute, as speaking "mute secret words" (10). The ghost of May Dedalus is also mute, urged by Stephen in "Circe" to "speak the word known to all men" (581). There is, however, no utterance forthcoming.

However, Joyce understood more fully the nature of the word, and it is Molly and the structure of language in the final episode that render a part of his meaning. Another clue is provided by Molly's name: Joyce says, "Moly is the gift of Hermes, a god of public ways, and is the invisible influence (prayer, chance, agility, *presence of mind,* power of recuperation) which saves in case of accident. . . . In this special case his plant may be said to have many leaves, indifference due to masturbation, pessimism congenital, a sense of the ridiculous sudden fastidiousness in some detail, experience."[15] With his eye on the personal, the mythic, the organic all at once, Joyce is still working with the alimentary process, for *moly* is food. It is something that must be ingested in order to be beneficial. In symbolic terms then, Molly has been the food of the book called *Ulysses*. And since Joyce is not about to render process static, she is also excrement, the end product of the work, and like all such end products bears the seeds of a new beginning.

Here is the coming together of all things. The associations of language with excrement and food, the characters' various ingestions on both a literal and metaphoric level, the physical and artistic transformations. According to Joyce, the "end" of *Ulysses* is "Ithaca." The last word of "Ithaca" is "Where?" but the last mark on the page is a period, a smudge that is both end and answer: home, Molly, Molly's end.

As he lies at her end, at the end of the day, at the end of his consciousness, Bloom is also lying at the beginning. Day is about to dawn; Molly's consciousness—intuitive, energizing consciousness based on ingestion, assimilation, and excretion—is awake. Molly's rump, the center of the world, is both object and symbol of the cyclical nature of life. This lump of lard, as Molly calls it, is not unlike Stephen's lump of earth, out of which will be fashioned art. Bloom, on the other hand, will continue to fashion his life around the worship of this lump by intuitively recognizing the sacred energies it represents, the important kinesis of the body, the presence of process, of emptying and filling, living, declining, and dying.

The priest's chalice, by which Stephen hopes to transmute the daily bread of experience into the radiant body of everliving life, the chalice that Mulligan mocks in the opening pages of the book, is only an objective vessel. Molly, asquat her chamberpot is the living vessel. She is subject and object, the source of all transformation mysteries for her creator, and it is she who represents communion, not as ritual but simply as being.

# NOTES

### CHAPTER 1

1. James Joyce, *A Portrait of the Artist as a Young Man* (New York: Viking Press, 1964), p. 221.

2. See particularly the work of Robert Boyle, S.J., "Miracle in Black Ink: A Glance at Joyce's Use of His Eucharistic Image," *James Joyce Quarterly* 10 (Fall 1972): 47-59; "The Priesthoods of Stephen and Buck," in *Approaches to "Ulysses": Ten Essays,* ed. Thomas F. Staley and Bernard Benstock (Pittsburgh: University of Pittsburgh Press, 1970), pp. 27-60; *James Joyce's Pauline Vision* (Carbondale: Southern Illinois University Press, 1978).

3. See Barbara Di Bernard, *Alchemy and "Finnegans Wake"* (Albany: State University of New York Press, 1980); William York Tindall, "James Joyce and the Hermetic Tradition," *Journal of the History of Ideas* 15 (January 1954): 23-29.

4. Frank Budgen, *James Joyce and the Making of "Ulysses"* (New York: Harrison Smith and Robert Haas, 1954), p. 21.

5. Stuart Gilbert, *James Joyce's "Ulysses": A Study* (New York: Vintage Books, 1956; see also a dissertation by Avel Austin entitled "*Ulysses* and the Human Body," *Dissertation Abstracts* 27 (1966): 1,778.

6. James Joyce, *Selected Letters,* ed. Richard Ellmann (New York: Viking Press, 1975), pp. 157-96. Some examples: "You had an arse full of farts that night, darling, and I fucked them out of you, big fat fellows, long windy ones, quick little merry cracks and a lot of tiny naughty farties ending in one long gush from your hole (185); and, "Are you offended because I said I loved to look at the brown stain that comes from behind on your girlish white drawers?" (189).

7. Clive Hart, *Structure and Motif in "Finnegans Wake"* (Evanston, Ill.: Northwestern University Press, 1962), pp. 202-3.

8. Mark Shechner, *Joyce in Nighttown: A Psychoanalytic Inquiry into "Ulysses"* (Berkley: University of California Press, 1974), p. 133.

9. Shechner, *Joyce in Nighttown,* pp. 133-35.

10. I am particularly indebted here to the work of Erik. H. Erikson, *Childhood and Society,* rev. ed. (New York: W. W. Norton, 1963), pp. 67-78.

11. Erich Neumann, *The Child,* trans. Ralph Manheim (New York: G. P. Putnam's Sons, 1973), pp. 33, 30.

12. Neumann points out that in many languages "to defecate" is translated as "to make" (*Child,* p. 118).

13, Neumann, *Child,* pp. 124-28.

14. Ibid, p. 126.

15. Sheldon R. Brivic, *Joyce Between Freud and Jung* (Port Washington, N.Y.: Kennikat Press, 1980), p. 5.

16. Brivic, *Joyce Between Freud and Jung,* p. 157. Brivic sees Bloom as a coprophiliac.

17. Elliott B. Gose, Jr., *The Transformation Process in Joyce's "Ulysses"* (Toronto: University of Toronto Press, 1980).

18. Gose, *Transformation Process in Joyce's "Ulysses,"* p. 11.

19. John B. Vickery, *The Literary Impact of "The Golden Bough"* (Princeton: Princeton University Press, 1973), pp. 283-84.

20. Vickery, *Literary Impact of "The Golden Bough,"* p. 330.

21. Theodor H. Gaster, *Thespis: Ritual, Myth and Drama in the Ancient Near East* (New York: Harper and Row, 1961). pp. 22-26.

22. Ernst Cassirer, *The Philosophy of Symbolic Forms, 1: Language* (New Haven: Yale University Press, 1955), p. 201.

23. See the work of Margaret Church, "*A Portrait* and Giambattista Vico: A Source Study," in *Approaches to Joyce's Portrait: Ten Essays,* ed. Thomas F. Staley and Bernard Benstock (Pittsburgh: University of Pittsburgh Press, 1976); also A. Walton Litz, "Vico and Joyce," in *Giambattista Vico: An International Symposium,* ed. Giorgio Tagliacozzo (Baltimore: Johns Hopkins, 1969), pp. 245-55. Litz says that Joyce was familiar with Vico as early as 1904. Although his use of Vico in *Ulysses* involves mostly "verbal detail," in *Finnegans Wake* Vico's ideas provide the foundation of the work. Although interested in Vico's ideas about etymology and cycles of history, Litz suggests that "it was Vico's creative interpretations of poetry and language that appealed to Joyce."

24. Giambattista Vico, *The New Science,* trans. Thomas Goddard Bergin and Max Harold Fisch (Ithaca: Cornell University Press, 1970), pp. 107-9.

25. Vico, *New Science,* p. 36.

26. Ibid., p. 88.

27. Jeanne McKnight, "Unlocking the Word-Hoard: Madness, Identity and Creativity in James Joyce," *James Joyce Quarterly* 14 (Summer 1977): 423.

28. Ibid., p. 432.

29. Vico, *New Science*, p. 260.
30. Cassirer, *Philosophy of Symbolic Forms, 1,* p. 90.
31. James Joyce, *Ulysses* (New York: Viking Press, 1961), p. 413.

CHAPTER 2

1. James Joyce, *A Portrait of the Artist as a Young Man* (New York: Viking Press, 1964), p. 221.

2. Philip E. Slater, *The Glory of Hera: Greek Mythology and the Greek Family* (Boston: Beacon Press, 1968), p. 88.

3. Slater, *Glory of Hera,* p. 92.

4. Chester G. Anderson, "Baby Tuckoo: Joyce's 'Features of Infancy,' " in *Approaches to Joyce's Portrait: Ten Essays,* ed. Thomas F. Staley and Bernard Benstock (Pittsburgh: University of Pittsburgh Press, 1976), p. 138.

5. Ibid.

6. Erich Neumann, *The Child,* trans. Ralph Manheim (New York: G. P. Putnam's Sons, 1973), p. 38.

7. Sheldon R. Brivic, *Joyce Between Freud and Jung* (Port Washington, N.Y.: Kennikat Press, 1980), p. 31. Brivic is right that Mrs. Dadalus is grouped with Dante.

8. Ibid. Brivic views the scene as one of castration since Dante has the last "spit."

9. Anderson argues that because Stephen's wishes to incorporate the mother have been repressed and sublimated into "epistemophelia"— an "intense desire to know"— any school failure is accompanied by a rejection of food. Hence Stephen's refusal to eat the damp bread is evidence of his "phobic attitude" (Baby Tuckoo," pp. 139, 155).

10. Neumann, *The Child,* p. 134.

11. Anderson, "Baby Tuckoo," p. 155.

12. William York Tindall, "Joyce's Chambermade Music," *Poetry* 80 (May 1952): 112.

13. Robert Briffault, "The Origin of Love," in *The Making of Man: An Outline of Anthropology,* ed. V. F. Calverton (New York: Modern Library, 1931), p. 487.

14. See Elaine Unkeless, "Bats and Sanguivorous Bugaboos," *James Joyce Quarterly* 15 (Winter 1978): 128-133. Unkeless points out that *bat* is a word for prostitute.

15. Jeanne McKnight, "Unlocking the Word-Hoard: Madness, Identity and Creativity in James Joyce," *James Joyce Quarterly* 14 (Summer 1977): p. 432.

16. James Joyce, *Ulysses* (New York: Viking Press, 1961), p. 5.

17. Robert Boyle's questions Buck's use of *Christine* instead of *Christ* and suggests that he "wants the rhythm and false rhyme which the—*ine* endings provide" ("The Priesthoods of Stephen and Buck," in *Approaches to "Ulysses": Ten Essays,* ed. Thomas F. Staley and Bernard Benstock [Pittsburgh: University of Pittsburgh Press, 1970, p. 44]). Boyle also thinks that *Christine* has a Hellenic ring. It may also be true that this is another example of one of Buck's sex reversals, the blurring of normal boundaries that is so much a part of this chapter.

18. Robert Graves, *The Greek Myths*, 2 vols., rev. ed. (Harmondsworth, Middlesex, England: Penguin, 1961), 2:167.

19. Weldon Thornton, *Allusions in "Ulysses,"* rev. ed. (New York: Simon and Schuster, 1973), p. 24.

20. William York Tindall, *James Joyce: His Way of Interpreting the Modern World* (New York: Charles Scribner's Sons, 1950), p. 23.

21. Suzette A. Henke, *Joyce's Moraculous Sindbook* (Columbus: Ohio State University Press, 1978), p. 41.

22. James H. Maddox, Jr., *Joyce's "Ulysses" and the Assault Upon Character* (New Brunswick, N.J.: Rutgers University Press, 1978), p. 32.

23. J. Mitchell Morse, "Proteus," in *James Joyce's "Ulysses": Critical Essays,* ed. Clive Hart and David Hayman (Berkeley: University of California Press, 1974), p. 30.

24. Thornton, *Allusions in "Ulysses,"* p. 51. Thornton says that the phrase *fleshpots of Egypt* was used by the sorrowing Children of Israel upon their exile from the land "where we did eat bread to the full" (Exodus 16:3).

25. Slater, *Glory of Hera,* p. 89. Slater notes children's desire to "gobble up the mother and keep her forever inside."

26. Ibid., p. 94. Quicksand fantasies of the child are a result of the mother's excessive need for nurturance.

27. Zack Bowen, *Musical Allusions in the Works of James Joyce* (Albany: State University of New York Press, 1974), p. 76.

28. Mark Shechner, *Joyce in Nighttown: A Psychoanalytic Inquiry into "Ulysses"* (Berkeley: University of California Press, 1974), p. 30.

29. Ibid., p. 31.

30. See Elliott B. Gose, Jr., *The Transformation Process in Joyce's "Ulysses"* (Toronto: University of Toronto Press, 1980), pp. 35-37. Gose's explication of this passage is illuminating. He views the last sentence as a description of "physical process, personal transformation, and spiritual metamorphosis," in which Stephen's submersion in existence is linked to his creator's acceptance of the threatening aspects of the female by way of Nora. Joyce has, he says, "put into Stephen's mind all the terms of a transformation cycle that he cannot yet appreciate."

31. Richard Ellmann, *Ulysses of the Liffey* (New York: Oxford University Press, 1972), p. 25.

32. Ruth von Phul, "The Boast of Heraldry in the 'Proteus' Episode of *Ulysses,"* *Journal of Modern Literature* 1 (March 1971): 403.

## CHAPTER 3

1. David Hayman, *"Ulysses": The Mechanics of Meaning* (Englewood Cliffs, N.J.: Prentice-Hall, 1970), p. 58.

2. William M. Shutte, "Leopold Bloom: A Touch of the Artist," *James Joyce Quarterly* 10 (Fall 1972): 122.

3. Shutte, "Leopold Bloom," p. 130.

4. Hayman, "*Ulysses*" p. 52.

5. Stuart Gilbert, *James Joyce's "Ulysses": A Study* (New York: Vintage Books, 1956), pp. 206-7.

6. William York Tindall, *James Joyce: His Way of Interpretating the Modern World* (New York: Charles Scribner's Sons, 1950), p. 43.

7. Frank Budgen, *James Joyce and the Making of "Ulysses"* (New York: Harrison Smith and Robert Haas, 1954), p. 106.

8. Erich Neumann, *The Origins and History of Consciousness,* Bollingen Series 42 (Princeton: Princeton University Press, 1954), p. 26.

9. Robert Graves, *The Greek Myths,* 2 vols., rev. ed. (Harmondsworth, Middlesex, England: Penguin, 1961), 2:366.

10. Gilbert mentions that Bérard, whom Joyce apparently drew on for much of his Homeric material, though *lot* to be a semetic word and that forgetfullness induced from the plant is partially a Homeric word play on *lethe,* the Greek river of oblivion *(James Joyce's "Ulysses,"* p. 156.).

11. Neumann, *Origins,* p. 307.

12. Ibid., p. 51.

13. Ibid.

14. William York Tindall, *A Reader's Guide to James Joyce* (New York: Farrar, Straus & Giroux, 1959), p. 156.

15. Robert Boyle, S.J., "Miracle in Black Ink: A Glance at Joyce's Use of His Eucharistic Image," *James Joyce Quarterly* 10 (Fall 1972): 55.

16. Zack Bowen states that this line is derived from an early 18th century song "The Roast Beef of Old England," that laments the weakening of English blood via French foods, and extols the days when "mighty roast beef" "enobled our hearts, and enriched our blood." If Bloom uses the song ironically, then the exploitation of Irish cattle for the purposes of invigorating English blood and abetting English imperialism, may also be suggested. The song seems to be another indication that Bloom is aware of Process, where things eat one another *(Musical Allusions in the Works of James Joyce* [Albany: State University of New York Press, 1974], pp. 108-9).

17. Robert M. Adams, "Hades" in *James Joyce's "Ulysses": Critical Essays,* ed. Clive Hart and David Hayman (Berkeley: University of California Press 1974), p. 97.

18. Gilbert, *James Joyce's "Ulysses,"* pp. 206-7.

19. Adolph E. Jensen's *Myth and Cult Among Primitive Peoples,* trans. Marianna Tax Choldin and Wolfgang Weissleder (Chicago: University of Chicago Press, 1963) is especially interesting. See also, Mircea Eliade's *Rites and Symbols of Initiation,* trans. Willard R. Trask (New York: Harper and Row, 1965).

20. Jensen, *Myth and Cult,* p. 165.

21. Ibid., p. 168, italics mine.

22. Weldon Thornton, *Allusions in "Ulysses,"* rev. ed. (New York: Simon and Schuster, 1973), p. 132.

23. "Yom Kippur," *Jewish Encyclopedia* (New York: KTAV Publishing, 1964).

24. Schutte, "Leopold Bloom," p. 124.

25. Bowen, *Musical Allusions,* pp. 131-32. Bowen stresses the importance of the association in Bloom's mind between women's toilets and female sexuality implicit in the lyrics of "The Meeting of the Waters."

26. Theodor H. Gaster, *Festivals of the Jewish Year* (New York: William Sloane, 1968), p. 136.

27. Roy Arthur Swanson, "Edible Wandering Rocks: The Pun as Allegory in Joyce's 'Lestrygonians,' " *Genre* 6 (December 1972): 391.

28. See also Gaster's discussion in *Thespis,* pp. 423-24.

29. Mircea Eliade, *Myths, Dreams, and Mysteries,* trans. Philip Mairet (New York: Harper and Row, 1960), p. 46.

30. See John B. Vickery's discussion of *Ulysses* in *The Literary Impact of "The Golden Bough"* (Princeton: Princeton University Press, 1973).

31. Sheldon R. Brivic, *Joyce Between Freud and Jung* (Port Washington, N.Y.: Kennikat Press, 1980), p. 137.

32. Erich Neumann, *The Child,* trans. Ralph Manheim (New York: G. P. Putnam's Sons, 1973), p. 37.

33. Ibid., p. 108.

34. J. C. Keogh, "*Ulysses:* 'Parable of the Plums' as Parable and Periplum," *James Joyce Quarterly* 7 (Summer 1970): 378.

35. Budgen, *James Joyce,* p. 106.

36. Stanley Sultan, *The Argument of "Ulysses"* (Columbus: Ohio State University Press, 1964), p. 225.

37. Jackson Cope, "Sirens," in *James Joyce's "Ulysses": Critical Essays:* ed. Clive Hart and David Hayman (Berkeley: University of California Press, 1974), p. 242.

38. Graves, *Greek Myths,* 2:249.

39. Sultan, *Argument of "Ulysses,"* p. 229.

40. Neumann, *Child,* pp. 124-26.

41. Suzette A. Henke, *Joyce's Moraculous Sindbook* (Columbus: Ohio State University Press, 1978), p. 130.

42. Sultan, *Argument of "Ulysses,"* p. 224.

43. Bowen, *Musical Allusions,* p. 179.

44. Ibid., p. 205.

45. "Foods," *Jewish Encyclopedia.*

46. "Foods," *Encylopaedia Judaica* (New York: Macmillan Co., 1971).

CHAPTER 4

1. Theodor H. Gaster, *Festivals of the Jewish Year* (New York: William Sloane, 1968), p. 34.

2. Marilyn French, *The Book as World: James Joyce's "Ulysses"* (Cambridge, Mass.: Harvard University Press, 1976), p. 100.

3. Gaster, *Festivals*, p. 32.

4. Ibid., p. 43.

5. Zack Bowen, *Musical Allusions in the Works of James Joyce* (Albany: State University of New York Press, 1974), p. 120.

6. See ibid., p. 119, for a complete discussion of the "Shema Israel," the "Krias Shema," and a complete rendering of the "Chad Gadya."

7. Bowen, *Musical Allusions,* pp. 80-81.

8. See also Robert Adams Day, "How Stephen Wrote His Vampire Poem," *James Joyce Quarterly* 17 (Winter 1980): 183-97.

9. Michael Seidel, "*Ulysses' Black Panther Vampire,*" *James Joyce Quarterly* 13 (Summer 1976): 419.

10. Ibid.

11. William York Tindall, *A Reader's Guide to James Joyce* (New York: Farrar, Straus & Giroux, 1959), p. 166.

12. M. J. C. Hodgart, "Aeolus," In *James Joyce's "Ulysses": Critical Essays,* ed. Clive Hart and David Hayman (Berkeley: University of California Press, 1974), p. 126.

13. J. C. Keogh, "*Ulysses:* 'Parable of the Plums' as Parable and Periplum," *James Joyce Quarterly* 7 (Summer 1970): 378.

14. James H. Maddox, Jr., *Joyce's "Ulysses" and the Assault Upon Character* (New Brunswick, N. J.: Rutgers University Press, 1973), p. 99.

15. Hodgart argues that Stephen's "Parable" is "true imaginative art, in contrast to merely brilliant oratory" ("Aeolus," p. 126); Maddox says that the "Parable" "tells us more about Stephen's direction as an artist than any other 'works' in the book" (*Joyce's "Ulysses,"* p. 99).

16. *Letters,* ed. Stuart Gilbert (New York: Viking, 1957), p. 139.

17. Weldon Thornton, *Allusions in "Ulysses,"* rev. ed. (New York: Simon and Schuster, 1973), p. 48.

18. Mark Shechner, *Joyce in Nighttown: A Psychoanalytic Inquiry into "Ulysses"* (Berkeley: University of California Press, 1974), pp. 136-38.

19. Frank Budgen, *James Joyce and the Making of "Ulysses"* (New York: Harrison Smith and Robert Haas, 1954), p. 217.

20. Gilbert, *Letters,* pp. 138-39.

21. "Oxen of the Sun" in *James Joyce's "Ulysses",* p. 324.

22. Suzette A. Henke, *Joyce's Moraculous Sindbook* (Columbus: Ohio State University Press, 1978), p. 175.

23. Robert Boyle, S.J., "The Priesthoods of Stephen and Buck" in *Approaches to "Ulysses": Ten Essays,* ed. Thomas F. Staley and Bernard Benstock (Pittsburgh: University of Pittsburgh Press, 1970), p. 48.

24. Robert Boyle, S.J., *James Joyce's Pauline Vision* (Carbondale: Southern Illinois University Press, 1978), p. 49.

25. Alan Watts, *Ritual and Myth in Christianity* (Boston: Beacon Press, 1968), p. 147.

26. Robert Boyle, S.J., "Miracle in Black Ink: A Glance at Joyce's Use of His Eucharistic Image," *James Joyce Quarterly* 10 (Fall 1972): 48.

27. Maddox, *Joyce's "Ulysses,"* p. 177.

28. See Don Gifford with Robert J. Seidman, *Notes for Joyce: An Annotation of James Joyce's "Ulysses"* (New York: E. P. Dutton, 1974), p. 342, for a discussion of the allusions to St. Bernard's homily, the Saturday Office, and the 11 October Feast.

29. Boyle, *Joyce's Pauline Vision,* p. 53.

30. Frank Zingrone, "Joyce and D'Annunzio: The Marriage of Fire and Water," *James Joyce Quarterly* 16 (Spring 1979): 257.

31. Theodor H. Gaster, *Thespis: Ritual, Myth and Drama in the Ancient Near East* (New York: Harper and Row, 1961), p. 222. According to Gaster, honey "features also in rites of regeneration," and is eaten at the time of the Jewish New Year. It is also associated with the Golden Age and the Promised Land.

32. Thornton, *Allusions in "Ulysses,"* p. 333.

33. Watts, *Ritual and Myth,* p. 98.

34. Stanley Sultan, *The Argument of "Ulysses"* (Columbus: Ohio State University Press, 1964), p. 297.

35. Ibid., p. 298.

36. Harry Blamires, *The Bloomsday Book: A Guide Through Joyce's "Ulysses"* (London: Methuen, 1966), pp. 163-64.

37. Gaster, *Festivals,* p. 63.

38. Ibid., p. 76.

39. "Festivals," *Jewish Encyclopedia.*

40. "Pentecost," *Catholic Encyclopedia* (New York: McGraw-Hill, 1967).

41. Maddox, *Joyce's "Ulysses,"* p. 177.

42. Shechner, *Joyce in Nighttown,* p. 101.

43. Shechner calls "Circe" "a boastful acknowledgment of sin" (*Joyce in Nighttown,* p. 32); French calls is a "nightmare sent by god-Joyce to the reader" (*Book as World,* p. 87).

44. Erich Neumann, *The Origins and History of Consciousness,* Bollingen Series 42 (Princeton: Princeton University Press, 1954), pp. 33-34.

45. Tindall, *Reader's Guide,* p. 156.

46. Blamires, *Bloomsday Book,* p. 168.

47. Tindall, *Reader's Guide,* p. 209.

48. Sheldon R. Brivic, *Joyce Between Freud and Jung* (Port Washington, N.Y.: Kennikat Press, 1980), p. 159.

49. John B. Vickery, *The Literary Impact of "The Golden Bough"* (Princeton: Princeton University Press, 1973), p. 381.

50. Elliott B. Gose, Jr., *The Transformation Process in Joyce's "Ulysses"* (Toronto: University of Toronto Press, 1980), p. 151.

51. Erich Neumann, *The Child,* trans. Ralph Manheim (New York: G. P. Putnam's Sons, 1973), pp. 127-28.

52. Vickery, *Literary Impact of "The Golden Bough,"* p. 395.

53. Thornton, *Allusions in "Ulysses,"* p. 381.

54. Neumann, *Origins,* p. 86.

55. Shechner describes this scene as a dramatization of "obeisance of a guilt-ridden ego before the terrible internalized parent, the stern superego . . . the phallic mother" (*Joyce in Nighttown,* p. 116); Brivic says that aggressive women are attractive to Bloom, and because they are "essentially men," Bella is turned into Bello (*Joyce Between Freud and Jung,* p. 188). "The root fantasy of submission to father, both attractive and terrifying, is exposed here without its usual disguise."

56. Shechner, *Joyce in Nighttown,* p. 110.

57. Blamires, *Bloomsday Book,* p. 195.

58. Vickery, *Literary Impact of "The Golden Bough,"* p. 403.

59. Thornton, *Allusions in "Ulysses,"* p. 359.

60. See Bowen's discussion, *Musical Allusions,* pp. 275-76; also Blamires, *Bloomsday Book,* pp. 184-85.

61. Maddox, *Joyce's "Ulysses,"* p. 139.

62. Boyle, "Miracle in Black Ink," p. 47.

63. Sheldon R. Brivic, "Time, Sexuality and Identity in Joyce's *Ulysses,*" *James Joyce Quarterly* 7 (Fall 1969): 35.

64. David Hayman, *"Ulysses": The Mechanics of Meaning* (Englewood Cliffs, N. J.: Prentice-Hall, 1970), p. 86; Gerald L. Bruns, "Eumaeus," in *James Joyce's "Ulysses",* p. 367; Gilbert, *James Joyce's "Ulysses,"* p. 361; French, *Book as World,* pp. 208-9.

65. French, *Book as World,* p. 212.

66. Boyle, "Miracle in Black Ink," pp. 52-53.

67. See John Henry Raleigh's excellent study, "On the Way Home to Ithaca: The Functions of the 'Eumaeus' selection in *Ulysses,*" in the *Irish Renaissance Annual,* 2 (Newark: University of Delaware Press, 1981). Raleigh sees the turds as "Joyce's comment on many things, past and present, in the public world of his times," and lists an impressive number of corresponding triads, stylistic, personal, political, sexual, and historical. He also views the turds as one of "two primary physical symbols of 'Eumaeus,'" a "culmination and conclusion to that galactic downward drift or movement of the episode."

68. Maddox, *Joyce's "Ulysses,"* p. 160.

69. Gifford, *Notes for Joyce,* p. 468.

70. Tindall, *Reader's Guide,* p. 222.

71. Hugh Kenner, *Joyce's Voices* (Berkeley: University of California Press, 1978), p. 96.

72. Gilbert, *Letters,* pp. 159-60.

73. "Ithaca," in *James Joyce's "Ulysses,"* p. 393.

74. Kenner, *Joyce's Voices,* p. 97.

75. Tindall, *Reader's Guide,* p. 222.

76. See Gifford, *Notes for Joyce,* pp. 491-92; also Thornton, *Allusions in "Ulysses,"* pp. 481-82.

77. "Burnt Offering," *Jewish Encyclopedia*.
78. Gifford, *Notes for Joyce*, p. 491.
79. Bowen, *Musical Allusions*, pp. 325-26.
80. Seidel, *"Ulysses' Black Panther Vampire,"* p. 423.
81. Ibid., p. 425.

## CHAPTER 5

1. Elliott B. Gose, Jr., *The Transformation Process in Joyce's "Ulysses"* (Toronto: University of Toronto Press, 1980). pp. 8-19, 166-70; also Joseph C. Voelker, "' Nature it is': The Influence of Giordano Bruno on James Joyce's Molly Bloom," *James Joyce Quarterly* 14 (Fall 1976): 39-48.

2. Voelker, " 'Nature it is,' " p. 46.

3. Gose, *Transformation Process in Joyce's "Ulysses,"* p. 183.

4. William P. Fitzpatrick, "The Myth of Creation: Joyce, Jung and *Ulysses,"* *James Joyce Quarterly* 11 (Winter 1974): 142.

5. Richard Ellmann, *Ulysses on the Liffey* (New York: Oxford University Press, 1972), p. 171.

6. Suzette A. Henke, *Joyce's Moraculous Sindbook* (Columbus: Ohio State University Press, 1978), p. 248.

7. Ellmann, *Ulysses on the Liffey*, p. 164.

8. Erich Neumann, *The Great Mother,* Bollingen Series 47 (Princeton: Princeton University Press, 1963), pp. 31, 291. See also Neumann's plates, especially nos. 3, 6, 20, 24-35, which show goddess figures as vessels or as seated on them.

9. Don Gifford, with Robert J. Seidman, *Notes for Joyce: An Annotation of James Joyce's "Ulysses"* (New York: E. P. Dutton, 1974) p. 512.

10. James Joyce, *Selected Letters,* ed. Richard Ellmann (New York: Viking Press, 1966), p. 285.

11. Ibid., p. 186.

12. See especially Diane Tolomeo, "The Final Octagon of *Ulysses,"* *James Joyce Quarterly* 10 (Summer 1973): 439-54, and James Van Dyck Card, " 'Contradicting': The Word for Joyce's 'Penelope,' "*James Joyce Quaterly* 11 (Fall 1973): 17-26.

13. Joyce, *Selected Letters*, p. 274.

14. Ibid., p. 278.

15. Ibid., p. 272.

# SELECTED BIBLIOGRAPHY

### JOYCE'S WRITINGS

Joyce, James. *Finnegans Wake.* New York: Viking Press, 1959.
———. *Letters,* Ed. Stuart Gilbert. New York: Viking Press, 1957.
———. *A Portrait of the Artist as a Young Man.* New York: Viking Press, 1964.
———. *Selected Letters.* Ed. Richard Ellmann. New York: Viking Press, 1966.
———. *Ulysses.* New York: Viking Press, 1961.

### SECONDARY SOURCES

Adams, Robert M. *James Joyce: Common Sense and Beyond.* New York: Random House, 1966.
———. *Surface and Symbol: The Consistency of James Joyce's "Ulysses."* New York: Oxford University Press, 1962.
Anderson, Chester G. "Baby Tuckoo: Joyce's 'Features of Infancy.' " In *Approaches to Joyce's Portrait: Ten Essays.* Edited by Thomas F. Staley and Bernard Benstock. Pittsburgh: University of Pittsburgh Press, 1976.
———. "Leopold Bloom as Dr. Sigmund Freud." *Mosaic* 6 (1972-73): 23-43.
———. "On the Sublime and Its Anal-Urethral Sources in Pope, Eliot, and Joyce." In *Modern Irish Literature: Essays in Honor of William York Tindall.* Edited by Raymond J. Porter and James D. Brophy. New York: Iona College Press, Twayne, 1972.
———. "The Sacrificial Butter." In *Portraits of an Artist.* Edited by William E. Morris and Clifford A. Nault, Jr. New York: Odyssey Press, 1962.
Austin, Avel. *"Ulysses* and the Human Body." *Dissertation Abstracts* 27 (1966): 1778.

Beausang, Michael. "Seeds for the Planting of Bloom," *Mosaic* 6 (1972-73): 11-21.
Blamires, Harry. *The Bloomsday Book: A Guide Through Joyce's "Ulysses."* London: Methuen, 1966.
Boldereff, Frances M. *Hermes to His Son Thoth: Being Joyce's Use of Giordano Bruno in "Finnegans Wake."* Woodward, Pa.: Classic Non-Fiction Library, 1968.
Bowen, Zack. *Musical Allusions in the Works of James Joyce.* Albany: State University of New York Press, 1974.
Boyle, Robert, S. J. *James Joyce's Pauline Vision.* Carbondale: Southern Illinois University Press, 1978.
―――. "Miracle in Black Ink: A Glance at Joyce's Use of His Eucharistic Image." *James Joyce Quarterly* 10 (Fall 1972): 47-59.
―――. "The Priesthoods of Stephen and Buck." In *Approaches to "Ulysses": Ten Essays.* Edited by Thomas F. Staley and Bernard Benstock. Pittsburgh: University of Pittsburgh Press, 1970.
Briffault, Robert. "The Origin of Love" In *The Making of Man: An Outline of Anthropology.* Edited by V. F. Calverton. New York: Modern Library, 1931.
Briskin, Irene Orgel. "Some New Light on 'The Parable of the Plums.' " *James Joyce Quarterly* 3 (Summer 1966): 236-51.
Brivic, Sheldon R. "James Joyce: From Stephen to Bloom." In *Psychoanalysis and the Literary Process.* Edited by Frederick C. Crews. Cambridge, Mass.: Winthrop, 1970.
―――. *Joyce Between Freud and Jung.* Port Washington, N. Y.: Kennikat Press, 1980.
―――. "Time, Sexuality and Identity in Joyce's *Ulysses.*" *James Joyce Quarterly* 7 (Fall 1969): 30-51.
Budgen, Frank. *James Joyce and the Making of "Ulysses."* New York: Harrison Smith and Robert Haas, 1954.
Burckhardt, Titus. *Alchemy: Science of the Cosmos, Science of the Soul.* Translated by William Stoddart. Baltimore: Penguin, 1972.
Cassirer, Ernst. *The Philosophy of Symbolic Forms, 1: Language.* New Haven: Yale University Press, 1955.
Church, Margaret. "*A Portrait* and Giambattista Vico: A Source Study." In *Approaches to Joyce's Portrait: Ten Essays.* Edited by Thomas F. Staley and Bernard Benstock. Pittsburgh: University of Pittsburgh Press, 1976.
Connolly, Thomas. *The Personal Library of James Joyce: A Descriptive Bibliography.* University of Buffalo Studies, vol. 22, no. 1, Buffalo: University of Buffalo Press, 1955.
Cope, Jackson I. "*Ulysses*: Joyce's Kabbalah." *James Joyce Quarterly* 7 (Winter 1970): 93-113.
―――. "Sirens." In *James Joyce's "Ulysses": Critical Essays.* Edited by Clive Hart and David Hayman. Berkeley: University of California Press, 1974.
Cornford, Francis MacDonald. *The Origin of Attic Comedy.* Cambridge: Cambridge University Press, 1934.
Curran, Stuart. " 'Bous Stephanoumenos': Joyce's Sacred Cow." *James Joyce Quarterly* 6 (Winter 1968): 163-70.
Day, Robert Adams. "How Stephen Wrote His Vampire Poem." *James Joyce Quarterly* 17 (Winter 1980): 183-97.
Di Bernard, Barbara. *Alchemy and "Finnegans Wake."* Albany: State University of New York Press, 1980.

Eliade, Mircea. *Myths, Dreams, and Mysteries.* Translated by Philip Mairet. New York: Harper and Row, 1960.
Ellmann, Richard. *The Consciousness of James Joyce.* Toronto: Oxford University Press, 1977.
———. *James Joyce.* New and rev. ed. New York: Oxford University Press, 1982.
———. *Ulysses on the Liffey.* New York: Oxford University Press, 1972.
Erickson, Erik H. *Childhood and Society.* Rev. ed. New York: W. W. Norton, 1963.
Evans, William A. "Wordagglutinations in Joyce's *Ulysses.*" *Studies in the Literary Imagination* 3 (October 1974): 27-36.
Fitzpatrick, William P. "The Myth of Creation: Joyce, Jung, and *Ulysses.*" *James Joyce Quarterly* 11 (Winter 1974): 123-44.
French, Marilyn. *The Book as World: James Joyce's "Ulysses."* Cambridge, Mass.: Harvard University Press, 1976.
Freud, Sigmund. *Three Essays on the Theory of Sexuality.* Translated by James Strachey. New York: Basic Books, 1962.
Gaster, Theodor H. *Festivals of the Jewish Year.* New York: William Sloane, 1968.
———. *Thespis: Ritual, Myth, and Drama in the Ancient Near East.* New York: Harper and Row, 1961.
Gilbert, Stuart. *James Joyce's "Ulysses": A Study.* New York: Vintage Books, 1956.
Gifford, Don, with Robert J. Seidman. *Notes for Joyce: An Annotation of James Joyce's "Ulysses".* New York: E. P. Dutton, 1974.
Goldberg, S. L. *The Classical Temper: A Study of James Joyce's "Ulysses".* New York: Barnes and Noble, 1961.
Gose, Elliott B., Jr. *The Transformation Process in Joyce's "Ulysses."* Toronto: University of Toronto Press, 1980.
Graves, Robert. *The Greek Myths,* 2 vols. Harmondsworth, Middlesex, England: Penguin, 1955.
Hart, Clive. *James Joyce's "Ulysses".* Sidney: Sidney University Press, 1968.
———. *Structure and Motif in "Finnegans Wake."* Evanston, Ill.: Northwestern University Press, 1962.
Hayman, David. *"Ulysses": The Mechanics of Meaning.* Englewood Cliffs, N. J.: Prentice-Hall, 1970.
Henke, Suzette A. *Joyce's Moraculous Sindbook.* Columbus: Ohio State University Press, 1978.
Hodgart, M. J. C. "Aeolus." In *James Joyce's "Ulysses": Critical Essays.* Edited by Clive Hart and David Hayman. Berkeley: University of California Press, 1974.
Jarrell, Mackie L. "Joyce's Use of Swift's *Polite Conversations* in the 'Circe' Episode of *Ulysses.*" *PMLA* 72 (June 1957): 545-54.
Jensen, Adolf E. *Myth and Cult Among Primitive Peoples.* Translated by Marianna Tax Choldin and Wolfgang Weissleder. Chicago: University of Chicago Press, 1963.
*Jewish Encyclopedia.* Edited by Isidore Singer. New York: KTAV Publishing, 1964.
Kenner, Hugh. *Dublin's Joyce.* London: Chatto and Windus, 1955.
———. *Joyce's Voices.* Berkeley: University of California Press, 1978.
———. "Molly's Masterstroke," *James Joyce Quarterly* 10 (Fall 1972): 19-28.
Keogh, J. G. *"Ulysses'* 'Parable of the Plums' as Parable and Periplum." *James Joyce Quarterly* 7 (Summer 1970): 377-78.

Kimball, Jean. "The Hypostasis in *Ulysses.*" *James Joyce Quarterly* 10 (Summer 1973): 422-38.
Klein, A. M. "The Black Panther (A Study in Technique)." *Accent* 10 (Summer 1950): 139-55.
Knuth, A. M. L. *The Wink of the Word: A Study of James Joyce's Phatic Communication.* Amsterdam: Rodopi, 1976.
Litz, A. Walton. "Ithaca." In *James Joyce's "Ulysses": Critical Essays.* Edited by Clive Hart and David Hayman. Berkeley: University of California Press, 1974.
―――. "Vico and Joyce." In *Giambattista Vico: An International Symposium.* Edited by Giorgio Tagliacozzo. Baltimore: Johns Hopkins, 1969, pp., 245-55.
Maddox, James H., Jr. *Joyce's "Ulysses" and the Assault Upon Character.* New Brunswick, N. J.: Rutgers University Press, 1978.
Magalaner, Marvin. *Time of Apprenticeship: The Fiction of Young James Joyce.* New York: Abelard-Schuman, 1959.
McCarthy, Patrick. "Further Notes on the Mass in *Ulysses.*" *James Joyce Quarterly* 7 (Winter 1969): 132-37.
McKnight, Jeanne. "Unlocking the Word-Hoard: Madness, Identity and Creativity in James Joyce." *James Joyce Quarterly* 14 (Summer 1977): 420-35.
Neumann, Erich. *The Child: Structure and Dynamics of the Nascent Personality.* Translated by Ralph Manheim. New York: G. P. Putnam's Sons, 1973.
―――. *The Great Mother.* Bollingen Series 47. Princeton: Princeton University Press, 1963.
―――. *The Origins and History of Consciousness.* Bollingen Series 42. Princeton: Princeton University Press, 1954.
Noon, William T., S. J. *Joyce and Aquinas.* New Haven: Yale University Press, 1957.
Ong, Walter J. *The Presence of the Word: Some Prologemena for Cultural and Religious History.* New Haven: Yale University Press, 1967.
Petta, Rochelle. "From Corpus to Corpse: 'Lotus Eaters' to 'Hades.' " *The Celtic Bull,* no. 3545, pp. 24-31.
Piaget, Jean. *The Child's Conception of the World.* London: Routledge and Kegan Paul, 1951.
Prescott, Joseph. "The Character of Leopold Bloom." *Literature and Psychology* 9 (Winter 1959): 3-4.
Raleigh, John Henry. "On the Way Home to Ithaca: The Functions of the 'Eumaeus' Section in *Ulysses.*" In *Irish Renaissance Annual, II.* Newark: University of Delaware Press, 1981.
Schutte, William M. "Leopold Bloom: A Touch of the Artist." *James Joyce Quarterly* 10 (Fall 1972): 118-31.
Seidel, Michael. *"Ulysses'* Black Panther Vampire." *James Joyce Quarterly* 13 (Summer 1976): 415-27.
Senn, Fritz. "Mullingar Heifer." *James Joyce Quarterly* 2 (Winter 1966): 36-37.
Shechner, Mark. "Joyce and Psychoanalyis: Two Additional Perspectives." *James Joyce Quarterly* 14 (Summer 1977): 416-19.
―――. *Joyce in Nighttown: A Psychoanalytic Inquiry into "Ulysses."* Berkeley: University of California Press, 1974.
―――. "The Song of the Wandering Aengus: James Joyce and His Mother." *James Joyce Quarterly* 10 (Fall 1972): 72-89.

Slater, Philip E. *The Glory of Hera: Greek Mythology and the Greek Family*. Boston: Beacon Press, 1968.

Steinberg, Erwin R. " 'Lestrygonians,' A Pale 'Proteus?' " *Modern Fiction Studies* 15 (Spring 1969): 73-86.

Sultan, Stanley. *The Argument of "Ulysses"*. Columbus: Ohio State University Press, 1964.

Swanson, Roy Arthur. "Edible Wandering Rocks: The Pun as Allegory in Joyce's 'Lestrygonians.' " *Genre* 6 (December 1972): 385-403.

Thomas, Brook. "The Counterfeit Style of 'Eumaeus.' " *James Joyce Quarterly* 14 (Fall 1976): 15-24.

Thompson, George. "Two More on 'Beef to the Heel.' " *James Joyce Quarterly* 9 (Summer 1972): 495-96.

Thornton, Weldon. *Allusions in "Ulysses."* Revised ed. New York: Simon and Schuster, 1973.

Tindall, William York. "James Joyce and the Hermetic Tradition." *Journal of the History of Ideas* 15 (January 1954): 23-29.

———. *James Joyce: His Way of Interpreting the Modern World*. New York: Charles Scribner's Sons, 1950.

———. *A Reader's Guide to James Joyce*. New York: Farrar, Straus and Giroux, 1959.

Tolomeo, Diane. "The Final Octagon of *Ulysses."* *James Joyce Quarterly* 10 (Summer 1973): 439-54.

Vickery, John B. *The Literary Impact of "The Golden Bough."* Princeton: Princeton University Press, 1973.

Vico, Giambattista. *The New Science*. Translated by Thomas Goddard Bergin and Max Harold Fisch. Ithaca: Cornell University Press, 1970.

Voelker, Joseph C. " 'Nature it is': The Influence of Giordano Bruno on James Joyce's Molly Bloom." *James Joyce Quarterly* 14 (Fall 1976): 39-48.

Von Phul, Ruth. "The Boast of Heraldry in the 'Proteus' Episode of *Ulysses."* *Journal of Modern Literature* 1 (March 1971): 399-405.

Wasson, Richard, "Stephen Dedalus and the Imagery of Sight: A Psychological Approach." *Literature and Psychology* 15 (Fall 1965): 195-209.

Watts, Alan W. *Myth and Ritual in Christianity*. Boston: Beacon Press, 1968.

Zingrone, Frank. "Joyce and D'Annunzio: The Marriage of Fire and Water." *James Joyce Quarterly* 16 (Spring 1979): 253-65.

# INDEX

Adams, Robert M., 61
A. E. *See* Russell, George
"Aeolus" episode, 40, 61, 76, 89–96, 103
Agendath, Netaim, 48
Alchemy, 1–2, 98, 101, 119
Alimentary process, 2, 4, 11, 24, 52, 69, 78, 102, 106. *See also* Digestive process; Process
Alimentary symbolism, 6, 11, 25–26, 44, 61, 78, 81
Anality, 2, 4–5, 16
Anderson, Chester G., 12–13, 15, 21
Animals: bat, 25–26; dog, 37–39, 76, 125–126; fox, 33–34; goat, 119; pig, 119
Aphrodite, 119
Armageddon, 140
Arnall, Father, 16–17
Art, 9–10; Joyce and, 1, 3, 27, 133, 154
Artist: as priest, 1, 11–12. *See also* Dedalus, Stephen
Atherton, J. S., 99

Barnacle, Nora, 2, 153
Beaufoy, Philip, 51–52, 69, 109, 112, 116–17

Bérard, Victor, *Les Pheniciens et l "Odyssee,"* 46
Bible, 108
Black mass, 125
Blamires, Harry, 106, 113, 120
Blavatsky, Helene, 44, 148
Bloom, Leopold: as artist, 45, 52, 64; and castration, 54–55, 117; as Christ, 119; and creativity, 27, 61, 73, 82, 90, 92, 109, 120, 122; and excrement, 51, 80, 115–17, 119, 121, 153; as Henry Flower, 54, 81; as ingester, 10, 48, 54, 84, 104, 106, 133, 136, 139, 144; and Martha, 55, 70, 74, 81–82; and memory, 8–9, 47, 74–76, 102, 104, 108, 119; and Milly, 50–51; and Molly, 8, 48–49, 51–52, 59, 64–65, 68, 72–80, 83–85, 87, 105, 111, 136, 143–44, 146–48, 150–52; as Moses, 91; and nature, 44, 50–51, 61, 65–66; as nurturer, 127–29, 136; and ritual, 9, 56–57, 65, 70, 99; and Rudy, 52, 60, 74, 83, 105; as sacrifice, 51, 57, 62, 64, 83, 89, 91–92, 96, 117, 140–41. *See also* Dedalus, Stephen: and Bloom

Bloom, Milly, 106, 149
Bloom, Molly, 55, 82, 106, 117, 144–45, 149, 154; and Howth, 8–9, 76–77, 81, 87, 95, 111, 113, 131, 151, 153, 155. *See also* Bloom, Leopold: and Molly
Body, 2, 6, 11, 27, 78–79, 116, 155; Bloom and, 2, 46, 51, 62, 86, 91, 113; Joyce's use of, 1, 2, 52, 133, 145, 154; Stephen and, 2, 15, 18, 20, 24, 38, 110, 123; upper/lower poles, 4, 17–19, 27, 79, 108, 110, 129. *See also* Language: and body
Bowen, Zack, 39, 92, 141
Boylan, Blazes, 50, 52, 55, 65, 68, 71–72, 74, 77, 81–84, 134, 137, 143, 147–49
Boyle, Robert, S.J., 99–101, 126, 128
Breen, Josephine, 69, 111–12
Brivic, Sheldon R., *Joyce between Freud and Jung*, 5, 14, 75, 115, 127
Bruno, Giordano, 5, 145–46
Bruns, Gerald, 128
Budgen, Frank, 1–2, 46, 98–99, 154
Burke, O'Madden, 93
Burnt offering, 139, 141

"Calypso" episode, 46–52, 57
Cannibalism, 24–25, 42, 57, 62–63, 71, 89, 92, 100, 132, 134
Carr, Pvt. 113
Casey, Mr., 13–15
Cassandra, 35
Cassirer, Ernst, 7–8
*Catholic Encyclopedia*, 107
"Chad Gadya," 90, 92
Christ, 14, 18, 42–43, 45, 56, 63, 101, 107–9, 126–29, 133, 140–41
"Circe" episode, 6, 29, 37, 40, 61, 109–27, 154
Coffey, Father, 59
Cohen, Bella, 114–15, 119, 126
Compton, Pvt., 113
Conmee, Father, 15
Cope, Jackson, 78
Cowley, Father, 78, 83–85
Cranly, 22–24
Crawford, Myles, 92, 117
Creative process: Joyce and, 1, 12, 76, 89, 97, 115, 132, 135. *See also* Digestive process: and creativity
Cunningham, Martin, 60–61

D'Annunzio, *The Marriage of Fire and Water*, 101
Dante Alighieri, 24; "Paradiso," 31
Davin, Michael, 25–26
Deasy, Garrett, 32, 34–35, 38, 40
Dedalus, May, 13, 95, 124, 154
Dedalus, Simon, 13–14, 60–61, 72, 78, 83–86
Dedalus, Stephen: as artist, 11–12, 21, 30, 35, 51, 101–2, 126, 141, 143, 155; and Bloom, 10, 89, 96, 105, 107, 113, 127, 133–35, 141–43, 145, 148, 151; and creative process, 23, 31–32, 43, 49, 89, 95, 103, 122, 133, 138; and devouring motif, 8–9, 16, 25, 27, 30, 36–37, 40, 43, 93, 95, 103, 109, 122, 132; and father, 15, 44, 106; and "Little Harry Hughes," 136, 141; and meals, 13, 21, 96, 100, 129, 138; and memory, 8, 24, 32, 39, 102; and mother, 30, 32, 89, 99, 104, 124; and nature, 17, 22, 33, 102, 125; and "Parable of the Plums," 90, 94–96, 130, 141; and vampire poem, 142; and water, 21, 29–30, 39, 42
Devouring motifs. *See* Dedalus, Stephen
Digestive process, 2, 8, 11, 13, 26, 35, 52, 62, 77, 87, 89, 103, 113, 117; and creativity, 2, 4, 9–10, 19, 26–27, 62, 79, 98, 100, 108; and elimination, 4, 9, 13, 15–16, 18–20, 23–24, 26, 41, 47, 131, 141, 153; and ingestion, 9, 15–17, 19, 24–25, 35, 47, 57, 59, 63, 90, 110, 114, 126, 131, 141, 146, 155; Joyce and, 2, 146; and peristalisis, 13, 18, 62; and urination, 41, 55, 85, 110, 136, 143, 153. *See also* Alimentary symbolism; Process
Dignam, Paddy, 58–59, 61, 64–65, 68, 89–90, 113, 124, 126, 137
Dolan, Father, 15
Dollard, Ben, 68, 78, 83–86
Douce, Lydia, 78, 81–82

Dublin, 16–17, 19, 21, 40, 76, 90, 108, 125

Egan, Kevin, 36
Eliade, Mircea, 63, 72
Elijah, 45, 63
Elimination. *See* Digestive process: and elimination
Ellmann, Richard, 42, 152
Emmet, Robert, 87
England, 58, 64, 95
Eucharist, 71
"Eumaeus" episode, 127–33, 146
Eve, 35, 40
Excrement, 2, 17–18, 40, 91, 109–11, 115–16, 130, 155. *See also* Digestive process: and elimination

Fasts, 6, 24, 67, 141; and Lent, 71, 74; and Yom Kippur, 67, 70–71, 118
Feasts, 7, 64, 66, 89–90, 91, 96–97, 101–3, 107, 134, 140; and Jesus' feeding of the multitudes, 96, 100; and Last Supper, 96, 99, 100, 103; and Passover, 90–91; and Pentecost, 96, 104, 106–9; and Shabout, 91, 96, 106–7, 109
Fertility, 2, 60, 63, 71, 78, 91, 96, 134, 148
*Finnegans Wake*. See Joyce, James
Fitzpatrick, William P., 149
Flynn, Nosey, 64
Food, 55, 81, 103, 145, 147–48; bread, 11–12, 97–98, 129–30, 140, 155; cheese, 71, 74, 107; cocoa, 133; eggs, 148; fish, 49, 97–98; honey, 98, 104; milk, 31–32, 47, 71, 98, 104, 148–49; wine, 99, 129, 140
Frazier, Sir James, *The Golden Bough*, 6
French, Marilyn, 91, 128
Freud, Sigmund, 3, 5, 13

Gaster, Theodor, 6, 107
Gea-Tellus, 152
Gifford, Don, 140, 153
Gilbert, Stuart, 2, 128
God, 19, 30, 40, 45, 98, 102–3, 106–7
Gose, Elliott B., Jr., 6, 145, 148; *The Transformation Process in Joyce's "Ulysses,"* 5

Goulding, Richie, 36–37, 81–84, 111
Graves, Robert, 29, 78
Greeks, 46, 62

"Hades" episode, 57–62, 104, 142
Haines, 32, 37, 104
Harrison, Jane Ellen, *Mythology*, 6
Hart, Clive, 2–3
Hayman, David, 45–46, 128
Heave offering, 139
Helen (of Troy), 35
Henke, Suzette A., 34, 82, 99, 152
Heracles, 29
Higgins, Zoe
Hodgart, M. J. C., 94
Holocaust, 139, 141
Holy Spirit, 107
Homeric parallel, 46, 62, 119. *See also Odyssey, The*
Hyde, Douglas, 45; "My Grief at Sea," 93

Ireland, 12, 27, 35, 58, 64, 65, 95–96, 102–3; sterility of, 14, 31, 78, 99
"Ithaca" episode, 128, 130, 133–44, 146, 155

Jeffrey, Charles, "M'Appari," 84
Jensen, Adolph, 63
*Jewish Encyclopedia*, 107
Jews, 35
John the Baptist, 24
Joyce, James, 27, 58, 67, 96, 100, 130, 132, 134, 136, 141, 150; *Dubliners*, "A Painful Case," 35; *Finnegans Wake*, 2–3, 110, 132; *A Portrait of the Artist as a Young Man*, 1, 4, 9, 11–27, 28, 36, 126, 146, 154; *Ulysses*, 1–3, 9, 16, 22–23, 27, 96–97, 128–29, 143–45, 153–55. *See also Ulysses:* Joyce's creation of; individual episodes
Jung, Carl Gustaf, 5

Kennedy, Mina, 78
Kenner, Hugh, 135–36
Keogh, J. C. 76, 94
Kissing, 24–25, 103, 114

Language, 2, 4, 7, 11–12, 14, 18, 25, 81–82, 132, 144, 154; and body, 7, 18, 27, 90, 144; Bloom and, 50, 55–56, 61–67, 70, 78–80, 82, 85, 87, 144; Joyce and, 130, 137, 154; Stephen and, 14, 18, 33–34, 37–38, 108, 122–23, 154. *See also* Word, the
"Last Rose of Summer, The," 86
Last Supper, the. *See* Feasts
Lenahan, T., 45, 93
Lent. *See* Fasts
"Lestrygonians" episode, 46, 51, 61, 62–77, 79, 104–5, 118, 131, 137, 147, 151
Lévy-Bruhl, Lucien, *L' Ame primitif, L'Éxperience mystique et les symboles chez les primitifs*, 6
Liffey, 58
Litz, A. Walton, 135
"Lotus Eaters" episode, 47, 52–57, 99, 106, 140
Lynch, Vincent, 22, 26, 28, 113, 122–23

McCable, Florence, 94
McCoy, 54–55
McDowell, Gerty, 112
MacHugh, 92–94
McKnight, Jeanne, 8, 12, 26
Maddox, James J., Jr., 35, 94, 101, 108, 125, 131
Mass. *See* Ritual: mass as
*Matcham's Masterstroke*, 51–52, 112
Milton, John, *Lycidas*, 32
Moore, Thomas, "The Meeting of the Waters," 69
Morse, J. Mitchell, 35
Moses, 101, 103–4, 107
Mulligan, Buck, 27–32, 34, 37–39, 80, 106, 124–25, 130, 136, 142, 155
Mulvey, Harry, 147, 152
Murphy, W. B. 130–35

"Nausikaa" episode, 148
"Nestor" episode, 32–35
Neumann, Erich, 4, 13, 16, 50, 53–54, 75–76, 110, 117, 152
New Testament, 100

*Odyssey, The*, 43, 52, 57, 62
Oedipal conflict, 12
Old Testament, 103
Omphale, 29
O'Shea, Kitty, 14, 35
Osiris, 118
"Oxen of the Sun" episode, 96–109, 113

"A Painful Case." *See* Joyce, James
Parnell, Charles Stewart, 14
Passover. *See* Feasts: and Passover
"Penelope" episode, 128, 145–55
Pentecost. *See* Feasts: and Pentecost
Peristalsis. *See* Digestive process: and peristalsis
Platonism, 43
Plumtree's potted meat, 54, 61, 65, 67, 114, 134, 137–38, 148
*A Portrait of the Artist as a Young Man*. *See* Joyce, James
Powers, Jack, 61
Process, 18, 30, 32, 37, 43, 90, 104, 155; and art, 94, 110, 122, 129–30, 154
Prodigal Son, 31
"Proteus" episode, 35–43, 94, 98, 103, 141
Purefoy, Mina, 51, 69, 86, 97, 104, 107–8, 125

Renan, Ernst, *Les Apôtres*, 6
Reuben J., 61, 72–73
Riordan, Dante, 13–14, 146, 150
Ritual, 1–2, 6, 29, 72, 90–91, 98, 119, 139; Eucharist, 52, 56–57, 62 John, rite of, 140–41; of *kenosis*, 6; mass, 20, 28, 63, 98, 136; Melchizedek, rite of, 140–41; mortification and purgation, 20, 60, 71, 118, 140–41; plerosis, 6, 107, 146; Samuel, rite of, 137. *See also* Fasts; Feasts
Rome, 95
Russell, George (A.E.), 43–44, 121

Sacrifice, 61–63, 72, 100, 118, 134. *See also* Bloom, Leopold: as sacrifice
Scapegoat, 6, 117, 120. *See also* Bloom, Leopold: as sacrifice

## Index

Schutte, William M., 45–46, 67
"Scylla and Charybdis" episode, 43–44
Seidel, Michael, 93, 142–43
Shakespeare, Ann, 44
Shakespeare, John, 43
Shakespeare, William, 45, 67, 73; *Hamlet*, 67, 73; *The Tempest*, 30
Shechner, Mark, 3, 12, 40, 109, 119
Shem, 110, 132–33
"Shira Shirim," 140
"Simchath Torah," 140
"Sirens" episode, 77–87
Slater, Philip, 12
Song of Moses, 98
Sterility, 90, 94, 96, 101, 103
Stuart, Gilbert, 46, 62
Sultan, Stanley, 78, 82, 105
Swanson, Roy Arthur, 71

"Telemachus" episode, 22, 27–32, 42
Thornton, Weldon, 31, 66, 118, 122
Tindall, William York, 46, 56, 94, 113, 115, 133–34, 136–37
Torah, 106
Twigg, Lizzie, 62, 68, 121

*Ulysses*: Joyce's creation of, 21, 46, 94, 98, 130–31, 135, 146, 149, 152–55. *See also* individual episodes

Uncle Charles, 15
Urim and Thummin, 139
Urination. *See* Digestive process: and urination

Vampirism, 25, 40, 73, 93, 132, 141–43
Venus, 44
Vickery, John B., 6, 118, 122
Vico, Giambattista, 8, 122, 154; *The New Science*, 7
Victoria, Queen, 36
Virag, Rudolph, 116
Virgin, 102
Voelker, Joseph, 145–46
Von Phul, Ruth, 42

Wandering Jew, 45
"Wandering Rocks" episode, 79
Watts, Alan, 100, 104
Word, the, 97, 100, 103, 106–7, 109, 145

Yom Kippur. *See* Fasts: and Yom Kippur

Zingrone, Frank, 101